NET SECURITY: Your Digital Doberman

Sure-fire Strategies for Wired Businesses

MICHAEL ALEXANDER

VENTANA

Net Security: Your Digital Doberman
Copyright ©1997 by Michael Alexander

All rights reserved. This book may not be duplicated in any way without the expressed written consent of the publisher, except in the form of brief excerpts or quotations for the purposes of review. The information contained herein is for the personal use of the reader and may not be incorporated in any commercial programs, other books, databases, or any kind of software without written consent of the publisher or author. Making copies of this book or any portion for any purpose other than your own is a violation of United States copyright laws.

Library of Congress Cataloging-in-Publication Data
Alexander, Michael, 1950–
   Net security : your digital doberman / Michael Alexander. — 1st ed.
     p. cm.
   Includes index.
   ISBN 1-56604-518-5
   1. Electronic commerce—Security measures. 2. Computer security. I. Title.
HF5548.32.A44 1996
005.8—dc20   96-35965
                              CIP

First Edition 9 8 7 6 5 4 3 2 1

Printed in the United States of America

Ventana Communications Group, Inc.
P.O. Box 13964
Research Triangle Park, NC 27709-3964
919.544.9404
FAX 919.544.9472
http://www.vmedia.com

Limits of Liability & Disclaimer of Warranty
The author and publisher of this book have used their best efforts in preparing the book and the programs contained in it. These efforts include the development, research, and testing of the theories and programs to determine their effectiveness. The author and publisher make no warranty of any kind, expressed or implied, with regard to these programs or the documentation contained in this book.

   The author and publisher shall not be liable in the event of incidental or consequential damages in connection with, or arising out of, the furnishing, performance or use of the programs, associated instructions and/or claims of productivity gains.

Trademarks
Trademarked names appear throughout this book, and on the accompanying compact disk. Rather than list the names and entities that own the trademarks or insert a trademark symbol with each mention of the trademarked name, the publisher states that it is using the names only for editorial purposes and to the benefit of the trademark owner with no intention of infringing upon that trademark.

   First Virtual, Virtual Tag and VirtualPIN are trademarks of First Virtual Holdings Incorporated.

Chief Executive Officer
Josef Woodman

**Vice President of
Content Development**
Karen A. Bluestein

Managing Editor
Lois J. Principe

Production Manager
John Cotterman

**Technology Operations
Manager**
Kerry L. B. Foster

**Product Marketing
Manager**
Jamie Jaeger Fiocco

Creative Services Manager
Diane Lennox

Art Director
Marcia Webb

Acquisitions Editor
Neweleen A. Trebnik

Project Editor
Jessica A. Ryan

Developmental Editor
Kat Turk

Copy Editor
Norma Emory

Assistant Editor
Patrick Bragg

Technical Reviewer
Russ Mullen

Desktop Publisher
Scott Hosa
Kristin Miller

Proofreaders
Ron Ferrell

Indexer
Ann Norcross

Cover Designer
Elena Skrinak

About the Author

Michael Alexander is author of *The Underground Guide to Computer Security*, as well as hundreds of articles about computer crime, security, hackers, cyberpunks, telephone phreaks, and other high-tech high jinks. The former editor-in-chief of *Infosecurity News* and senior editor of advanced technology at Computerworld, he is also special sections editor of *Datamation* and Home Tech columnist for *The Boston Globe*.

Acknowledgments

I would like to thank the many folks at Ventana Communications Group who worked on this project, especially the project editor, Jessica Ryan; the developmental editor, Kat Turk; and the copy editor, Norma Emory for editing the manuscript and catching all of my mistakes. Thanks also to desktop publishers Kristin Miller and Scott Hosa for guiding this book to its publication. I also would like to thank Laura Belt, my agent at Adler & Robin Books.

Dedication

To my wife Lorri and my daughters Leigh and Jessie for their love and support and in memory of my mother Ginette Alexander and my mother-in-law Dolores Weinstein.

Contents

Introduction xv

Chapter 1: Electronic Commerce & Security 1

New Ways of Doing Business 2
    Malling the Internet

New Ways of Cashing In 5

What Is Electronic Commerce? 6
    Advantages ■ Disadvantages

A Brief History of the Internet 8

World Wide Web 10

Internet & WWW Security 11
    WWW Hacks ■ Growth Equals Security Problems ■ Challenges to Security ■ Hack & Enter ■ Insecurity Begins at Home ■ Unwillingness to Take Security Seriously

Legal Issues 19
    Privacy in Cyberspace ■ Assault on Encryption

EDI Over the Internet 21

Chapter 2: Risky Business 25

Attractive Targets 26

It's the Employees 27
    Internet + Employees = Trouble ■ Disgruntled Employees ■ Dishonest Employees ■ Motto: Be Aware ■ Wild & Crazy Employees

Outsiders Looking In 31
    Outlaw Hackers ■ No Lex Luthors ■ I Spies ■ Organized Crime
    ■ Cyberterrorists ■ Competitive Intelligence Gatherers ■ Attack
    Scenarios ■ Sniffing Out Passwords ■ IP Spoofing ■ Sendmail Attacks
    ■ Network Scanning ■ Denial-of-Service Attacks ■ Anonymous FTP
    ■ E-mail Bombing ■ Forging E-mail & News

Cybermicrobes Are Out to Getcha 51
    Viruses Multiply ■ The Bug Is Born ■ What Is a Virus? ■ No Easy
    Answers ■ How Are PCs Infected? ■ Telltale Signs ■ Virus Antidotes
    ■ Worms, Trojan Horses, Bombs ■ Logic & Time Bombs

Chapter 3: Encryption & Digital John Hancocks 69

Banking on Encryption 70
Encryption Crash Course 71
    Plain Talk About Text ■ The Secret Is in the Keys ■ Crooks Do Simple
    Crypto ■ One for You, One for Everybody Else ■ The Best of Both Worlds
    ■ Digital Envelopes ■ Digital John Hancocks ■ Public Servers for Keys

Common Crypto Systems 79
    Data Encryption Standard ■ RSA ■ Pretty Good Privacy 84

A Few More Code Systems 89
    RIPEM ■ Kerberos ■ Clipper

Buyer Beware 91
    It's Good Business

Encrypting Electronic Mail 93
    Acting on MIME ■ Close, But Not Foolproof

Make It a Policy to Protect Yourself 97

Chapter 4: Digital Money 99

No Credit Card Safeguards in Cyberspace 100
    Credit Where Credit Is Due ■ Cashing In on Credit Cards

Setting Standards for Security 105
    Secure Electronic Transactions

Contents

Two Other Credit Card Crypto Standards 113
    Secure Sockets Layer ■ Secure HyperText Transfer Protocol

Checking Out the Web 118

Gimme Digital Money (That's What I Want) 119
    Conspicuous Consumers? ■ One Micropayment at a Time

E-wallets 124
    Mondex ■ E-cash Obstacles

What's Needed for Digital Money to Work? 127
    Privacy Concerns ■ Regulating E-money

Chapter 5: Digital Money Makers 133

CyberCash 134
    For Consumers Considering CyberCash ■ Shop Setup With CyberCash ■ Advantages & Disadvantages

CheckFree 140

DigiCash 141
    Digital Dollar Deals ■ U.S. Consumer Accounts ■ Becoming an Ecash Merchant ■ Advantages & Disadvantages

First Virtual Holdings, Inc. 146
    Nothing, Not Even Net ■ Getting Set Up to Use First Virtual ■ Shop Basics ■ Advantages & Disadvantages

Could-Be Contenders 152
    Citibank's Electronic Monetary System ■ NetCash & NetCheque ■ Online Pocket Change ■ NetCash/NetBank Merchants ■ NetChex

Chapter 6: Safe Shopkeeping on the WWW 161

Attack Modes 163

Web Server Security 163
    Do It Yourself, or Not

Storefronts in a Box 165
    Microsoft Merchant System

Cracking Web Sites 170
  Common Gateway Interface Scripts ■ Security Precautions
  ■ Sacrificial Lamb ■ Narrow World Webs

Security in Browsing 176

Java 177
  Java's Own Security ■ Java's Security Flaws ■ Hostile Applets
  ■ JavaScript

Active Software Components 182

Last But Not Least 184

Chapter 7: Airbags & Seat Belts for the I-way 185

Cyberguardian at the Gates 186
  The Objectives of Firewalls ■ Firewall Basics

Filtering Out Packets 188
  Put It on a Table ■ Block to Protect

Proxies With Moxie 191
  SOCKS

Firewalls Aren't Cure-alls 192
  Maginot Line of Defense ■ Inside Out ■ Firewalls & Viruses
  ■ The Terror of the Unknown

Authentication & Identification 195
  Passwords Are a Factor ■ One, Two Factors ■ Smart Passwords

Encryption 197
  Link-level Encryption ■ Network-level Encryption

Comparing Firewall Features 200
  Identification & Authentication ■ Encryption ■ Proxies ■ Address &
  Machine Name Hiding ■ Auditing ■ Administration ■ Pricing
  ■ Vendors ■ Personnel

Attack Simulators 202
  Get SATAN

Intrusion Detection 205
Hack Attack Aftermath 207
    No Trespassing

Tools for Firewall Builders 210
    COPS ■ Crack & Cracklib ■ Passwdplus ■ SATAN ■ SOCKS ■ Tiger ■ TIS Internet Firewall Toolkit

Overall Look at Security 212
    Security Awareness ■ Operating System Security ■ Application Security ■ Network Security

Chapter 8: The Law Comes to Cyberspace 217

Legal Gray Areas 218
Call Your Attorney 220
Changing Copyright Law 220
    Copyright Rewrite

Cryptographic Copyright Containers 223
Digital Vending Machines 224
Digital Boxes & Other Containers 226
    IBM Cryptolope Containers ■ InterTrust DigiBoxes ■ Xerox Usage Rights Language ■ Standards Battle ■ IMPRIMATUR

Privacy Is Good for Business 230
Cookies for Consumers 232
    Persistent Cookies

Keeping Track 233
Floppy Copy Concerns 234
Digital Shrink Wrap 236
    Electronic Licensing & Security Initiatives

May You Have Many Employees 237
Make it a Policy to Protect Yourself 239
The Right & Wrong of Using Computers 240

Top Down View of Policies 240
   Permission ■ Responsibilities ■ Keep Passwords & Accounts
   Confidential ■ Unauthorized Access to Files & Directories
   ■ Unauthorized Use of Software ■ Use for For-profit Activities
   ■ Electronic Mail ■ Harassment ■ Attacking the System ■ Theft
   ■ Waste & Abuse ■ Networks ■ Enforcement ■ Your Responsibility
   ■ Workplace Monitoring

Last Rights & Wrongs 246
   Caveat ■ Policy Helpers

Computer Awareness Training 247

Who Has the Right to Surf? 248

Appendix A: Using the Internet to Stay Ahead of the Bad Guys 249

Appendix B: Firewall & Secure Web Server Buyer's Guide 259

Index 269

Introduction

Everyone from Mom and Pop to Amalgamated Inc. is looking to strike it rich in cyberspace. But before you set up your electronic storefront or other online business you should know that setting up shop on the Internet and the World Wide Web can be risky business. There are all sorts of crooks, ranging from outlaw hackers to your own employees, who aim to pilfer your wares and cause mischief in more ways that you ever imagined. What's more, the ways these crooks and others can compromise company information systems are multiplying almost daily.

For example, in August 1996, while this book was being written, researchers at universities in the United States and Europe uncovered three significant security flaws in the two popular Web browsers, Netscape Navigator and Microsoft Internet Explorer, and in Sun Microsystem's Java programming language used to create special effects on Web sites. Also that month, computer hackers broke into Web sites maintained by the U.S. Justice Department and the Central Intelligence Agency and altered their home pages with electronic graffiti, pornographic images, and links to other Web sites that neither agency would willingly choose to be associated with.

What's This Book About?

Net Security: Your Digital Doberman is a watchdog for your cyberbusiness. It explains what the risks are of doing business on the Internet and World Wide Web and what you can do to protect your enterprise. It also takes a look at the new and emerging standards for electronic payments systems, ranging from secure credit card transactions to digital money.

This book covers topics such as:

- the risks of doing business on the Net and the World Wide Web
- the many ways that security and privacy can be compromised
- who is committing crimes (often it's the employees)
- transacting business safely with credit cards
- digital cash, checks, and other forms of digital money
- how to reduce security exposures in electronic mail
- how to use the Internet to shore up your defenses
- setting up pilfer-proof storefronts on the World Wide Web
- strategies for signing electronic documents
- the steps to take to protect business and personal affairs
- what to do to beat off an attack and who to contact for help

Who Needs This Book?

Is setting up shop on the Internet and World Wide Web worth the risk? You can count on it, but only if you know what security precautions to take. *Net Security* is for anyone who has or plans to set up shop on the Internet and World Wide Web and is worried about protecting their assets. The book provides digital merchants with technology strategies and guidelines for securely transacting electronic commerce over the Internet and the World Wide Web.

What's Inside?

Chapter 1: Electronic Commerce & Security

The Internet, I-way, the Net—call it what you like—is the modern equivalent of California's mother lode region where the forty-niners found gold in 1849 and later. The Internet is a huge matrix of computer networks, spread all over the planet (and beyond if you listen to the cyberspace zealots).

More recently, thousands of companies have discovered the Net, seeking to strike it rich in electronic commerce. Large corporations—especially banks and other financial institutions—have been doing business electronically for several years. But thanks to the growth of the Net, and the World Wide Web in particular, electronic commerce is expanding to include individuals and small businesses and will soon become part of everyday life.

Buying and selling goods and services online is expected to grow dramatically over the next five to seven years. According to Input, an information technology market research firm based in Mountain View, California, worldwide sales of goods and services traded over the Internet will increase from $70 million in 1995 to $255 billion in the year 2000, a compounded growth rate of more than 400 percent.

This opening chapter introduces readers to electronic commerce and the notion of setting up shop on the Internet and the World Wide Web. It is a crash course on what doing business in cyberspace is all about; what kinds of businesses are being established; and the benefits of doing business electronically.

Chapter 2: Risky Business

Security takes on an entirely new dimension when a business puts its employees on the Internet. For example, a well-meaning but naive employee may download files that contain viruses or post copyrighted material on a Web site. Disgruntled employees have used the organization's systems to launch attacks against other systems and to download cracking tools that can be deployed against internal systems.

Does the value of conducting business over the Internet outweigh the risks? Yes, but only if a business is aware of the pitfalls and avails itself of current and emerging technologies to protect itself and its transactions.

This chapter explores the many risks of doing business on the Internet and provides readers with insight on who's committing crimes, why and how. In subsequent chapters, would-be digital entrepreneurs find out what they need to do to protect their organization's systems and Web sites once connected to the Internet.

Chapter 3: Encryption & Digital John Hancocks

Encryption is one of the key ways that electronic business operators can protect themselves. Savvy digital merchants can use encryption to

- scramble credit card numbers and other sensitive financial data so that even if intercepted, they cannot be read and used;
- encode electronic mail messages and important documents whose contents must remain confidential;
- sign documents, providing irrefutable proof of the authenticity of buyers and sellers involved in financial transactions, or anyone else who creates a document.

This chapter is a nontechnical crash course in encryption, intended to help readers sort out the leading encryption techniques for financial transactions and electronic mail; explain the benefits of using encryption; and the technical and legal challenges of using encryption. It also provides a complete rundown on the prevailing and emerging encryption standards and how they are being applied in digital cash payment systems.

Chapter 4: Digital Money

Concern about security is the primary factor inhibiting consumers from conducting transactions online, according to an ongoing survey of 23,000 Internet users done by Georgia Tech and the

University of Michigan. What will it take to turn Web window shoppers into online buyers? There are several emerging standards and protocols for using credit cards and transferring money across the Net. These standards include: ecash or electronic cash, Payment Transaction Application Layer, Secure Electronic Payment Protocol, among several others.

Chapter 5: Digital Money Makers

Several companies are vying to be among the early leaders in providing safe credit card transaction systems and electronic cash. Some methods use encryption; others do not. Some methods use certificates and repudiation to verify and vouch for the parties involved in the transactions; others do not. Is one approach better than the other? What are the risks? This chapter will address these and many other questions that would-be online merchants are sure to have.

Chapter 6: Safe Shopkeeping on the WWW

The fabulously successful World Wide Web is electronic commerce's equivalent of a killer app, that is, an application that makes a technology skyrocket. The Web has been in existence for only a couple of years, yet it is the fastest growing segment of the Net. Most of the digital merchants are going about their business on the World Wide Web.

Not surprising, outlaw hackers also have discovered the Web. Gangs with monikers like the Chaos Merchants and the Internet Liberation Front are regularly attacking WWW sites, altering information and causing mischief in other ways.

Web sites are among the easiest to attack and plunder, mainly because Webmasters and site administrators pay little, if any, attention to security. Web sites are designed for easy access and typically offer features such as online form entry and electronic mail—both features that can be readily exploited.

There are three angles of attack favored by intruders and mischief makers: Web browsers, Web servers, and the network itself. This chapter takes a look at the ways Web sites are compromised and what to do about them.

Chapter 7: Airbags & Seat Belts for the I-way

In other chapters, we discussed the many ways that computer systems connected to the Internet can be attacked and compromised. In this chapter, we take a look at the best defenses available to online entrepreneurs: firewalls, attack simulators, intrusion detection mechanisms, and access control devices such as smart cards.

Chapter 8: The Law Comes to Cyberspace

If you're planning to set up shop on the Net, better call your lawyer first. The laws of cyberspace are still developing and for that reason entrepreneurs and other businesses should be wary. Doing business in cyberspace is fraught with many new and novel legal issues that entrepreneurs on Main Street, Anytown, never have to be concerned about.

What are the legal requirements and liabilities for businesses who set up shop on the WWW? This section examines the legal responsibilities related to maintaining and operating a Web site. These include: copyright infringement, defamation, pornography, rights of privacy, First Amendment concerns, and related issues. It will also include a discussion of the need for employee policies that spell out what sorts of activities are permissible (and those that aren't) when using Internet accounts. Since most computer crimes are committed by insiders, businesses should have policies in force in the event they must prosecute offending employees or have other legal recourse.

Appendices

Information security and electronic commerce are volatile topics, changing rapidly from one day to the next. Appendix A, "Using the Internet to Stay Ahead of the Bad Guys," provides readers with tips such as

- where to find free and almost-free security software;
- what are the best newsgroups covering security and electronic commerce;
- what are the top security sites on the WWW;

- where to find industry bulletins about late-breaking security events;
- where to find the groups that track security-related issues;
- where to find advisories, security tools, and information of interest to all Webmasters;
- where to find how-to documents, white papers, and FAQs (Frequently Asked Questions).

Firewalls and secure Web servers are two key defenses available to organizations that wish to protect its internal computer networks and Web sites from outsiders. A firewall also provides a secure way of enabling insiders to access the Internet, exchange e-mail, and so on.

There is a dizzying array of firewall and secure Web server vendors and products. Appendix B, "Firewall & Secure Web Server Buyer's Guide," provides readers with a handy overview of the major firewall and Web server vendors and their products so readers can more readily start shopping.

As we all know, the Internet is constantly changing. As hard as I've tried to make our information current, the truth is that new sites and information will come online as soon as this book goes to press (and continually thereafter). Ventana provides an excellent way to tackle this problem and to keep the information in the book up-to-date: the *Net Security* Online Updates. You can access this valuable resource via Ventana's World Wide Web site at http://www.vmedia.com/updates.html. Once there, you'll find updated material relevant to *Net Security* as well as other security issues.

—*Michael Alexander*

1 Electronic Commerce & Security

Not long after gold was discovered in Sutter's Mill in 1848, some 100,000 hopeful prospectors headed for the mother lode region of California. Although most people today are apt to think many forty-niners became wealthy, the majority of prospectors never struck it rich. The forty-niners were preyed upon by crooks, who through all manner of trickery, were able to steal the mines away from those who first owned them. Indeed, the prospectors found life was hard in Hell's Half Acre, Hangtown, and other mining camps. In the first year of the gold rush, 10,000 miners died as a result of inadequate shelter, poor food, lack of medical supplies, dysentery, and other diseases.

Today, there is a new gold rush underway, with everyone from small family businesses to major corporations looking to stake a claim in cyberspace. Like those early prospectors, these electronic entrepreneurs must contend with high-tech thievery, computer viruses and bugs, and other hardships.

Is setting up an online business worth the risk? You bet! Buying and selling goods and services online is expected to grow dramatically over the next five to seven years. According to Input, an information technology market research firm based in Mountain View, California, worldwide sales of goods and services traded over the Internet will rocket from $70 million in 1995 to $255 million in 2000, a compounded annual growth rate of more than 400 percent.

If you're already operating a business or planning to set up shop on the Internet, you can certainly minimize your risks. If you were to open a business on one of those congested miracle-mile shopping strips common in many urban communities in the United States, you probably would buy a solid lock for the front door, install a burglar alarm, obtain property and liability insurance, and get yourself the biggest, meanest guard dog you could find.

Setting up an electronic business is no different in that respect. You need a digital Doberman and electronic equivalents of other protective mechanisms to guard your wares from thieves entering your establishment through the Internet. A smart merchant doesn't wait to get robbed but takes proactive steps to protect the business.

More than a hundred companies are setting up Internet connections each week, according to Input. Large corporations—especially banks and other financial institutions—have been doing business electronically for several years. But, thanks to the growth of the Net and the World Wide Web (WWW) in particular, electronic commerce is expanding to include individuals and small businesses. Soon it'll be a part of everyday life.

New Ways of Doing Business

Much of what passes for electronic commerce over the Internet today is geared toward what businesses have always done—only faster, with fewer employees, and over a wider area than ever before.

That's only the beginning of a brave new electronic world in which consumers and digital merchants can specify exactly what they want to buy, acquiring bids from several vendors who will compete for their business. Before long, anyone will be able to transmit a global request for a product or service, customizing it to very specific requirements; gather competing quotes; and buy from the lowest bidder within a matter of hours. Think of it as made-to-order buying and selling.

We're now moving into an era in which electronic entrepreneurs are launching the sorts of businesses that were impossible and even unimaginable only a few years ago.

Electronic auction houses sell goods and services to the highest bidder in real time, video arcades allow gamers to sample the latest games and pay by the minute, bakery/cafes sell breads and pastries with a serving of conversation on the side, and publishers sell technical reports a page at a time.

Companies noted for their catalog marketing skills are busily setting up virtual storefronts to cater to customers around the world. Most are still content to offer what I call *brochureware*, electronic versions of the marketing materials stuffed into mailboxes and Sunday newspapers, but that is changing as companies become more Net-savvy.

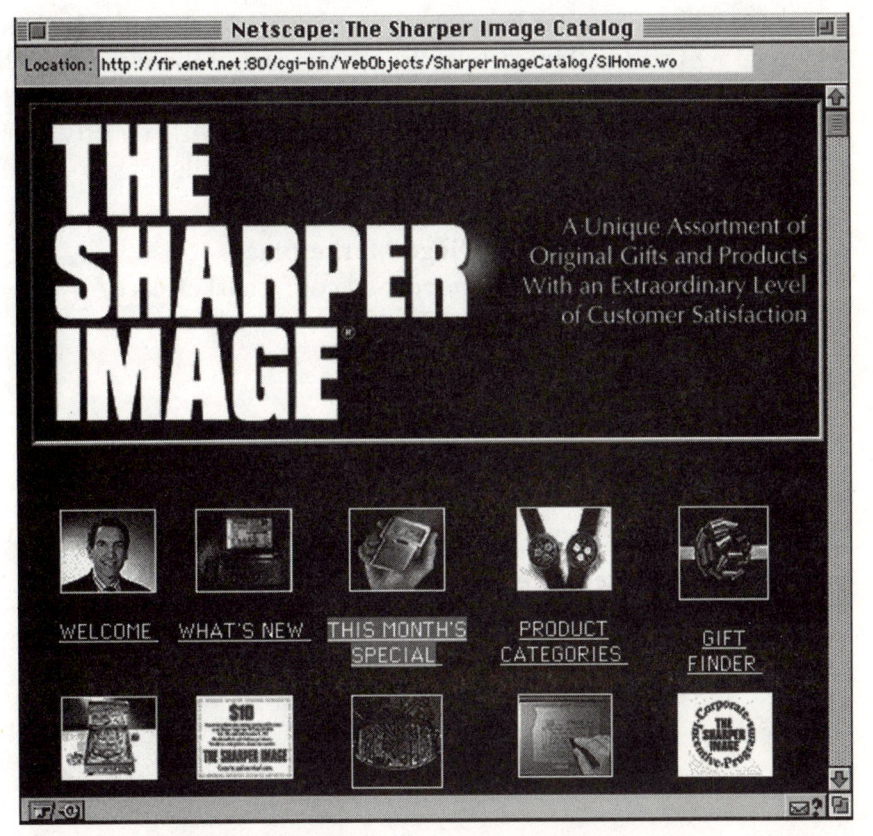

The Sharper Image catalog online.

For example, an upscale retailer, The Sharper Image, has had a Web site since mid-1995. The company is one of only a few to link its Web site with its ordering system in a bid to speed its handling of online sales and delivery of the purchased goods. The company is angling to triple its online business (from $500,000 in 1995) over the next year.

Even L.L. Bean, widely admired for its catalog marketing success, is online. The Freeport, Maine, company, with some help from IBM, is setting up a virtual storefront on the Internet.

Malling the Internet

Not everyone wants to go it alone. Many digital merchants believe there is safety in numbers and have opted to set up shop in one of the many electronic malls opening up on the WWW.

Forrester Research, a market research company based in Cambridge, Massachusetts, estimates that there are more than six hundred malls on the WWW, housing some seventy-five hundred retailers. The number of malls is growing by fifty to a hundred per month, Forrester adds. Here's a short list of some of the more established online shopping malls:

HomePort San Diego Marketplace
http://www.homeport-sd.com/marketplace/

IndustryNet Marketplace
http://www.industry.net

InfoHaus
http://www.infohaus.com

InterWeb
http://www.interwebinc.com

Marketplace
http://www.cts.com

Shopping2000
http://www.shopping2000.com

Village Potpourri Mall
http://www.vpm.com

Chapter 1: Electronic Commerce & Security 5

Homeport San Diego Marketplace.

New Ways of Cashing In

Along with new goods and services are new ways of paying for them based on *encryption*. Encryption, a mixture of science and art, can be used to scramble credit card numbers, e-mail messages, and other private information so that, even if intercepted, they cannot be read.

Encryption also can be used to create:

- Digital signatures and digital certificates that provide irrefutable proof of your identity

- Digital money, which can never be stolen or counterfeited

- Digital envelopes, which can be opened only by the person to whom they are addressed

- Digital vending machines, which can dispense information for a fee

Whether the smallest coin in your pocket is a cent or a centime, some forms of electronic commerce will deal in even smaller units. Imagine being able to make micropayments equal to fractions of a cent and pay for only the portion of a product used or the amount of time a service is used. Digital money, based on encryption, makes that possible.

A number of these electronic cash systems are being proposed for electronic commerce over the Internet. When you purchase an item in a store and use a credit card to pay for it, the merchant can verify your identity, get the card issuer's approval for the sale, and require you to sign the credit card receipt to prove that you are a willing participant in the transaction.

Electronic commerce over the Internet needs the same safeguards used in face-to-face business transactions.

These safeguards can be accomplished with digital signatures and digital certificates. Together, the two can provide irrefutable proof of a seller's or a buyer's identity. I describe in detail how this encryption works in Chapter 3, "Encryption & Digital John Hancocks."

What Is Electronic Commerce?

Electronic commerce is using networks to facilitate the selling and buying of goods and services and related activities involved in the transaction of business. Big business has been conducting electronic commerce for several years using *Electronic Data Interchange (EDI)*. More about that later.

Now wide-scale electronic commerce over the Internet and the World Wide Web is becoming possible. Global electronic commerce and payments business on the Internet will reach $800 billion within five years (an annual growth rate of 16 percent), says Killen Associates, a research and consulting company. By the year 2000, revenues from electronic payments will account for two-thirds of all noncash transaction revenues in the United States, Killen says.

Advantages

Electronic commerce over the Internet has several advantages over traditional commerce. Digital merchants can:

- Cut the costs of finding customers and suppliers
- Expand trading areas from local to global
- Speed the time it takes to purchase and receive goods and services
- Pay for and receive goods as they are needed without having to rely on large inventories
- Reduce or even eliminate the cost of creating documents and other printed materials
- Enhance customer service with faster response

Disadvantages

Several hurdles must be resolved before electronic commerce really takes off, but two stand out: (1) the perception that transacting business is risky for both buyers and sellers and (2) the lack of standards for digital money and other electronic payment systems.

Security concerns are the primary factor inhibiting consumers from conducting transactions online, according to an ongoing survey of 23,000 Internet users by Georgia Tech and the University of Michigan. The Hermes Project found people are less likely now than early in 1996 to post credit card information online. The most common reason given is a lack of security: 60 percent of those surveyed agreed "somewhat strongly" or "strongly" that security concerns are a primary reason for not buying.

The survey indicates that Web travelers are using the network more to gather information about products and services than to actually buy them. This is a key issue that virtual businesses must contend with, at least for the foreseeable future.

A Brief History of the Internet

The Internet began as an experimental network called Arpanet, established in 1969 by the Department of Defense's Defense Advanced Research Projects Agency (DARPA). The prototype network was created in response to questions then being posed by the Pentagon, which was worried about the prospect of a nuclear strike on the U.S. military communications systems. Pentagon officials wanted to know if it were possible to devise a network that could withstand sabotage or even an all-out war.

A small group of computer scientists at defense laboratories and universities discovered a way to give the military what it wanted, using a technique called *packet switching*.

The idea was to create several paths on which information could travel, break up the information into small chunks called packets, and arrange for these packets to get to their destination independently, where they would be reassembled.

If one path were cut, the packet automatically would find another route. It's like sending someone a 10-page letter, one sheet at a time. Each sheet is numbered and put into a separate numbered envelope. The 10 envelopes are sealed, addressed, and mailed. When all envelopes arrive, the recipient opens them in the proper order to read the pages of the letter in sequence.

On the Internet, packets also are numbered and addressed before being transmitted. Along the way, packets pass through *routers*—computers that check the address and send the packets along. If one route is too busy or is blocked, the router sends packets along another path. The process is similar to the way that letters sent by the U.S. Postal Service travel from the local post office, through the distribution system, and to your mailbox.

DARPA also sponsored several other packet-switching networks. In the 1970s, recognizing the need to link these networks, DARPA supported the development of a set of procedures and rules for addressing and routing messages across separate networks. These procedures and rules, called the Internet Protocol (IP), provided a universal language allowing information to be routed across multiple interconnected networks.

In the 1980s, the number of networks attached to Arpanet grew as technological advances facilitated network connections. By 1983 Arpanet had become so heavily used that the Department of Defense split operational military traffic into a separate system called Milnet, funded and managed by the Defense Communications Agency. Both Arpanet and Milnet are unclassified networks. Classified military and government systems are isolated and physically separated from these networks.

Building on existing Internet technology, the National Science Foundation (NSF), responsible for nurturing U.S. science infrastructure, fostered the proliferation of additional networks. In 1985, NSF made the Internet Protocol the standard for its six supercomputing centers and in 1986 funded a backbone network, NSFnet, linking the centers. NSF also supported a number of regional and local-area campus networks. Regional networks include partial statewide networks, such as the Bay Area Regional Research Network in northern California, statewide networks such as the New York State Educational Research Network, and multistate networks such as the Southern Universities Research Association Network.

Other federal agencies funding research networks include the Department of Energy, the National Aeronautics and Space Administration, and the Department of Health and Human Services.

This loosely organized web of interconnected networks—including Arpanet, Milnet, NSFnet, and the scores of local and regional networks that use IP—make up the Internet. The Internet supports a vast multidisciplinary community of computer scientists, physicists, electrical engineers, and many other researchers.

These researchers use the Internet for such functions as electronic mail, file transfer, and remote access to computer data banks and supercomputers. Increasingly, the Internet is being used by business organizations to communicate with customers and to disseminate information about products and services.

In the last 10 years, the Internet has grown to tens of thousands of networks. In 1988 the NSF estimated that there were more than half a million Internet users; today, that organization estimates

30 million people around the world use the Internet. Some market researchers predict 100 million users will be connected by 1998.

It is both a key strength and a key weakness that no one agency or organization is responsible for the Internet's overall management. No one owns or controls it.

Early in the Internet's development, responsibility for managing and securing host computers was given to end users—the host sites that owned and operated them, such as college campuses and federal agencies. It was believed that the host sites were in the best position to manage and determine a level of security appropriate for their systems.

The Internet is largely free of bureaucratic control and burdensome regulation. Management of the Internet is decentralized and informal, residing primarily at the host-site and individual-network levels.

Each of the Internet's thousands of networks maintains operational control over its own network, whether it is a backbone, regional, or local area network. According to DARPA, this decentralization provided the needed flexibility for the Internet's continuing growth and evolution.

World Wide Web

The fabulously successful World Wide Web is electronic commerce's equivalent of a *killer app*—one that makes a particular technology skyrocket. The Web has been in existence for only a few years yet is the fastest growing segment of the Net. Most digital merchants are conducting business on the World Wide Web.

The underpinnings of the World Wide Web were created by Tim Berners-Lee at CERN, the European Particle Physics Laboratory in Geneva, Switzerland.

Everything is *hyper* on the Web:

- Web travelers use browsers to access Web sites using a language called HyperText Transfer Protocol (HTTP), which regulates how documents are retrieved and displayed.

- Web pages are created using a language called HyperText Markup Language (HTML), used to define each page's look and feel.

- Hyperlinks allow WWW travelers to connect quickly from one Web page or Web site to another.

The WWW makes it possible for even newcomers to travel the Internet, gather information, and make purchases. Along the way, their shopping experience is enlivened by colorful graphics, audio, moving images, 3D, and virtual reality. In fact, the WWW did for the Internet what MTV did for a generation of TV-watching music lovers.

WWW users are also the sort of people digital merchants love to do business with. They're upscale, with annual household incomes of more than $80 thousand dollars, according to an Internet demographics survey conducted by CommerceNet and Nielsen in 1996. About half of WWW users say they are in professional or managerial positions, and 64 percent say they have at least bachelor's degrees. In all, approximately 2.5 million people have purchased products or services over the WWW.

Internet & WWW Security

Protecting your internal computer systems and Web site starts in layers, beginning with employee awareness of methods used by intruders and other employees to compromised information systems.

One of the primary ways that organizations can protect their internal information systems, including their Web servers, is with one or more computers that comprise a *firewall*. The firewall allows or blocks data traffic according to rules created by the system administrator.

Digital merchants also use Web servers designed for electronic commerce. These servers use Secure Sockets Layer (SSL) and other encryption technologies to protect credit card numbers and other sensitive information needed to conduct business.

WWW Hacks

As you might expect, the WWW also has become a favorite of assorted crooks and computer crackers. One of the most common antics of hackers these days is to break into a Web site and scramble the information.

In this book I use the term *hacker* to describe a person who breaks into computer systems, today's commonly accepted definition. At one time, a hacker was anyone who was interested in finding creative ways to solve system problems; the term had nothing to do with breaking into systems. I sometimes use the term even more loosely to describe anyone from the stereotypical teenager who browses systems for fun to the wily intelligence operative engaged in paid economic espionage.

No matter who these outlaws really are, they are becoming bolder and more adept, thanks to the proliferation of how-to hack information and computer burglary tools that make it possible for even rank amateurs to enter computer sites.

In August 1996, a hacker who apparently opposes Net censorship and gun control attacked the Department of Justice's Web site. The DOJ's pages were replaced with pages bearing Nazi swastikas, pictures of Adolf Hitler, sexually explicit material, and a picture of George Washington with the caption, "Move my grave to a free country! This rolling is making me an insomniac." Whoever doctored the pages asserted that the Justice Department wants to take apart the Constitution "one amendment at a time," starting with the rights of free speech and gun ownership.

The following month, The Swedish Hackers Association (SHA) decided to protest the treatment of five of their members, who were on trial for a variety of computer-related crimes, by trashing the Central Intelligence Agency's Web site. They changed the CIA's logo to the "Central Stupidity Agency," as well as posted "Stop lying Bo Skarinder" in English and Swedish. Skarinder is the trial prosecutor. They also changed the CIA's links to connect to Playboy's site, as well other sites frequented by members of the computer underground.

Ironically, the day before the SHA's attack on the CIA's site, the U.S. Senate passed, by unanimous consent, legislation that would provide harsher penalties for criminal hacking. The National

Information Infrastructure Protection Act provides for stiffer penalties for hackers who steal files or tamper with computer systems in other ways. It also amends the Computer Fraud and Abuse Act, adding a section that provides penalties for transmitting threats against computer systems over networks that cross state or national boundaries. Among the actions covered by the legislation are threats to deny access to authorized users, erasing or corrupting files, and encrypting files and demanding a ransom in exchange for the key. Outlaw hackers who break into computer systems and use computer time worth more than $5,000 in any one year would be charged with a felony.

Growth Equals Security Problems

Just as the Internet is providing digital merchants with new ways of doing business, it also is providing outsiders and employees alike with new ways to compromise business. Obviously, when businesses connect to the Internet, they expose themselves to attack by a wide variety of outsiders, ranging from outlaw hackers to former Cold War spies who have turned to economic espionage. The number of Internet-related security breaches has risen in tandem with the increase in the number of organizations plugging into the Internet.

Connecting to the Internet only increases a company's exposure to security breaches. An *InformationWeek*/Ernst & Young survey of 1,290 information services (IS) executives conducted in October 1995 found that one in five companies suffered break-ins through the Net. The actual number of break-ins probably is much higher, since only half the surveyed managers felt confident they could detect a break-in through the Net.

Although many companies have installed such security precautions as firewalls to restrict access by outsiders and encryption to protect the confidentiality of vital documents, the number of security breaches continues to rise.

The Computer Emergency Response Team (CERT), an Internet watchdog organization based at Carnegie Mellon University's Software Engineering Institute, reports that it handled 2,412 computer security incidents (affecting 12,000 sites) in 1995. That's up from six such incidents in 1988, when the group was formed.

The rapid increase in commercial traffic also is making it more difficult to track and stop breaches. Although there is yet little hard evidence of companies with Internet links having suffered significant losses as a result of security breaches, it is only a matter of time, say many security experts.

The Federal Bureau of Investigation, for example, says the Internet is used to break into systems in more than 80 percent of the computer crime cases it investigates. For the most part, these attacks have been aimed at universities, research centers, and other noncommercial sites. Obviously such attacks have financial implications associated with them but are still difficult to quantify. Many victim organizations are reluctant to report security-related incidents to law enforcers.

Still, it is easy to envision some of the potential consequences of a security breach through the Internet for commercial organizations. Given the enormous reliance most organizations now place on information systems technology, unauthorized tampering with those systems or the theft of the information they contain could have serious financial impact. In a survey conducted this year by *Infosecurity News*, a trade magazine about information systems security, 34 percent (169) of respondents estimated that if their organizations' computerized data were lost, tampered with, erased, or stolen, the loss would amount to more than $5 million. An additional 25 percent (125) of respondents said the loss would be between $1 million and $5 million.

Challenges to Security

Whether committed by disgruntled employees on the inside or outlaw hackers on the outside, computer crime through the Internet is on the increase. There are many reasons for this:

- *The Internet is inherently insecure.* The Internet was never designed with electronic commerce in mind. Internet protocols have a number of flaws that can be exploited, and most are well known to hackers.

- *The Internet has grown rapidly.* The number of crimes are increasing in sync with the number of people and companies that attach themselves to the Internet.

- *Technical ability has grown, too*. Outlaw hackers and other intruders are more knowledgeable and more proficient than ever at breaking into computer sites.

- *Risks are not recognized*. Many companies fail to take adequate measures to protect their internal systems from attacks by insiders and outsiders because they don't take the risks seriously or choose to downplay them.

- *Security precautions are expensive*. Firewalls, secure Web servers, encryption mechanisms, and other security measures can be costly and difficult to administer.

- *Security is difficult to achieve*. Networks are a jumble of platforms, operating systems, applications, and protocols. Providing seamless security is impossible.

- *Competition is great*. Companies are scrambling to adopt new technology that they hope will make them more competitive, without understanding the security implications.

- *Some products are flawed and vendors unresponsive*. Too many companies are introducing products without regard to whether they are adequately protected against attack. Those aware of potential security vulnerabilities overestimate their products' features or are slow to respond with patches and information when security holes are uncovered. For example, in 1996 alone, computer researchers at universities in the United States and Europe found more than a dozen security loopholes in Netscape Navigator and Microsoft Internet Explorer—the two most popular browsers.

- *Recourse may not be possible*. Computer attacks often cross national boundaries. In many countries, breaking into computer systems is not against the law. If a hacker in a country that does not have laws prohibiting computer intrusion breaks into a computer site in the United States, what recourse does the victim have (assuming you're able to identify the intruder, which is highly unlikely)?

Hack & Enter

In mid-September 1996, Public Access Networks Corp., a New York Internet service provider (ISP) otherwise known as Panix, found its computer systems being assailed by unknown hackers. Someone was flooding the ISP with 50 packets of information per second, nearly five times as much as the systems were designed to handle.

The computer systems tried to acknowledge a wake-up call sent from computers manipulated by the hackers asking to make a connection to the Internet site. The problem was the hackers concealed the true addresses of the computers initiating the connections, tricking the Panix computers into trying to synchronize with computers that essentially did not exist.

The Panix computers were to wait for 75 seconds for the initiating computers' response to their acknowledgments before they stopped trying to establish the connection. The attackers flooded the ISP's computers with so many of these unacknowledged wake-up calls that the Panix computers suspended all further processing.

Although this kind of attack was known to computer security experts, this was the first time that it had succeeded. Only days before, such an attack had been described in two publications that cater to hackers, *2600* magazine and *Phrack*, an online newsletter.

No company with an Internet connection is immune to this kind of assault, more commonly known as a *denial-of-service attack.* Although possible, prevention requires extraordinary cooperation among the Internet sites from which the attacks originate and through which they flow. In addition to denying service, outsiders can attack a system by *network scanning, IP spoofing*, and *password sniffing*. I define these attack methods in Chapter 7 and describe the ways in which computer systems are compromised, who breaks into systems, and why and how they do it. I'll also explain what you can do about it.

Chapter 1: Electronic Commerce & Security

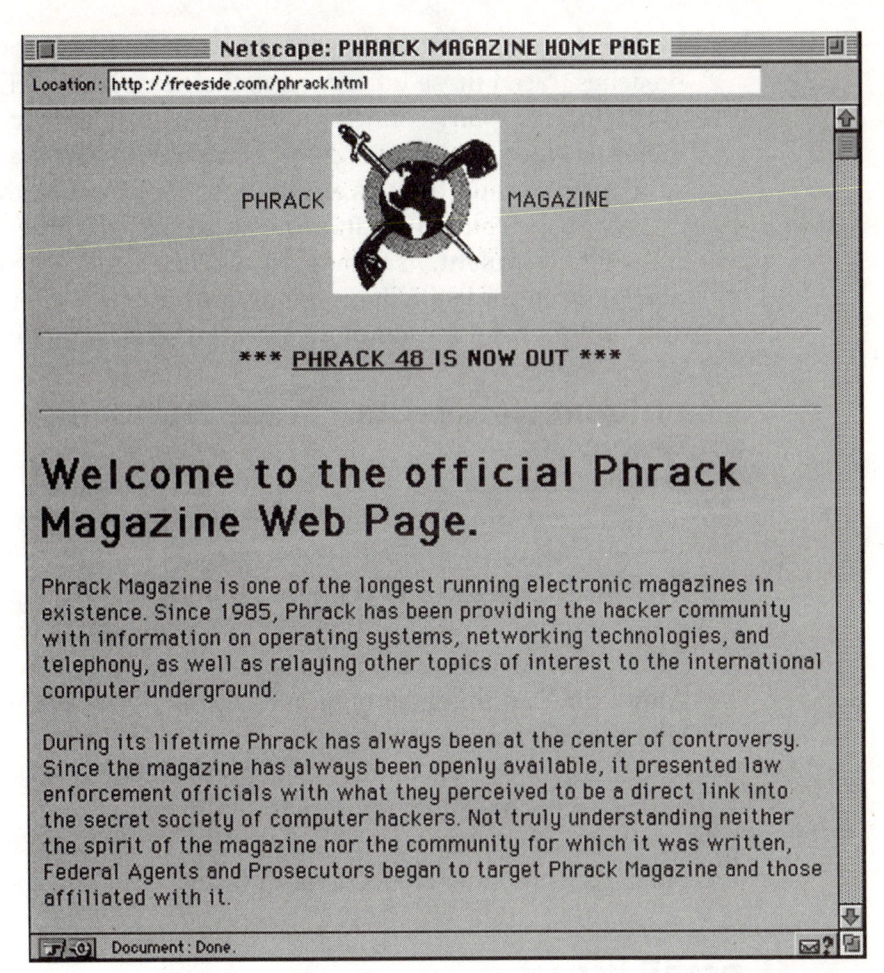

Phrack Magazine for hackers.

Insecurity Begins at Home

Despite the publicity generated by the antics and arrests of outlaw hackers, up to 80 percent of computer crimes are inside jobs, according to some estimates.

In a survey of 428 organizations conducted in 1996 by the Computer Security Institute (CSI), an association for information systems security professionals, 42 percent of respondents confirmed having experienced some form of intrusion or other unauthorized use of computer systems within the past 12 months.

More than 50 percent of those who experienced computer security breaches traced those intrusions to their employees, the CSI said.

When a company connects to the Internet, its security problems increase. Not until it's too late do companies learn that most problems are caused by its employees. For example, they might use the company's Internet access to hack other sites; transmit fraudulent, harassing, or obscene e-mail; download pornography and store it on the organization's computer system; and commit similar unauthorized or criminal activities.

Unwillingness to Take Security Seriously

Despite the proliferation of secure Web servers and digital transaction schemes, digital merchants aren't quick to embrace available security measures. Quite the opposite, in fact. After all the years I've covered the security beat, I've learned that most people do not take the threat of a security breach seriously until something bad happens—they lose a lot of business or nearly go bankrupt. Although "bad things only happen to the other guy," sooner or later we become the other guy.

Commerce servers tend to be expensive, and it takes a certain amount of technical know-how to set up and run a secure Web site. That's why the vast majority of Web merchants still are doing business using unencrypted credit cards.

Legal Issues

Digital merchants operating electronic storefronts and other Web sites must address such issues as copyright violation, defamation, pornography, privacy, and several other issues that traditional merchants seldom get involved with.

First Virtual Holdings Inc., one of the pioneers in developing a secure way to take credit cards over the Internet, is developing an applet that would turn a banner advertisement on a Web page into a point-of-sale system.

Created with a programming language called Java by Sun Microsystems, *applets* are small programs downloaded from Web pages and run on a desktop machine. They can perform various tasks to help digital merchants build Web sites with scrolling marquees, rotating 3D figures, stock market quotes that are updated in real time, and other razzle-dazzle effects.

First Virtual's applet, called VirtualTag, would let consumers buy a product simply by clicking on an advertisement. While that sounds like a great idea, Java has a number of security holes. If a thief broke into a Web site, substituted the VirtualTag with a phony tag that uploaded an applet that would pry open security doors or cause mischief in other ways on the shopper's machine, what would the merchant's liability be?

Doing business on the Internet poses many similar potential dilemmas. The bottom line is this: If you plan to set up shop on the WWW, consult your attorney first.

Privacy in Cyberspace

In cyberspace, will everyone know your business? If you're smart, they won't. The privacy of consumers is rapidly becoming one of the key issues that will shape the way you will do business online.

Consumer advocates are pushing federal regulators to clamp down on attempts by digital merchants, Internet service providers, advertisers, and marketers to gather information about Net travelers that later can be used to fuel marketing campaigns.

In a report entitled "Privacy and the NII," the National Telecommunications and Information Administration warns that, unless online industry voluntarily adopts uniform privacy guidelines, government-mandated privacy regulations or standards will result.

The message is clear: Digital merchants and others doing business on the Internet must devote more attention to protecting the privacy of their customers. That's where security comes in.

Assault on Encryption

Encoding messages to keep secrets from spies goes back at least to the time of Julius Caesar. Today, encryption is perhaps the single most important security tool digital merchants have to protect proprietary and other valuable information from crooks and snoops.

There are no restrictions on using secure encryption products in the United States, although the federal government and Congress have made several attempts to change that . . . and they're still working on it.

The Clinton administration has been pushing for a national encryption standard, based on technology called the Clipper Chip, with a backdoor that would permit federal investigators, armed with a court order, to decipher the encrypted communications of suspected wrongdoers.

In June 1996, Senator Charles Grassley (R-Iowa) introduced the Anti-Racketeering Act. The act contains provisions that could outlaw encryption that does not allow for government agencies to read the documents. The law would make it illegal to "distribute computer software that encodes or encrypts electronic or digital communications to computer networks that the person distributing the software knows, or reasonably should know, is accessible to foreign nationals and foreign governments, regardless of whether such software has been designated as nonexportable."

As you might expect, any encryption system with a provision that would permit someone to tap could not be truly secure. There has been quite a bit of opposition to the government's encryption laws by civil libertarians, computer industry groups, and several other organizations.

The federal government also has long been reluctant to grant export licenses for really good crypto products. The National Security Agency—the government's supersecret spy agency—must approve export licenses. So far, they're willing to do that only for crypto products they can crack.

In October 1996, the U.S. Department of State proposed letting software companies export products with more robust security features if they give the U.S. government a means to decode the data. The draft of the State Department's new criteria would let companies export with 64-bit keys to encrypt data, rather than the 40-bit keys permitted now. The keys would be 17 million times more difficult to break. The keys to decode the software would have to be placed in a special escrow account where federal investigators could access them under a court order to decode encrypted communications.

The State Department classifies encryption products as munitions, and requires you to obtain an export license to take a crypto product out of the United States to use while you're traveling on business or to install at one of your subsidiaries overseas.

That restriction has severely hampered U.S. companies from selling overseas products with encryption mechanisms that are widely thought to be bulletproof. Until these restrictions are lifted, there is no hope for universal standards for a wide variety of proposed electronic transactions systems based on digital money.

EDI Over the Internet

Many large companies use Electronic Data Interchange (EDI) to order goods and services and to process payments. Many businesses choose EDI as a fast, inexpensive, and safe way to send purchase orders, invoices, shipping notices, and other frequently used business documents. General Motors, Wal-Mart, and several other large corporations insist their suppliers and trading partners operate over EDI, to completely automate purchasing and inventory record keeping.

Networks managed by GE Information Systems, IBM Global Network, MCI Communications, Sterling Software, and other EDI companies are *private*—inaccessible by outsiders—and that's one of the main reasons they're secure. Lately, there's been a lot of talk about using EDI on the Internet, which would be far cheaper but less secure.

Information is transmitted from one computer to another without having to rekey it. When a retailer like Kmart needs to replenish its inventory, it doesn't issue a purchase order. Instead, the EDI system provides regular reports on inventory levels, and when the levels reach a certain threshold, the goods are shipped automatically. The system cuts weeks off the order-fulfillment process and makes it possible for retailers to get goods as they need them rather than pay to store warehouses full of inventory.

EDI also saves money by eliminating paperwork. The Giga Information Group, a research and consulting firm based in Norwell, Massachusetts, says U.S. companies spend $250 billion processing commerce-related paper documents such as purchase orders, invoices, and checks. In one year alone, U.S. banks process more than 60 billion checks.

So far, EDI has been too costly for most companies, but that might change soon, thanks to the growing popularity of the Internet. EDI's proponents envision that the Internet will become a universal communication medium among businesses all over the world, permitting, for instance, a microwave maker in Shanghai to automatically replenish depleted inventories at a regional distributorship in Springfield, Massachusetts.

An example is the GE Information Systems service called GE TradeWeb, launched in 1996, that operates entirely on the WWW to provide EDI for small businesses. The service allows anyone on the WWW to swap business documents and conduct electronic commerce with any of the network's 40,000 trading partners, each of which pays $1,000 per year for the privilege.

TradeWave Corp. in Austin, Texas, is selling Internet security tools for companies that want to create their own EDI setups over the WWW. The tools, marketed under the name TradeSecret, let companies build Virtual Private Internets (VPIs) using an encryption system called public-key cryptography.

With such activity, the WWW will eliminate use of EDI over proprietary networks, according to Forrester Research. In a recent report, the market research firm, based in Cambridge, Massachusetts, said the Web will give small companies the same benefits that large companies enjoy using proprietary EDI networks. Some 100,000 companies worldwide use EDI software and value-added networks, Forrester says, which is only about 5 percent of the potential market.

Many obstacles must be cleared first, not the least of which is security. Also of concern is a lack of standards that restrict companies from doing business with those in other industries.

EDI is expensive but private and secure; the Internet is cheap but wide open and not as secure. Although being open might seem to be a good thing, for digital merchants it isn't. If your company is connected to the Internet, almost anyone, anywhere in the world can travel to your doorstep. Not everyone visiting you is there to give you money. Some are there to pilfer your wares, disrupt your business, or snoop in your files. What's illegal in your country might be perfectly legal elsewhere, so you might have no recourse.

Moving On

Electronic commerce over the Internet and WWW is exploding, but computer crime is also on the rise. While many digital merchants worry about outlaw hackers and others breaking into their Web sites, they should be at least equally concerned about their own employees.

Is going into business on the WWW and the Internet worth the gamble? Definitely. However, prudent digital merchants will take advantage of whatever computer security solutions are available and remember that there are no magic bullets. Security is achieved in layers that include encryption, firewalls, secure Web servers, and more.

Throughout this book are many Internet addresses of sites you can visit to get security-related advice, software, and help when trouble strikes. Refer to Appendix A for many of these addresses.

Net Security: Your Digital Doberman

2 Risky Business

Does the value of conducting business over the Internet outweigh the risks? Yes, but only if you're aware of the pitfalls and are willing to take appropriate steps to protect the business and its affairs. In this chapter, I'll tell you about the many risks of doing business on the Internet, along with insight on who's committing crimes and how. In subsequent chapters, digital entrepreneurs will find out what they need to do to protect their organizations' systems and Web sites while connected to the Internet. I'll cover Internet security risks in general in this chapter and go over World Wide Web (WWW) security issues (and what to do about them) in a later chapter devoted to the WWW.

A survey of executives at 1,290 North American companies conducted in October 1995 by *InformationWeek*, a trade magazine, and Ernst & Young found that one in five companies suffered break-ins via the Net. The actual number of break-ins probably is much higher, since only half of the surveyed managers said they felt confident they would be able to detect a break-in via the Net, according to the survey report's authors.

Especially worrisome is that the Internet break-ins are occurring despite the widespread use of security measures. According to the survey, 70 percent of companies already protect themselves on the

Net with firewalls, about 60 percent with virus protection, and 15 percent with encryption. A firewall is a computer system or a combination of systems that sits between the organization's internal network and the Internet. Most (sometimes all if security is exceptionally tight) of the computer traffic in and out of the organization passes through this firewall, which is designed to scrutinize the traffic to see that it adheres to a set of security restrictions determined by the system administrator. For example, the system administrator can set up the firewall so that everyone in the organization can access the Internet to send e-mail but only certain employees are able to browse the WWW.

Why aren't these measures working? For one thing, the attacks are coming from a variety of sources, often from within the organization itself. Two, the intruders increasingly are able to find or develop sophisticated cracking tools. Even novice hackers are able to penetrate corporate sites successfully with some of these tools. Three, the need for security is not adequately appreciated by top executives in most companies, and as a result, security often is underfunded and understaffed.

Attractive Targets

There's no doubt that the risks to computers and information are on the rise. More people, including crooks, are using computers, which means that there also are more people capable of learning how to get around security barriers. Computers are being tied into networks, especially the Internet, making it possible for more people to get to your computer. Also, computers are being used for increasingly important things—financial records, secret formulas, and such—so they're becoming increasingly attractive targets for crooks.

What's to worry about?

- Disgruntled or dishonest employees and former employees
- Hackers, industrial spies, organized crime, and other crooks
- Viruses, worms, and other sorts of malicious software

It's the Employees

Real-life horror stories: A convicted child rapist working in a Boston-area hospital uses a former employee's computer password to retrieve telephone numbers stored in confidential patient files and makes obscene calls to girls. An employee at one of the nation's three nuclear weapons labs stores more than thirty thousand images of hard-core pornography on the lab's computers and distributes them over the Internet. And at the San Francisco national headquarters of a major stock brokerage firm, employees use the company's computer systems to buy and sell cocaine.

The vast majority of computer crimes—whether unauthorized tampering with company's files or planting a time bomb designed to destroy programs and data—are inside jobs. What's more, the ways employees are able to exploit or sabotage company computer systems are multiplying rapidly.

Internet + Employees = Trouble

Security takes on an entirely new dimension when a business puts its employees on the Internet. Even well-meaning employees pose risk to the enterprise: A naive employee may download files that contain viruses, post copyrighted material on the company's Web site, or provide links from the company's site to sites displaying offensive content.

Unhappy employees are even turning to the WWW to air their grievances and gripes about their current or former employers. One employee created the Kmart Sucks site, and at First Boston, a former employee posted the salaries of key employees, information that was previously a closely guarded company secret.

To what extent computer crimes committed by current and former employees are occurring is hard to say with any precision because many go undetected, and even when they are discovered, many companies keep quiet because they fear negative publicity. The best guess, by the Federal Bureau of Investigation (FBI), is that probably 80 percent of all computer crime is carried out by insiders.

In the same *InformationWeek*/Ernst & Young (IW/E&Y) survey mentioned earlier, more than half of 1,290 respondents reported financial losses. The cost of each security breakdown exceeded $100,000, and 17 respondents reported suffering losses of more than a million as a result of a single security incident. The greatest threat is not hackers, viruses, natural disasters, or other calamities but rather unauthorized access to information by insiders, IW/E&Y reports.

Disgruntled Employees

Companies should worry most about disgruntled employees who are intimately familiar with the inner workings of their employers' businesses and the computer systems they've installed. For example, in 1991 at General Dynamics in San Diego, a programmer—unhappy about the size of his paycheck—planted a destructive program called a *logic bomb,* designed to erase a missile parts inventory program. Another programmer found the program—named CleanUp—before it activated, after checking a list of programs queued up to run during a maintenance session. A Texas firm was less fortunate: After losing his job, a bitter programmer planted a logic bomb that wiped out thousands of critical financial records, nearly ruining the company.

Most disgruntled people are motivated by some emotional concern. They're unhappy about something the boss said or because they lost their jobs as the result of poor performance, layoffs, or other reasons. Dishonest employees, on the other hand, are motivated by the smell of money.

Dishonest Employees

Increasingly, employees are using company computer systems to engage in illegal activities or businesses on the side. Officials at Charles Schwab & Co. in San Francisco, for example, discovered in 1991 that a cocaine ring was operating among its headquarters employees. It turned out that sales were being arranged via the e-mail system. In another case in 1990 involving AT&T's London office, three employees were accused of setting up an outside company with a 900 number, which charges anyone who makes the call. They then programmed an AT&T computer to call the number repeatedly, ringing up huge bills, which AT&T paid.

With accounting and other functions on computers, any employee who has access to the systems could abuse them. Usually employees will manipulate data to cover up a theft of dollars or inventory, a technique that is sometimes called *data diddling*. If the company handles a large number of transactions involving fractions of cents, a crooked insider may round down numbers and siphon off the difference, a technique that is sometimes called *salami slicing*.

If you're a manager and you have key technical or financial staff members who never take vacations or regularly decline promotions, it may be because they are engaged in computer fraud. These people often are fearful that evidence of their fraudulent activity may be uncovered by other employees filling in while they are away.

Motto: Be Aware

Computer security would be less of a concern if senior managers took it more seriously and were aware of the risks, many security experts say. Smart companies, no matter how small or how large, recognize that information—and not just computers and related systems—is a strategic and competitive tool. At the same time, top executives at many major corporations also recognize that company information falling into the wrong hands may lead to lawsuits for failing to protect the privacy of company data, missed marketing opportunities, or even more disastrous consequences. Unfortunately, too many managers seem unaware how important their information is until they lose it.

One reason some companies are reluctant to implement proper security controls is out of concern that these controls tend to get in the way of productivity. The trick is to find the right balance between reasonable security limits without the sort of controls that would seriously impair productivity and lax security that would permit a disgruntled employee from tampering with or stealing the firm's data.

Not all information needs to be stored under lock and key. There's little sense, for example, in protecting information that is routinely handed out at trade shows. On the other hand, it makes a lot of sense to protect information related to a new product that the company plans to launch. Somewhere between the two extremes is a level of security that is right for your firm. Security experts say that the typical company needs to protect only about 5 to 10 percent of its data. In fact, protecting up to 80 percent of a company's data would use up only 20 percent of a security budget; it is the final 20 percent of data that would be most costly to protect, the experts say.

Wild & Crazy Employees

Who says there is never anything new under the sun? Today's computer-using employees are coming up with new and increasingly novel ways to squeeze a buck out of employers' information systems. Here are some of the more prevalent scams and mischief:

- Data diddling—entering false data to falsify records, say to cover up the theft of inventory or embezzlement. It is by far the most common way employees use computers to rip off the boss.

- Eavesdropping on e-mail and voice mail messages.

- Using e-mail to anonymously send coworkers and others sexually explicit, racist, or other offensive messages.

- Deliberately planting a virus or some other form of malicious software or using the company's system to transmit viruses to other sites.

- Salami slicing—stealing a zillion dollars one cent (or even a fraction of a cent) at a time by rounding down numbers and siphoning off the difference. That's not worthwhile in most companies, but if you work in a bank or a financial institution that handles lots of financial transactions, it might be something to worry about.

- Stealing information that can be resold to a competitor or held for ransom.

- Using the computer system to run a business on the side or to engage in illegal activities such as gambling, drug dealing, or distributing of hard-core pornography.

- Stealing computers, peripherals, or copyrighted software that the company has paid for or created for its own use.

Outsiders Looking In

There are all sorts of people who might want to get into your company's information systems or Web site.

They range from curious computer users who probe simply to find out what's stored there to outlaw hackers who want to destroy data or cause mischief in other ways. There are industrial snoops as well as ex-cold war spies now working for their countries' foreign intelligence agencies. Then there are organized crooks who want to steal information that may be useful in committing crimes or that they can hold for ransom.

Generally, the hackers will take advantage of known weaknesses such as systems running File Transfer Protocol (FTP), old versions of Sendmail with security holes, or other system utilities with loopholes. They also will try things like default user IDs and passwords and tools such as Crack (for cracking UNIX system passwords) or Security Analysis Tool for Administering Networks (SATAN) to look for vulnerabilities. Internet administrators should run these tools against their own systems before someone else does.

Traditional criminals also have discovered the Internet, using it to facilitate illegal drug transactions, child pornography distribution, fraud and the exchange of information related to criminal enterprises. In many cases, it's simply criminals using a new means of communications just as they have used the telephone and mail systems.

Potentially, this group may target financial and ordering systems to obtain money or merchandise through outright theft via the network.

The industrial espionage aspect is one of the most troublesome, because these groups have resources generally not available to hackers and ordinary crooks.

Both the traditional criminal and the industrial espionage agent tend to be very sophisticated. Rather than try to access systems direct, they may scoop up huge amounts of data traveling the Net—like a whale sucking up plankton. If you analyze enough data, no matter how innocuous, revealing patterns start to emerge.

Outlaw Hackers

Outlaw computer hackers have gotten a lot of attention in recent years—probably more than they deserve. They've been featured in movies such as *Sneakers*, starring Robert Redford and Sidney Poitier, and in books such as *The Cuckoo's Egg*, a tale about three hackers who worked for the KGB in exchange for cash and cocaine.

Their latest exploits also are chronicled on the front pages of most of the major newspapers in the country. Most recently it was Kevin Mitnick, a notorious hacker who was captured early in 1995 after being on the run for two years. His chase and capture were the subject of three books and led to at least one movie deal.

According to the FBI, during the time that Mitnick was on the run, he allegedly broke into dozens of computers—in one case downloading twenty thousand credit card numbers belonging to customers of an Internet service provider. The company, Netcom On-Line Communication Services, did not know that the theft had occurred until contacted by subscribers. Mitnick also is accused of breaking into the computer of Tsutomu Shimomura, a noted security expert, and downloading thousands of security-related files and programs. His eventual capture in Raleigh, North Carolina, made the front page of *The New York Times*. Shimomura and John Markoff, a *Times* reporter, detailed the chase and capture of Mitnick in a book called *Takedown*.

Call it Billy the Kid on the Electronic Frontier. However, just like the tale of William Bonney, it's at least equal parts fantasy and fact.

No Lex Luthors

Contrary to the popular view, the average outlaw computer hacker is not some super-evil genius like Lex Luthor in Superman comics or even some above-average technical wizard. He (and they are almost always young men) doesn't get the information he needs to break into systems by diligently probing the systems' electronic innards and then vaulting the electronic fences designed to keep him out. Most often, he'll cajole or wheedle an unsuspecting employee into giving him a password. He'll say he's a new employee and needs help logging in to the system, or he may masquerade as a service technician and need the employee to help him test the system in some fashion. (Hackers call this "social engineering.") If that technique fails, he'll rummage through refuse containers looking for computer manuals, disks, or scraps of paper with access codes written on them. This decidedly low-tech approach of "dumpster diving" or "trashing" is one of the productive sources of information that hackers and other outsiders can use to penetrate systems.

Sweet Talk & Social Engineering

Despite the whole arsenal of technical tools in their kit bags, hackers often will resort to using the telephone to get the information they need to break into your computer. Hackers call it "social engineering", and it's one of their most potent ploys to get passwords and collect information about the systems they intend to attack and more.

Here are some social engineering scams that you should be aware of:

The New Kid on the Block

The hacker assumes the role of a new employee unfamiliar with the organization's information systems and procedures for logging into the systems. He'll say that he's new on the job and ask for step-by-step instructions on how to log in. Perhaps he'll say that he's tried hard to follow the directions he's been given for logging in but has been unable to do it. He may play on the employee's ego in hopes that the employee will be induced to show off just how well he or she really understands system procedures.

Hackers often use this ploy right before or right after business hours. This gives the caller what would appear to be a legitimate reason for asking someone outside of his own department for assistance.

The Boss
The hacker acts like the man or woman in charge. In a corporate setting, that person might be a department head or a personal assistant to a chief executive, while in a military setting, it's probably a high-ranking officer. Typically, the hacker will angrily make demands, pressuring the employee into doing whatever it takes to get the nasty boss off the phone.

The Helpful Hand
In this scenario, the hacker pretends that something has gone wrong with the organization's computers and he is a technician calling to fix it. In all likelihood, he will attempt to create a sense of rapport, perhaps engaging the unwary employee in conversation about the fallibility of computers and expressing annoyance at how much trouble they are. Most people can relate to this—nearly everyone has had a problem with his or her computer. Usually, the hacker will ask the employee to log in and enter his or her password, all the while telling the hacker exactly what is being keyed in so that the "technician" can pinpoint the difficulty. This call is likely to come during a busy time of the day—often late afternoon—so that the harried employee will cooperate in order to get back to work quickly.

This last scenario often is carried out via e-mail. An employee receives a message, purportedly from the system administrator, asking the employee to send the impostor passwords, or change his or her password to something that the impostor can use to penetrate the system, for example. It is such a common ploy that America Online must regularly remind its customers that system administrators will never ask subscribers for their passwords and not to send anyone their passwords.

Although it certainly helps to be a whiz kid, many hackers succeed in breaking into systems simply by following instructions provided in publications such as Phrack, a free electronic newsletter for hackers. Also, people are fairly predictable, and hackers know this. They know that most people are going to choose passwords that remind them of a person, pet, place, or personal interest so that they are easy to remember. Try using such passwords as SEX and LOVE to get into half the computer systems in the country, and you'll probably be inside poking around within minutes.

Hackers are persistent. They don't mind trying hundreds of different keystroke combinations until a computer door clicks open.

Hackers also stay on top of the latest developments in their field, and they have good tools—just like many young business professionals these days.

Hackers thrive on information in the same way that other people thrive on sumptuous cuisine. What sort of information? Stuff like how to crack passwords that open the portals of computers, how to make a red box with which to make free telephone calls, how to masquerade as someone else when you send e-mail on the Internet, and how to boldly go where no one has gone before. Information is a currency in many places in hackerdom. To get a look at some of the better files on cracking computer systems stored on bulletin boards frequented by hackers, you might be asked to pay up first with a purloined long-distance telephone credit card number.

Hackers are apt to target systems during holidays and other times when they are less likely to be noticed. It also gives them more time to crack systems and rummage around. During the year-end holiday season in 1995, for example, a group calling itself the Internet Liberation Front broke into computers operated by IBM and Sprint. They also clogged some business sites with e-mail warning corporate America against turning into a "cesspool of greed."

I Spies

Glasnost may have occasioned a thaw in East-West relations, but many of the spies who have come in from the cold are as busy as ever. Instead of spying on one another, however, foreign intelligence agencies are focusing on industrial espionage, with U.S. companies as one of the prime targets.

Foreign intelligence operators have turned to industrial espionage aimed at helping their domestic corporations better compete in a global marketplace. The FBI estimates that up to 20 foreign nations are actively engaged in industrial spying. Many of those countries, such as Japan and France, are U.S. allies.

The theft of information gleaned from computers and communications networks may be costing U.S. corporations billions of dollars per year; no one really knows for sure. There's no way to find out because information theft is difficult to detect, and companies that find out the hard way seldom talk publicly about it.

Organized Crime

Criminals are getting computer smarts along with the rest of us and are setting up operations in cyberspace with the intent of infiltrating and robbing businesses.

In hearings before the House Committee on International Relations, Louis Freeh, the director of the Federal Bureau of Investigation, warned that Russian organized crime has been busily engaged in computer crime, along with terrorism, nuclear smuggling, and a whole string of other criminal activities.

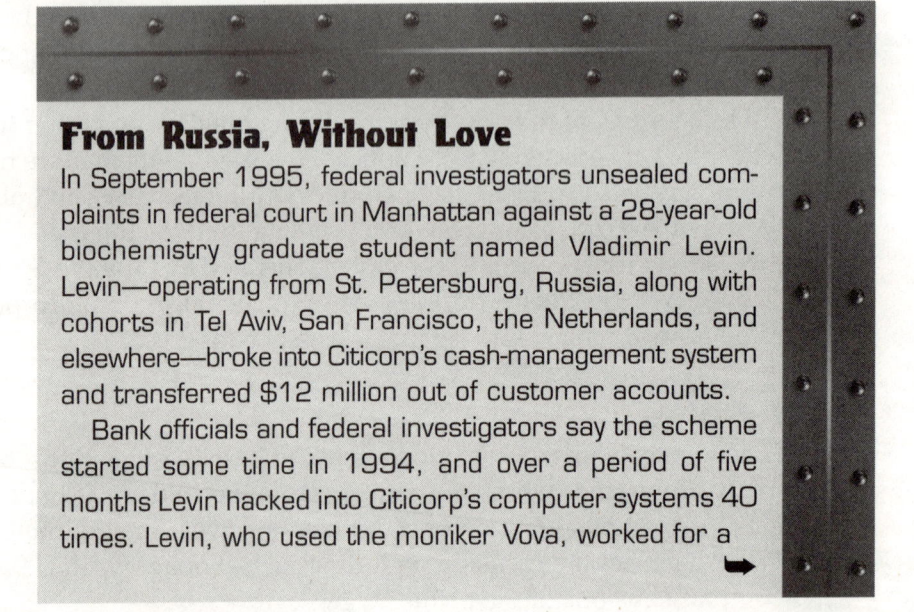

From Russia, Without Love

In September 1995, federal investigators unsealed complaints in federal court in Manhattan against a 28-year-old biochemistry graduate student named Vladimir Levin. Levin—operating from St. Petersburg, Russia, along with cohorts in Tel Aviv, San Francisco, the Netherlands, and elsewhere—broke into Citicorp's cash-management system and transferred $12 million out of customer accounts.

Bank officials and federal investigators say the scheme started some time in 1994, and over a period of five months Levin hacked into Citicorp's computer systems 40 times. Levin, who used the moniker Vova, worked for a ➡

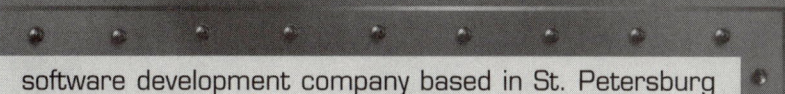

software development company based in St. Petersburg called AO Saturn.

From his office at AO Saturn, Levin went to work on Citicorp's cash-management system computers at 111 Wall Street in Manhattan. He posed as one of Citicorp's customers and succeeded in diverting funds belonging to the customer to a bank account in Finland. One of his cohorts went to the bank and withdrew the stolen funds.

Later that year, in July, Levin transferred funds from Citicorp's system to a bank account in St. Petersburg. The take up to that point was about $300,000, according to court documents. Then in August, Levin moved $522,000 from two banks—one in Jakarta, Indonesia, the other in Buenos Aires, Argentina—to a BankAmerica account in San Francisco that belonged to two confederates, Eugene and Katerina Korolkov.

The two banks discovered the illegal transfers and tracked them to the Korolkov accounts. Although Citicorp notified BankAmerica and asked the bank to freeze the funds, someone managed to withdraw tens of thousands of dollars out of the Korolkov account. Up to this point, some $400,000 had been withdrawn from bank accounts in the United States and overseas.

When Korolkov learned that his access to the funds had been blocked, he flew to St. Petersburg, according to the FBI, to confer with Levin. The two apparently concluded that their system had a few flaws and decided to open several new accounts and redirect the funds they stole to those accounts.

Meanwhile, Citicorp, aware that someone was illegally moving funds out of its electronic funds transfer (EFT) system, alerted the FBI and set up a war room in Manhattan to track and ensnare the criminals, whoever they were.

Citicorp also secretly asked customers around the world to keep an eye out for unusual activity and to alert the bank as soon as any funds were diverted.

In August, Katerina Korolkov opened accounts at five banks in San Francisco and passed the account numbers to Levin. Soon after, Levin again starting moving funds—about $200,000 in all—into the Korolkov accounts. That activity caught the attention of officials at a bank in Buenos Aires, who notified Citicorp. Citicorp in turn froze the five new accounts and alerted the FBI in San Francisco, according to court documents.

Katerina Korolkov appeared at one of the banks and attempted to withdraw $31,000 but was told that the accounts had been frozen because there was suspicion that the funds were obtained illegally. When Mrs. Korolkov left the bank, the FBI followed her to her apartment and a day later arrested her.

The FBI says that while Mrs. Korolkov was under surveillance in San Francisco, a Levin confederate was busy opening accounts at five banks in Tel Aviv. On August 24, the same day that funds were being diverted into the San Francisco accounts, $940,000 was moved from a bank in the Bahamas to the Tel Aviv accounts.

The following day, Tel Aviv police, notified by the FBI, arrested a Russian named Alexi Michailovich Lachmanov when he attempted to withdraw some of the diverted funds.

According to the federal criminal complaints, from the end of August to October the bank robbers succeeded in transferring funds to bank accounts in the Netherlands and Switzerland. Citicorp quickly moved to have the funds frozen. In Rotterdam, Dutch police arrested two men, Frans Bul, a Dutch citizen, and Vladimir Voronin, a Russian, when they appeared to withdraw at least some of more than $1.6 million in stolen funds.

By reviewing telephone records, investigators were able to determine that the hacker was working from AO Saturn in St. Petersburg, but they still didn't know precisely who they were after. In December, Mrs. Korolkov, still sitting in jail since her August arrest, began cooperating with authorities and laid out the robbery scheme to the FBI. She gave the FBI the information it needed to go after Levin and Korolkov (who were obviously already known to the FBI).

Lacking an extradition treaty with Russia, the FBI could not ask Russian police to arrest the two men. But they caught a break in the case several months later. In September 1995, the FBI received a tip that Levin was planning to travel to Great Britain and Korolkov to the United States. Scotland Yard picked up Levin as he stepped off a plane at Stansted airport, near London. The FBI got their man at Kennedy Airport.

With the exception of Bul, the Dutchman, the bank robbers are either already in jail or awaiting extradition to the United States. Bul is free and likely to remain so because the Dutch refuse to extradite one of their citizens to face prosecution in the United States.

Just how Levin managed to break into the electronic funds transfer system remains unclear, even now. Hacking EFT systems is thought to be nearly impossible because of the many security checks and balances that such systems depend upon. Levin, however, was somehow able to obtain valid user IDs and passwords, which he used to carry out his scheme. For that reason, the FBI suspects that Levin may have had help from people inside the company. Citicorp denies that any of its employees were involved. What is known is that Levin made his transfers during normal business hours in order not to draw attention to his activities.

In all, the bank robbers succeeded in moving $12 million. Citibank says that all but $400,000 has been recovered.

Cyberterrorists

The federal government is becoming increasingly concerned that terrorists eventually will mount attacks on financial networks, air traffic control systems, power grids, defense computers, and other systems that are at the core of the country's economy and well-being.

The Pentagon revealed in 1996 that the previous year it had suffered some two hundred fifty thousand attempted intrusions into its computer systems by hackers on the Internet, more than twice the number detected in 1994. Nearly a hundred sixty thousand of the break-ins were successful, the Pentagon added. This alarming number of attacks prompted the White House to set up a task force called the Critical Infrastructure Working Group, staffed with representatives of law enforcement and defense agencies. The panel's mission is to recommend policy and draft legislation for protecting national interest networks and computer systems from attacks and mishaps that might shut them down.

Thus far, there has been little hard evidence of terrorist attacks aimed specifically at key information systems. In Europe and elsewhere, information systems have been shut down by terrorists armed with low-tech weaponry such as explosives, but it probably is inevitable that terrorists will target business and other systems using viruses and other high-tech methods.

Competitive Intelligence Gatherers

Competitive intelligence operators, for a price, will gather information about a company or an industry, tailor-made for your interests. Partly because of the growth of computer networks, which makes it easier than ever before to collect information, competitive intelligence (CI) is a booming business. CI operators usually can find out an awful lot just by digging through publicly accessible databases, newspapers, market research reports, and a wide variety of other sources.

However, there's no reason to believe that every CI operator is honest and would never resort to illegal or at least questionable practices to get a look at some of your bet-the-business information. The lesson here is: If you can't afford to lose it, take care of it.

Attack Scenarios

No matter whether it's a teenage hacker or an ex-KGB spy who's trying to pick your pockets or steal your wares, there are numerous ways to go about it. In fact, there's no way that I could tell you about all of the ways that a system can be compromised, even if I knew them all (and I certainly don't).

The Computer Emergency Response Team (CERT) gathers reports from Internet sites that have been or are under attack and keeps track of the sort of attacks that are most common. I'll give you a run-down on those and a few others.

According to CERT, some of the top techniques that hackers use to break into computers connected to the Internet are:

- Password attacks either by means of sniffers or Trojan horses
- IP spoofing
- Attacks aimed at Sendmail, the mail handler in UNIX
- Network scanning

Sniffing Out Passwords

Many of the tools that hackers use to crack computer systems were designed originally for troubleshooting, tweaking performance, and assessing security measures. A *sniffer*, for example, is used to evaluate the performance of a *local area network (LAN)*. While it's doing things like checking the flow of packets on a LAN, it's also collecting passwords.

Here's the scenario: A hacker breaks into a machine and installs a packet sniffer, specially designed to harvest user names and passwords when users log in.

The sniffer grabs the first dozen or so characters entered during these sessions, which contain the logons and passwords, and stores them in a hidden file. Later the hacker will retrieve the secret file and use the logons and passwords to break into the system and attempt to get root access through a cracked root password or by exploiting another vulnerability.

This attack is one of the most common. It's difficult to spot, in part because sniffer programs are tiny in comparison to most. In one episode, a system's administrators were unaware that a sniffer had been installed until it had captured so many logons and passwords that the machine's hard drive became full and crashed the machine.

These sniffers often are installed along with a *Trojan horse*, a program that appears to be benign but in fact is designed to mask its evil intent: to hide sniffer activity on systems on which they are installed.

Protecting Passwords

What can be done about password attacks? System administrators can shut off Telnet, FTP, and other services that require users to authenticate themselves first by logging in with a user name and password. That means they will not be able to download files, which might not be such a bad thing. However, they still will be able to send and receive e-mail, read newsgroup postings, and search the World Wide Web, among other I-way activities that don't require authentication.

System administrators also should be alert that an intruder or unauthorized insider may attempt to install a sniffer and regularly scan the system for unexplained files. The administrators should scan the system for files that were installed without their knowledge or whose purpose is unknown. There are several tools that can help in this sort of monitoring, such as Tripwire, which can be used to monitor inexplicable changes in files and directories.

Passwords should not be sent over your network in clear text— that is, in plain English. Instead, they should be encrypted so that they cannot be read even if intercepted.

Passwords are the first line of defense in most systems, and attackers will try to crack passwords if they are not able to install a sniffer. If your company runs a UNIX-based network, your system administrator should run Crack, an automated program that tries to guess user passwords.

Make sure that this activity is sanctioned by the company: An employee who runs Crack risks being prosecuted for attempting to break in. That's what happened to Randal Schwartz, a former Intel employee who was convicted in July 1993 in Oregon under a state law that makes it a felony to alter a computer system without authorization and to gain access to a system with the intention of theft. Schwartz claims that he was merely attempting to test security limits and intended to inform company officials of flaws that he uncovered. Schwartz was placed on probation for five years and assessed $170,000 in legal fees and 480 hours of community service, among other penalties.

If you do nothing else, make sure that your employees use common sense in selecting their passwords. That means no passwords like SEX and LOVE or passwords that are the same as user names. Here are some additional guidelines for your employees:

- You should instruct employees to choose passwords that are at least six characters long and have a mix of uppercase and lowercase characters and symbols like @#$%^&*.

- Employees can create passwords that are easy to remember but tough to crack, by using acronyms or pass phrases. For example, TA5WTLYL is easy to remember if you know that it stands for "There are 50 ways to leave your lover"! For even stronger security, they can create a pass phrase such as "ShepicksSHEllsbyTheCshore" that includes a combination of uppercase and lowercase characters.

- Employees who have a hard time remembering their passwords might want to trying creating passwords by picking out a pattern on the keyboard. Hackers know that many people like to use things like FRED and QWERTY, so you need to be particularly imaginative and try something like 1=q]a'z/g (figure it out).

- Make sure employees know they are not to share passwords or give them out to anyone.

- Require employees to change passwords at least every 90 days. Change them immediately if you suspect that any password has been compromised.

- Instruct employees not to key in their passwords while others watch.

- Employees should not use the same password for all of the computer systems they use—including their automatic teller machine (ATM), commercial online account, desktop computer, and laptop computer.
- Don't allow an unlimited number of attempts to crack a password. There are password programs that will shut someone out after three unsuccessful attempts to enter the correct password.

IP Spoofing

Data travels in "packets" over the Internet. Each packet is contained in an electronic envelope and, like any envelope, has "from" and "to" addresses—Internet Protocol (IP) addresses. If my machine regularly connects to your machine, we set up a trusted system that basically says: I know you're a good guy; and you know I'm a good guy, so we don't have to continually check each other out every time we want to send messages back and forth.

Hackers can take advantage of this trusting relationship in order to break into one of our machines: They create packets with, for example, my address and send them to your machine. Your machine thinks I sent the packets and allows the connection.

CERT says there was a surge in IP spoofing in 1995. The year began with an advisory about IP spoofing, and attacks continued throughout the year. In a matter of weeks during the summer, CERT says that it received more than 170 reports of IP spoofing attacks or probes, many resulting in successful break-ins. CERT also found that several sites mistakenly believed that they were blocking such packets, and other sites had planned to block them but hadn't yet done so.

Once inside your system, interlopers can modify it so that they can nab user logons and passwords. They can also install a *back door*, a secret entryway into the machine that they can use later. What makes this attack so sneaky is that the hackers can circumvent security measures such as those used by systems that require people on the system to use password generators before connecting to other machines. The hackers are able to hijack the connection after authentication takes place.

Spoof Proof

If you monitor packets using network-monitoring software such as netlog, look for a packet on your external interface that has both its source and its destination IP addresses in your local domain. If you find one, you are currently under attack.

Another way to detect IP spoofing is to compare the process accounting logs between systems on your internal network. If the IP spoofing attack has succeeded on one of your systems, you may get a log entry on the victim machine showing a remote access; on the apparent source machine, there will be no corresponding entry for initiating that remote access, CERT says.

When the intruder attaches to an existing terminal or login connection, users may detect unusual activity, such as commands appearing on their terminals that they did not type or a blank window that will no longer respond to their commands. CERT says that you should encourage your users to inform you of any such activity. In addition, pay particular attention to connections that have been idle for a long time.

Sendmail Attacks

One of the most compelling reasons that people want a connection to the Net is to send and receive e-mail. If you have a direct connection to the Internet using a UNIX machine, you'll be using Sendmail, the electronic mail handler in UNIX.

Attacking Sendmail is a common technique, and there are many ways to do it, with more being uncovered every day. The goal, of course, is to trick Sendmail or to *hamstring* it in some way that will enable the intruder to get into the system and take control.

System administrators often rig Sendmail to suit their own needs, blindly unaware of the security implications. What Ellis Island was to generations of immigrants, Sendmail is to UNIX. It's how you get into the system. A number of loopholes have been exposed in Sendmail in recent years. For example, a savvy user can exploit the debug option to get root access or use a loophole in the error message header option to read any file on the system, thereby attacking Sendmail in an attempt to get the password files.

If that's what you're planning to use, make sure that you have a current release with all of the known fixes.

Stay Awake

The main thing is to make sure that your system administrator stays abreast of upgrades and patches designed to make Sendmail more secure.

Most Internet connections are made via systems running UNIX or its clone Linux. The good thing about UNIX and Linux is that they are exceptionally flexible and can be tailored in Tinkertoy fashion in a variety of unique ways.

It's this openness that many system administrators find so appealing. Unfortunately, this openness also makes UNIX and Linux difficult to secure. Fortunately, many of the loopholes are known, and patches to close them are widely available. There also are many security tools such as Tripwire, Computer Oracle, Password System, and COPS, a collection of utilities, that can be used to spot potential security vulnerabilities in a UNIX system. Best of all, most are free. You can get COPS, Tripwire, and other tools from ftp://info.cert.org/pub/tools/ and many university sites.

Network Scanning

One method that has become popular among computer intruders is a freeware network-scanning tool called Security Administrator Tool for Analyzing Networks (SATAN) or its commercial counterpart, Internet Security Scanner (ISS). SATAN scans several computers within a predetermined range of IP addresses, looking for certain types of configurations that are known to make these systems vulnerable to attack.

Suppose your company has set up an anonymous FTP server to make it easy for outsiders to download demo software, files containing product descriptions, and the like. SATAN will look at how an anonymous FTP server is configured; misconfiguring it is common. For example, it may be possible for an intruder to seize a copy of the complete file containing passwords from the server and execute a command to mail it back to himself or herself.

SATAN was the subject of considerable scrutiny and controversy when it was released in 1995 by Dan Farmer and Wietse Venema. SATAN was to be used by security and network managers to examine their own networks for security holes. Critics countered that SATAN could be used as readily by hackers to probe for weaknesses through which they could enter and attack sites.

SATAN is like a security system that constantly monitors all the entryways into your house and then sends an alert that the front door has been left ajar. However, the alert can be sent just as readily to the burglars as to you.

Smarter Scanning

Okay. What can you do to make sure that your organization's systems are safe from these attack scanners? Run SATAN or ISS against your own system, pinpoint any weak spots, then close the loopholes.

Don't be lulled into a false sense of security, however. Automated scanning programs identify only about a dozen potential problem areas. There are many other loopholes that you need to worry about.

Denial-of-Service Attacks

Not all attacks on computer systems are intended to steal information or carry out any of the other sorts of crimes that immediately come to mind. There are also attacks that rob the system owner of the use of the system itself, perhaps by crashing it, consuming disk space or resources, or jamming it with packets. In security-speak, these sorts of attacks are called *denial-of-service* attacks.

Two common denial-of-service attacks are breaking into anonymous FTP servers to use the system's disk storage and other resources and e-mail bombing. Both disrupt systems and, if left unchecked, can shut them down. There are other ways to make systems inaccessible or unusable, of course. I mention some others in Chapter 6 on WWW security and risks.

Anonymous FTP

Many companies set up anonymous FTP servers that outsiders can access, usually to upload and download files of various kinds. For example, Ventana Communications has an anonymous FTP server for its authors to send book chapters. You might be thinking of offering a similar service.

I mentioned earlier that these servers often are misconfigured and thus easier for an outsider to tamper with.

Hackers break into FTP servers and use them to exchange secret pirated software, passwords, and tips for breaking into other systems and files. Once the word is out that a server has been compromised, it quickly becomes an electronic meeting place where intruders swap software, messages, and so on. If enough of this activity takes place, the system may crash or run out of disk space, thereby making it inaccessible to legitimate users.

Hackers also may use an anonymous FTP server as a backdoor or jumping-off place to break into other systems inside the target company.

Go Figure, Configure

The obvious thing to do is make sure that your anonymous FTP server is properly configured. You can use SATAN or ISS, for starters, to identify potential trouble areas.

Internet Security Scanner (the company, not the software) also publishes a Frequently Asked Questions (FAQ) on FTP loopholes and how to close them. The FAQ is available from info@iss.com, as well as on many Web sites (see Appendix B).

There are other monitoring tools, such as Tripwire, that flag files that have changed without explanation and alert you to unusual activity.

Ensure that your site is using the latest software and that all available patches have been applied.

Keep an eye on server activity and regularly check directories where software is uploaded. Also check for hidden directories, which typically begin with spaces or special characters, as these may conceal unwanted information or files.

E-mail Bombing

Authors Joshua Quittner and Michelle Slatalla wrote a book called *Masters of Deception: The Gang that Ruled Cyberspace* in 1995, chronicling the antics of the Masters of Deception, a once-notorious gang of hackers.

Despite the book's sympathetic portrayal of the group and its activities—which led to the arrest of its members by the U.S. Secret Service and the imprisonment of some—it was not well received by some in the hacker community.

In the fall of 1995, a group calling itself the Internet Liberation Front hijacked routers on the Internet and directed them to flood Quittner's e-mail address and that of *Wired* magazine, which had run an excerpt of the book. Some 30 megabytes worth of messages (actually a copy of the group's manifesto, sent to the same address many times over) jammed Quittner's e-mail box on America Online, causing it to "sink like a stone," in Quittner's words.

Pump massive amounts of data into a single site, and the site's network connections may fail, the system may run out of disk space, or it may crash. Any person or company may find themselves on the receiving end of an e-mail bomb attack. Unfortunately, there is little you can do to prevent it.

The attacker does not use a personal e-mail account to send the mail, and it is nearly impossible to trace the sender's identity.

If your organization relies on e-mail over the Internet for business communications, you would be wise to have a backup plan all set to go in the event that your site or your service provider is the target of an e-mail attack. You could set up a few MCI mail accounts for this purpose, for example.

E-mail *spamming*, when an outsider may send everyone at a site the same message, has consequences similar to e-mail bombing, although it may not originate as a deliberate attack. The problem can be compounded if everyone receiving the message decides to respond, rebounding messages over the network like a sort of electronic tidal wave.

Unlike an e-mail bomber who uses a phony account, many e-mail spammers use legitimate accounts, at least long enough to send the spam, and then change accounts. Many spammers, obviously, use phony names when they open accounts to protect themselves from the ire of those who receive their unwanted messages.

Close-Shave Protection

Denial-of-service attacks via e-mail probably are impossible to prevent. Once the attack is launched, however, you can configure your router to reject any messages with the address from which the attack originated.

Forging E-mail & News

An attacker can cause all sorts of mischief by masquerading as a legitimate employee of your company and by forging e-mail, newsgroup postings, or both.

The attacker might assume the identity of a company executive and send e-mail to employees, asking for the release of sensitive or proprietary information. This ploy often is used to trick employees into revealing their passwords, for example. Or the attacker may send offensive or otherwise damaging e-mail to customers, suppliers, and others the company does business with.

There are at least a few ways an attacker can make it appear that an e-mail message originated from your company's Simple Mail Transfer Protocol (SMTP) server: The most common one is for the attacker to connect to the SMTP port and send e-mail messages; no passwords or other codes are needed to make the connection. Fake e-mail originating from the site will seem legitimate, at least to recipients who do not know how to read or don't bother to read the message header, which contains the sites that the message passed through before reaching the intended target.

Keep E-mail Private

Sensitive or proprietary e-mail should never be sent in plain English. The message should be encrypted and signed with a digital signature. The next chapter will tell you everything you need to know about encryption and digital signatures using Pretty Good Privacy (PGP) and other public-key encryption programs.

Make sure your employees are alert to the prospect that e-mail may be spoofed and instruct them not to reveal passwords or other sensitive information just because they received an e-mail message asking for it.

Configure the mail server so that no one can connect to the SMTP port. Transmission Control Protocol (TCP), the communications protocol used by the Internet, uses an abstract object called a port to identify a destination within a computer system. Each port is given a unique number. You can prevent someone from connecting to the SMTP port by preventing someone from listening to or originating connections from that port number. Also ensure that incoming mail is logged to facilitate tracing suspect e-mail messages back to their origin.

If your employees receive several messages purportedly from other employees, look at e-mail message headers for clues as to where the messages are coming from. That's not always possible, especially if the messages were sent by an intruder who connected to your site's SMTP site.

Also instruct employees not to use the company's systems to post messages to newsgroups; if you permit it, set limits on what may appropriately be posted. Offensive messages signed by *employee@yourcompany'snamegoeshere*.com reflect badly on your company.

Cybermicrobes Are Out to Getcha

There are two kinds of people: Those who have been hit by a virus and those who will be hit by a virus. The experts reckon that new viruses are being created at the rate of two to three a day. According to the National Computer Security Association (NCSA), a trade group for information systems security professionals based in Carlisle, Pennsylvania, there are some 8,000 viruses on the loose. There are several ways that your PC can be infected, including getting the virus from commercial, shrink-wrapped software.

There are all sorts of cybermicrobes—viruses, worms, Trojan horses, bombs (both logic and time)—that are capable of trashing your data faster than a New York minute.

If you give your employees Internet access or you accept uploads from outsiders, it is not a matter of if but when your site will be tagged by a virus or some other sort of cybermicrobe.

Viruses Multiply

The chances of your personal computer becoming infected are greater than ever, according to NCSA and many virus experts. One reason is that personal computers and networks also are multiplying rapidly, making it even easier for viruses to spread. Another reason is that virus creators are devising increasingly sophisticated *stealth* viruses that are more difficult to detect and more difficult to eradicate once they have been discovered.

Ominously, new viruses are becoming increasingly more insidious and more destructive than were prior generations.

The Bug Is Born

Fred Cohen was a student at the University of Southern California in 1983 when he decided to construct what many experts now say was the first computer virus. Cohen told me he created the virus to demonstrate the need for computer security. These days no one knows for sure what motivates virus writers.

What Is a Virus?

Cohen, the virus guru, came up with this definition: "A virus is a program that can infect other programs by modifying them to include a, possibly evolved, version of itself." What does that mean? Basically: Viruses latch on to programs like leeches and replicate themselves like bunnies.

There are three basic parts to any virus: a mechanism that permits it to go forth and multiply, a trigger that causes it to activate, and a payload—sometimes harmless, often not.

Send in the Clones

Viruses are not programs in the sense that they are not able to do things on their own the way real programs do. Computer viruses work much like their biological counterparts. That flu bug you caught last month, for example, needed a host (the cells in your body) to thrive. Computer viruses also are like that: They need a host (a program) in order to work.

Virus Launchpads

Typically, viruses clone themselves by preying on computer programs, which they use as launchpads to replicate themselves. Most viruses fall into one of two categories: those that infect files and those that infect the boot sector of a floppy or hard disk. Some viruses latch on, like parasites, to files ending in .EXE or .SYS; others attack only files ending in .COM. Viruses that attack both files and boot sectors are called *multipartite* viruses.

File Infectors

Programs in IBM PCs and compatibles that use either the MS-DOS or PC-DOS operating systems are called executable files because that's what they do when they're opened: They execute. File-infecting viruses attach themselves to these *executable files*, and when a file executes, they go along for the ride. Most of these files end with .COM or .EXE, although some viruses can infect executables ending with .DLL, .SYS, .OVL, .OVR, .PRG, or .MNU.

Boot Infectors

Boot-sector viruses infect the area of a floppy or hard disk that contains the information the machine needs to boot or start up. Without a boot sector, your computer will not "pull itself up by its bootstraps," which is where the term "boot" comes from.

The boot sector is the first thing that loads into memory when you turn on the PC. A boot-sector virus replaces a portion of the boot sector with its own code so it loads before DOS when you turn the system on. Usually, these viruses load themselves into memory and infect other programs as they are called. Boot-sector viruses get into your system only if you boot from an infected floppy. I would have figured that few people boot from floppies these days. However, a list published by an IBM research lab of the 15 most prevalent viruses revealed that all were boot-sector viruses.

Pulling the Trigger

A virus may activate as soon as the program is run, may wait until a particular date (such as March 6—the trigger date of the infamous Michelangelo virus), or may activate after a certain number of times a file is accessed or some other activity takes place. During the entire time before the virus delivers its payload, it is busily infecting every program it comes in contact with.

Delivering the Payload

Once a file is infected, what happens next? It's payload time. If all that viruses did was attach themselves to files, most people wouldn't care much and would go on to worry about more important things. It's what happens when the virus drops its payload that gets everyone's attention.

The Jerusalem virus attaches itself to a file and does nothing more, but it does it over and over again, making the infected program swell. Eventually it fills the PC's memory and causes it to crash. Even leeching onto a file can be bad sometimes, but usually it's the payload that is most worrisome.

No Easy Answers

With so many viruses on the loose, there is no generic way to describe what they do. Their actions range from the relatively innocuous, such as displaying a message such as "Have a nice day," to the catastrophic, such as causing your hard disk to reformat itself and wipe clean programs and data.

Here are a few viruses to give you an idea what some of them do:

- Cannabis, a poorly written virus, displays the message: "Hey man, I don't wanna work. I'm too stoned right now."

- Ripper, a particularly mean-spirited virus, randomly trades pairs of numbers of an electronic spreadsheet.

- Ping-Pong virus (also called the Italian and the Vera Cruz) causes a ball to bounce back and forth, from one side of the screen to the other. It is quite common.

- Disk Killer displays the message: "Disk Killer, Version 1.00 from Ogre Software. Now killing disk. Please do not power down the machine." The virus then causes the hard drive to start formatting itself.

- Prank is one of the new breed of viruses written in Microsoft Word Basic, the computer language used in Word to create macros (macros are sequences of commands that can be triggered using one or two keys). Prank infects Word documents and causes them to be saved as templates. What is unique about this virus is that it was the first to infect documents and to also work across both PCs and Macs.

By the way, although many viruses are designed to delete files or cause the PC to malfunction, the fact that these beasts can cause damage is not what makes them viruses. Some are intended as harmless pranks, although they're seldom funny to those whose PCs happen to be infected.

It's going to get worse before it gets better.

How Are PCs Infected?

The single most frequent way viruses get into PCs is on an infected floppy disk. However, it's also possible to download a program with a virus attached from a bulletin board system or even one of the nationwide commercial online services. It's also possible to download documents that have been infected with a macro virus that has been attached to an e-mail message. Downloading alone is not enough to infect the computers; opening the attachment is what causes the virus to activate.

Usually, one of the programs on the disk has been infected. The disk is inserted into the PC, the infected program is opened, and the virus begins infecting whatever programs reside on the PC's hard disk drive. Stick another disk into an infected PC, and there's a good chance that disk will be infected, too.

Even a blank disk can harbor a virus. Any disk that has been properly formatted contains an executable program in the boot sector. Where there's an executable program, there could be a virus.

You should be wary of any floppy disk—no matter where it came from. I've seen viruses on commercial, shrink-wrapped software; on setup and utility disks that came with modems, printers, and other peripherals; on demo disks from manufacturers; and on disks used by well-meaning coworkers who shuttle work between home and office. If you're unsure where the disk came from, don't insert it in your machine or at least protect your PC with the different kinds of antivirus software that I'll tell you about shortly.

Telltale Signs

Virus writers want their creations to spread as widely as possible before they deliver their payloads. So your machine can be infected by a virus for a while before you actually notice it.

Let's say you're trying to complete an important project when, suddenly, strange or inexplicable things start happening. Here are the telltale signals that a virus has invaded your PC or Mac:

- The size of programs increases dramatically, but you didn't do anything to change them.

- The date or time stamp on files and programs has changed and isn't what it should be.

- Programs take longer to load or run than normal or simply stop working altogether.

- The hard or floppy disk drive starts up even though you haven't touched the keyboard for some time.

- You have less hard drive space or memory than before.

- You get more than the expected number of error messages on the screen.

- Strange objects start appearing on the screen. You might see a bouncing ball; a message demanding you free Eddie, Frodo, or some other person you've never heard of; or worse, a message such as "Your hard drive is being formatted."

- You can no longer print.

- The computer reboots for no reason.

- The computer keeps crashing (and it has nothing to do with those mail-order memory chips that you just installed).

Virus Antidotes

The only way you can be sure if the problems you're having are being caused by a virus is to run antivirus software.

You'll need four virus antidotes in your kit bag: a scanner, file-change detector, virus-activity monitor, and disinfectant. You want to be able to:

- Identify both known and unknown viruses
- Stop them before they infect your PC
- Get rid of those that manage to slip through the radar

Most antivirus software being sold today offers a combination of these features. For example, some scanners detect and remove viruses, and some file-change detectors also include virus-activity monitors. Terms such as scanner, file-change detector, and so on may be easy to understand, but they're not universal or standardized.

Scanning for Trouble

Scanners are designed to look in files, boot sectors, and other places viruses are known to hide for strings of code or signatures that are unique to each virus. Some scanners can pick up on these signatures even if the file containing the virus has been compressed using PKLite or LZEXE, two popular shareware programs, to compress and decompress files.

The advantage of scanners is that they are able to tell you exactly what virus has invaded your system, usually before the virus has a chance to deliver its payload.

The drawback is that, if the virus is unknown, a scanner's library will not contain the unique bits of code needed to run an ID. Also, if the scanner must check thousands of files against its database of thousands of virus signatures, it could be a long time before you can actually get to work. Last, a scanner cannot readily detect *polymorphic* viruses because they are continually forging new signatures. To get around that, those who sell antivirus software are working on scanners that use *heuristics*—an artificial intelligence of sorts—to aid in detection of polymorphic viruses.

Signatures Need Updates

Scanners are only as good as yesterday's virus.

You also need to be able to keep up with new viruses as they come along. One way to do that is to periodically download the signatures of new viruses as they are discovered. Antivirus software vendors routinely provide these signature updates as a service to their customers. The updates usually are released quarterly, although some companies such as McAfee Associates release them as often as every couple of weeks. They're mailed to you if you registered the software or they are available for download from the vendor's bulletin board system and from online services such as America Online, CompuServe, and Prodigy. Keeping current with updates can be time-consuming and, in some cases, costly, however.

Looking for Changes in File Sizes

A *file-change detector* takes a snapshot of a file's contents using either the unique *checksums* or *cyclic redundancy check (CRC)* characters contained in the file's code. The detector periodically checks to see whether the checksum or CRC has changed, indicating a virus may have attached itself to the file.

A file-change detector will check the entire disk, check every program as it launches, or check just the files you specify. You want to be able to exclude files that change frequently for legitimate reasons. Otherwise, you'll be alerted all the time that something wacky is going on, requiring you to stop what you're doing to investigate. Before long, you start to ignore the warnings, and that's when the wolf shows up.

The beauty of a file-change detector is that you can use it to ensnare unknown viruses; it's one of the few weapons in your armory that can.

Virus Watchdogs on the Alert

Virus-activity monitors also act as watchdogs on the alert for suspicious activity signaling a virus on the grounds. These monitors are said to *terminate and stay resident (TSR)*, meaning they sit in memory and check files before they run to alert you when executable files are modified, among other things. Most folks refer to them simply as TSRs.

TSR monitors are not very effective against unknown viruses. Another problem with them is that, because they reside in memory, they can slow system performance or take up space better used by applications. Worse, they can be outsmarted by a well-designed virus, such as a boot-sector virus that runs before the TSR has had a chance to load.

Like file-change detectors, monitors tend to set off false alarms easily.

Removing Viruses

Some antivirus programs will automatically disinfect or remove viruses from your system, but they should be used cautiously. There is some debate just how well these programs actually work. Viruses sometimes only partially infect programs and other times they may damage applications so that they will no longer run, even after the virus has been removed. Assuming that you have backups, the most effective approach is to erase infected programs completely and restore them from your backups.

Help Ward Off Cybermicrobes

Your best protection against viruses is to make regular backups of programs and valuable data. That said, here are some tips for coping with the virus problem:

Establish a company policy about downloading. If you permit it, set up a quarantine machine on which all new programs can be checked out before loading them on to one or more of the company's regular machines.

Use antivirus software that scans, detects changes in files, and monitors for viruslike activity. Make sure that your employees use scanners with up-to-date signatures. Instruct them to run the scanner whenever they suspect a problem, load new software, or insert disks of questionable origin. Insist that they do not circumvent the antivirus software's system of checks and balances or turn off its features to save time when they boot up.

Be wary of shareware and other software that has been downloaded from bulletin board systems because you can't be sure they're clean. And stay away from pirated software. Copyright violations aside, you have no idea where the software originated.

Write-protect your disks so that no virus can attach itself to a program on the disk. Store the disks in a secure place when they're not in use. It's still worthwhile to check these disks from time to time; someone may have removed the write-protect tab or the disk could have been infected before the tab was put on.

Also write-protect documents, directories, and operating system files. If a virus tries to modify a file, it will trigger an error message, alerting you that something might be awry. Use ATTRIB to make all of your .EXE and .COM files read-only. This will protect you from many poorly written viruses. Caution: Some programs will not work in read-only mode.

If your system administrator manages to spot a virus before it causes damage, try to trace it back to its source and close that entry point. That's not always possible, of course, because many viruses will have been lurking undetected for months.

Consider the prospect that the antivirus software itself has been infected. Some viruses specifically target antivirus software (after all, they're programs too), and some virus creators think it's funny to upload to bulletin board services (BBSes) copies of an antivirus shareware program in which they have embedded a virus. Top-shelf antivirus software will do a self-check for viruses. If yours does not, get one that does.

Although it helps to purchase software only from a reputable vendor, that is by no means a guarantee of getting a virus-free disk. Microsoft, Aldus, Novell, and countless other companies have distributed shrink-wrapped software that was infected by a virus, which often happens while the disks are being duplicated at an outside disk-duplicating service.

Never copy software from other computers, because you don't know where that software came from.

Scan before backing up. You run the risk of backing up a virus at the same time you're backing up everything else. If the backups are infected (and it happens a lot), you're out of luck and may be out of business. To be safe, do a full scan of the hard disk just before every backup to make certain that your backups are virus-free.

Worms, Trojan Horses, Bombs

There are other forms of malicious software in addition to viruses. They include Trojan horses, worms, and logic and time bombs. Fortunately, they're rare. Unfortunately, they're not always easy to defend against, as you'll see.

Trojan Horses

You know the story about the mythical Trojan horse, right? A malicious software program called a Trojan horse can ostensibly be useful but also contains hidden functions such as a virus, a trapdoor permitting intruders to enter a system, or a time or logic bomb that, when triggered, causes damage. The most famous, if you can call it that, was the AIDS Information Introductory Disk, Version 2.0, which was distributed free with copies of a U.K. computer magazine. That program was designed purportedly to help a person evaluate his or her susceptibility to being infected by the AIDS virus. It did that, but it also contained a virus that in some cases destroyed data and programs. In other instances, it altered file names and shifted them into hidden subdirectories. The Trojan horse was activated randomly after it had been installed on the user's hard disk drive.

If you unluckily plug a Trojan horse into your PC or Mac, there's no telling what will happen or just what you should do about it. If it's carrying a virus, you should be able to detect and remove it using any of the popular antivirus programs on the market. However, the Trojan may do something else, such as locking or scrambling files unless you register the program or send money or something else. In many cases, Trojans do their damage the minute they are run, so you may not have much opportunity to react.

What you may have to do is erase a few programs and reload them from your backups. Luckily, you don't see many Trojan horses harboring viruses.

Worms

Worms differ from viruses in at least one significant way: They're programs that don't need other programs to deliver their payloads. They tend to travel networks, like the Internet, and are sophisticated enough to try different password combinations and look for loopholes in programs that are running on the targeted system. They don't infect other programs, although they may carry a virus that does. You don't see a lot of worms in the wild, and it's unlikely you will if your PC is not connected to a network.

The Worm That Ate the Internet

Internet security was propelled into the national consciousness in November 1988 after a Cornell University computer science graduate student shut down thousands of computers with a worm program that he had crafted. Robert Tappan Morris, the son of a National Computer Agency computer expert, later testified at his trial that it was an experiment gone awry. He set out to prove that he could deposit a single copy of his worm on every Internet host the program could connect to. Instead, a programming error caused the worm to replicate wildly, clogging computer memories and causing the computers to shut down. When the dust cleared about three days later, it was estimated that more than six thousand computers had been attacked and crippled. The worm did little damage, but system downtime and the time used to combat and eradicate the worm have been estimated in the hundreds of thousands of dollars.

The worm program exploited well-known loopholes in system software based on the Berkeley Software Distribution UNIX system and by taking advantage of vulnerabilities in host-site security policies. Despite the many months of ensuing publicity about the Internet and the ease with which the worm traveled from one host to another, Internet security remains poor. In fact, many installations have yet to close the loopholes the Morris worm was able to wriggle through.

There's no standard way to get rid of a worm. In the case of the Internet worm, the solution simply was to turn off the machine and disconnect it from the network to keep the worm from returning.

Worms currently aren't a problem on PCs and Macs.

Logic & Time Bombs

True story: A programmer created a customized database under contract for a small importing company. Sometime during the project, the programmer began to suspect that he wasn't going to get paid for his work, so he planted a set of instructions that, when activated, would wipe out his program. Evidently, the importing company was not satisfied with the work and refused to pay the programmer the entire amount agreed upon. One day, the programmer phoned the company and, under the pretense of making some final adjustments to the program, directed an employee to activate his hidden instructions. In a matter of minutes the custom database program and all of the company's data that had been laboriously entered into it were wiped clean. The programmer had planted a logic bomb, one designed to activate under a precise set of circumstances.

The Logic of Bombs

A *logic bomb* monitors the system's activity. When a defined event takes place—such as opening a particular file X number of times—it detonates. It often, but not always, causes damage. A time bomb is a variation of the logic bomb—the difference being that it detonates at a certain time or on a certain date.

There may not be a lot you can do to stop a logic or time bomb from being planted in your system because they're usually hard to detect.

The Computer Emergency Response Team

The Internet worm heightened awareness of the key vulnerabilities of the Net: In times of crisis, system administrators had no central coordinator to turn to for assistance. CERT, established within weeks of the worm attack, now provides that badly needed support. Funded by the Department of Defense Advanced Research Projects Agency, it is based at the Software Engineering Institute at Carnegie Mellon University in Pittsburgh. The group's charter is to:

- Provide Internet-wide security policy, direction, and coordination

- Support ongoing efforts to enhance Internet security

- Obtain involvement of Internet users, software vendors, technical advisory groups, and federal agencies regarding security issues

- Become an integral part of the structure that emerges to manage the National Research Network

CERT tracks security incidents, issues security alerts, and distributes bulletins on how to close loopholes and other useful information. Check ftp://info.cert.org to find a treasure trove of information. While writing this book, I visited the site to find out how many security incidents CERT logged in 1995, the most significant security problems they found, and their problem-fixing suggestions. I would like to acknowledge their help in writing this chapter.

Moving On

Several recent research studies by information systems security associations and law enforcement agencies confirm that the risks to computers and information are on the rise. More people, including crooks, are using computers, which means that there also are more people capable of learning how to get around security barriers. Computers are being tied into networks, especially the Internet, making it possible for more people to get to your organization's computer systems. Also, computers are being used for increasingly important work—financial records, secret formulas, and such—so they're becoming increasingly attractive targets for crooks.

Does the value of conducting business over the Internet outweigh the risks? Yes, but only if you're aware of the many ways that security can be compromised and willing to take appropriate steps to protect the business and its affairs.

The vast majority of computer crimes—whether unauthorized tampering with company's files or planting a time bomb designed to destroy programs and data—are inside jobs. Security takes on an entirely new dimension when a business puts its employees on the Internet. Even well-meaning employees pose risk to the enterprise: A naive employee may download files that contain viruses, post copyrighted material on the company's Web site, or provide links from the company's site to sites displaying offensive content.

The chances of your organization's personal computer becoming infected by computer viruses are greater than ever, according to professional associations such as the NCSA. One reason is that personal computers and networks also are multiplying rapidly, making it even easier for viruses to spread. Another reason is that virus creators are devising increasingly sophisticated stealth viruses that are more difficult to detect and more difficult to eradicate once they have been discovered.

There are many outsiders who are intent on peering inside corporate systems, especially those that are being used for electronic commerce. They range from curious computer users who probe simply to find out what's stored there to outlaw hackers who want to destroy data or cause mischief in other ways. There also are industrial snoops as well as ex-cold war spies now working for their countries' foreign intelligence agencies. Then there are organized crooks who want to steal information that may be useful in committing crimes or that they can hold for ransom.

Many of the ways that outsiders can penetrate computer systems are well known. Generally, the hackers will take advantage of known weaknesses such as systems running File Transfer Protocol (FTP), old versions of Sendmail with security holes, or other system utilities with loopholes. They also will try things like default user IDs and passwords and tools such as Crack (for cracking UNIX system passwords) or Security Analysis Tool for Administering Networks (SATAN) to look for vulnerabilities. Internet administrators should run these tools against their own systems before someone else does.

3 Encryption & Digital John Hancocks

When you buy a microwave oven in a department store and pay for it with a credit card or check, one of the first things the clerk may ask for is some form of identification. If you offer your driver's license, the clerk may check to see that the name on the card or check is the same as the one on your license. Then the clerk gives your face a once-over and compares it to the mug shot on your license. And a particularly conscientious clerk may compare the signature on the credit card or check with that on your license.

In security-speak, this process is called *authentication and verification*. You proffer your license to authenticate yourself (establishing that you are indeed Joe Jones), and the clerk verifies your identity by comparing your name, address, photo, and signature.

This process works reasonably well when you do business with someone face-to-face. But what happens when the credit card number or check travels electronically? How does the customer authenticate himself or herself and how does the merchant verify the customer's identity?

Electronic commerce requires additional safeguards that generally are not needed for face-to-face commerce. What happens if the credit card number or check is intercepted en route from the customer to the seller? What's to prevent someone from adding a couple of extra zeroes to the amount and diverting the funds to a Swiss bank account? What about the confidentiality of the transaction? If the check were used to buy weapons, for example, for a would-be Third World dictator, that's not something you want made public. How do you maintain the confidentiality of financial transactions and other sensitive information that you wish to remain private?

The answer in a single word is *encryption*. Encoding messages to keep secrets from spies goes back to at least the time of Julius Caesar. Today it is perhaps the single most important security tool that digital merchants have to protect proprietary and valuable information from crooks and snoops.

Banking on Encryption

Encryption is at the core of a wide range of new and emerging digital money technologies, whether it's digital cash, digital checks, or digital coupons. Encryption is being used to:

- Scramble credit card numbers and other sensitive financial data before sending them across networks so that even if intercepted, they cannot be read and used

- Encode electronic mail messages and important documents, the contents of which must remain confidential

- Sign documents, providing irrefutable proof of the authenticity of buyers and sellers involved in financial transactions or of anyone else who creates a document

- Protect private or confidential information stored on your desktop or notebook computer

Even if someone steals your computer or circumvents security controls in other ways and manages to get a peek at your files, proper encryption means he or she will be unable to read them.

And that's just for starters! In this chapter, I'll introduce you to the basic concepts of encryption and digital signatures, and I'll talk about how encryption is being used in securing financial transactions and the emerging security standards on the Internet and World Wide Web. Encryption is so deeply ingrained in the security of electronic commerce that you'll also read about it in chapters covering digital cash technologies and the companies involved in setting up digital cash systems, as well as in several other places throughout this book.

Encryption Crash Course

Encryption is the process of scrambling a message so that only the people you want to read the message are able to do so. The military and banks are the most active users of encryption, for pretty obvious reasons. Both have a lot to lose if someone intercepts important messages such as "The troops will land at Calais at dawn" or "Transfer 8 million francs to Swiss bank account 876-5434-000."

Encryption can be accomplished with hardware, software, or a combination of the two. Generally speaking, the process of encryption and *decryption* is faster with hardware than software, which is an issue if you do a lot of it over networks. Even so, in the past decade, software encryption applications have become quite common.

What are the basic objectives of encryption? In security-speak, encryption can be used to provide for privacy, identification, authentication, verification, and nonrepudiation. Here's the translation into plain English:

- *Privacy*: Protecting the confidentiality of financial transactions and other sensitive data in the event they are intercepted

- *Identification*: Proving that the sender and recipient of important information are indeed who they claim to be and not impostors

- *Authentication*: Ensuring that payment instructions and other critical information has not been tampered with
- *Verification*: Affirming the trustworthiness of a message by positively identifying the message sender and the authenticity of the message
- *Nonrepudiation*: Preventing the sender of an encrypted message from denying having sent a message or claiming that the message was sent by someone else

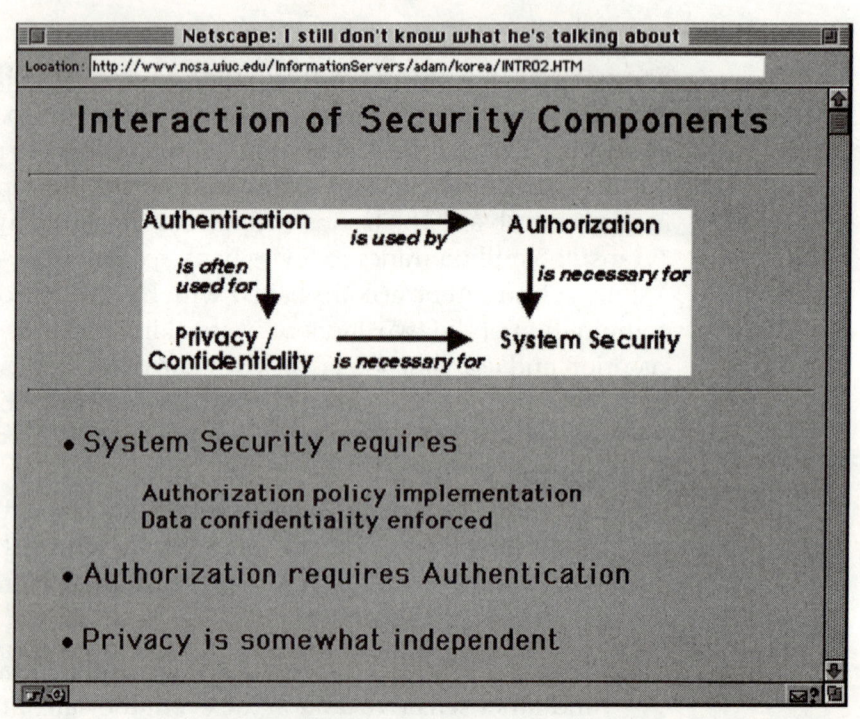

Interaction of security components.

As you can see, there is some overlap in the terms. Authentication applies to the process of authenticating a message sender and recipient, as well as the process of verifying that the integrity of the message remains unbroken.

Plain Talk About Text

Crypto experts define encryption as the process of taking *plaintext* and scrambling it into *ciphertext*. Decryption is just the opposite: transforming ciphertext back into plaintext.

Plaintext is just what it sounds like—plain English, or any other language; ciphertext looks like gibberish. Sometimes plaintext is called *cleartext* because it is sent in the clear, in readable form.

Plaintext is scrambled into ciphertext by either transposing or changing the order of the plaintext characters or by substituting cipher characters or symbols for plaintext characters. A formula or algorithm is used to scramble the message, usually by translating the messages into a series of numbers.

Cryptanalysts—people who specialize in breaking codes—have become quite adept at figuring out how algorithms are put together. As a result, *cryptographers*—people who specialize in creating codes—hit upon the idea of using a key along with the algorithm. The key is a number—typically several digits long—that is used with the algorithm, to specify precisely how plaintext characters should be transposed or arranged. To make it even tougher to crack, some systems use one key to encrypt and another key to decrypt.

The Secret Is in the Keys

There are two basic types of crypto schemes widely used today: Symmetric and Asymmetric.

Symmetric algorithms are based on using the same key to scramble and unscramble messages. This technique is also called *secret-key, single-key,* and *one-key crypto*.

Asymmetric algorithms are based on using one key to encrypt and another key to decrypt. This technique is more commonly called *public-key crypto* because one key is kept private and the other is widely or publicly distributed.

Keys used in single- and public-key cryptography are generated by the encryption program. Often, you have the option of deciding how many digits long the key will be. The longer the key, the more difficult it is to crack. For example, if you tried every possible combination of numbers in an 8-bit key, it would take fractions of a second to crack it, even using the typical home computer. In comparison, if you tried every possible combination in a 56-bit key, it would take some two thousand years, using a super-computer capable of a million calculations per second. Doubling the number of keys would not take twice as long, but infinitely longer (billions of years) using the same supercomputer.

Crooks Do Simple Crypto

Here's how encryption works in its simplest form: Let's say Bonnie and Clyde are crooks who want to swap messages that only the two of them can read. First, they choose the single-key encryption scheme they'll use. Then they decide what key they'll use to scramble and unscramble messages. The key is used to change letters to their corresponding numbers so that ABC is 123 (an obviously simple key).

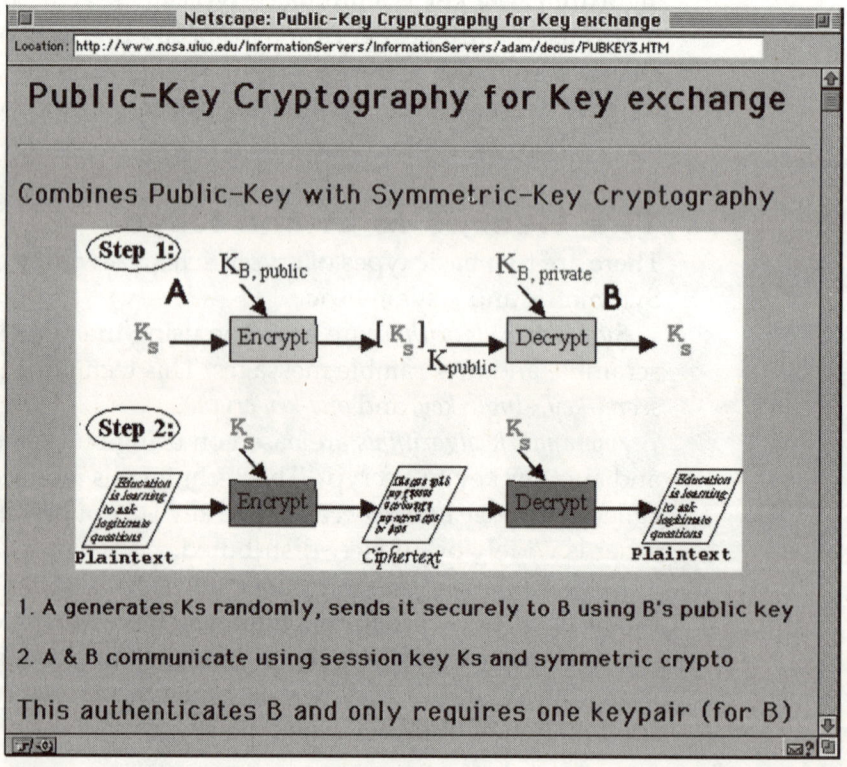

Public-key cryptography for key exchange.

Later, Bonnie sends Clyde a message that in plaintext reads something like this: "The bank job will go down at 10 o'clock tomorrow. Bring your gat." Before sending the message, Bonnie scrambles it using both the crypto scheme and the key she and Clyde decided upon. Now the message appears to be unreadable gibberish. When Clyde gets the message, he runs it through the decryption, using the same key Bonnie used to scramble it.

Suppose a rival crook discovers the key Bonnie and Clyde are using and has eavesdropped on their electronic mail. Since he knows the key that Bonnie used to scramble the message, he too can read the message. The fink calls the police explaining the crooks' plans to rob the bank. How does the fink know the key? Perhaps he overheard Bonnie and Clyde talking while sitting in the booth behind them; or maybe one of them wrote the key on a scrap of paper and carelessly left it in a bar, where their rival found it; or perhaps their key was simply too easy to crack. In any case, Bonnie and Clyde did not manage their secret key very well. The process of deciding on a key and keeping it safe from prying eyes is called *key management*. Poor key management equals poor (or no) security. That's one of the big problems with one-key crypto systems.

One for You, One for Everybody Else

Because the secret-key idea is not feasible for electronic commerce, *public-key (PK) cryptography* is used instead. PK crypto was invented in 1976 by Whitfield Diffie and Martin Hellman as a way to solve the problem of managing keys.

Here's how it works: Each person gets two keys, a public key for scrambling messages and a private key for unscrambling them. You guard the private key with your life, while everyone else uses your public key to scramble their messages before sending them to you.

Once the messages are encrypted, only you—the person with the corresponding private key—can read them. Not even the person who wrote the message can read it once it has been encrypted with your public key.

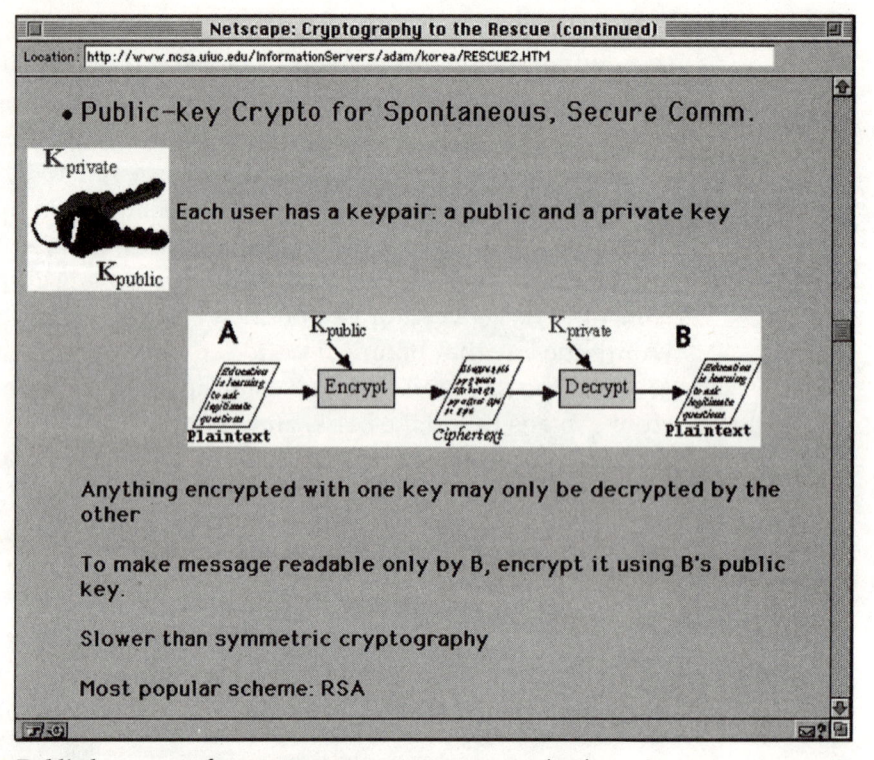

Netscape: Cryptography to the Rescue (continued)

Location: http://www.ncsa.uiuc.edu/InformationServers/adam/korea/RESCUE2.HTM

• **Public-key Crypto for Spontaneous, Secure Comm.**

Each user has a keypair: a public and a private key

Anything encrypted with one key may only be decrypted by the other

To make message readable only by B, encrypt it using B's public key.

Slower than symmetric cryptography

Most popular scheme: RSA

Public-key crypto for spontaneous, secure communication.

    The private key doesn't have to be shared with anyone, which is a big improvement over single-secret-key crypto systems. You should store your private key in a safe place so that it can't be used by someone other than yourself. The best way to do that is to encrypt the key itself (using a secret-key crypto scheme), assign a password to it, and store it on a disk. As a further precaution, lock the disk in a cabinet or some other secure storage unit.
    If you lose your private key or forget the password assigned to it, you're out of luck. You won't be able to encode or decode messages. You'll need to generate a new key using your public-key encryption program and let everyone know not to use the old public key to scramble messages they intend to send to you because you won't be able to read them.

The Best of Both Worlds

Although public-key cryptography is industrial-strength security, that does not mean private- or secret-key crypto is no longer useful. PK crypto's scrambling and unscrambling are slow in comparison to secret-key crypto, which is certainly a concern for anyone who has to send and receive a lot of long messages.

One solution is to combine the best of public-key and secret-key crypto system security. The public-key system is used to encrypt a secret key, which is in turn used to scramble the message. Earlier I mentioned that PK crypto was devised to make it possible to securely exchange keys. It is still very good for that purpose.

Digital Envelopes

When you can use both single-key and public-key cryptography in this way, you are creating what amounts to a *digital envelope*. The secret key is encrypted using the public key of the person you are sending the message to. That creates the digital envelope for the encrypted message. The message and envelope are sent to the recipient. The recipient opens the digital envelope by decrypting it with his or her private key, retrieves the secret key, and uses that key to decipher the message.

Digital John Hancocks

If I send you a message (even an encrypted one), how do you know that it is really me, not someone else, who has intercepted and changed the message? For that matter, how do I know that you are who you say you are and not someone masquerading as you in order to intercept my messages?

Normally, there is no way for the sender and recipient to know for sure that the other really is who he or she claims to be and that the message hasn't been intercepted or tampered with while in transit.

That's where *digital signatures* come in. They serve to identify you, much in the same way as your real signature on your credit card, checks, and driver's license. It's a bit of data unique to you. The experts call this notion of verifying the identity of both message sender and recipient *authentication*.

You can put more faith in a digital signature than in a handwritten signature. The recipient of your message can verify both that the message originated from you and that it wasn't accidentally altered or tampered with after it was electronically posted. What's more, the digital signature cannot later be repudiated or disowned by the signer as a forgery.

In addition to encoding messages, you can use PK crypto to create this digital signature, one that may even hold up in court. Let's say Bonnie decides to send Clyde and their gang the message, "Don't forget to bring the dynamite and safe-cracking tools." Bonnie uses her private key to scramble the message, at the same time creating a digital signature based on a calculation with the private key and the message itself. Only a piece of the message—a unique sequence of characters—is encrypted with the private key. This unique sequence is the equivalent of a digital fingerprint, and that's what is sent as the signature along with the original message. It's done that way because it's faster than sending the entire message twice.

Everyone in the gang can read the message. Because only Bonnie has the private key, the gang also knows that only she could have sent the message. Later, if the cops arrest the gang for conspiring to rob a bank, Clyde and the other gang members can point to Bonnie, claiming that she was the one to devise the scheme. Bonnie can't deny sending the message or claim someone impersonated her because the message has her unique digital signature.

The experts call this process of not being able to deny having signed and sent a message *nonrepudiation*. This is a key concept for digital merchants, because digital signatures can be used not only to establish someone's identity but also to ensure that, once a deal is signed, sealed, and delivered, neither party can deny it.

Public Servers for Keys

How can you find someone else's public key? Usually, you can ask him or her (usually through e-mail) for the key, and that's all there is to it. You can also check one of the *public-key servers*.

If you're using a public-key scheme, you want as many people as possible to be able to find out what your public key is so they can exchange encoded messages with you. The best way to do that is to register your public key with a certifying authority called a public-key server. This certifying authority will ask you for certain information that can be used to establish your identity and will send you a certificate to verify that this key is actually yours. The certificate also keeps someone from masquerading as you. There are several thousand public-key servers, but you don't have to send your key to every one of them. Just send it to one server, which will in turn send it to the others. To get a list of current key servers, see the FAQ on alt.security.pgp.

Next, I'll cover the popular encryption systems currently in use.

Common Crypto Systems

There are several encryption systems in use today. There are single-key systems like Data Encryption Standard (DES) and public-key systems like Pretty Good Privacy (PGP). The ones I'll cover in this chapter are fairly common, which makes them a kind of standard. For reasons I'll explain later, the last thing you want is a proprietary encryption scheme that few organizations or individuals use.

Data Encryption Standard

DES, the most widely used secret-key crypto scheme, is an encryption scheme developed by IBM and officially endorsed by the U.S. government. It's been the number one crypto standard since 1977. DES has never been cracked—at least not by anyone willing to talk about it—although many people have tried and some are reportedly closing in on the elusive solution.

DES is a one-key (symmetric) system, similar to the one described in the Bonnie and Clyde example previously. The same key is used to scramble and unscramble messages. And with the Bonnie and Clyde encryption scheme, the key is susceptible to being intercepted and used to unscramble supposedly secret communiqués.

One way to better protect yourself or your company, if you use DES, is to change the keys often.

Of course, you could encrypt your message three times, each time using a different key—a technique called *triple encryption*. Why three times? That effectively doubles the size of the DES key, making it nearly impossible for anyone to crack. Obviously, triple encryption takes three times as long as single encryption, which can be a problem if you send a lot of messages.

Changing the DES key frequently is not practical if you're just using DES to scramble files stored on your PCs. You would have to unscramble and then rescramble all of your files every time you decided to change the key. If you have lots of files, this can be very time-consuming. A better approach is to store all of the different keys in a single file and encrypt the file with a master key, every so often changing the master key.

Another problem with DES is that it can't be exported. The federal government classifies many encryption schemes as munitions, mainly because they don't want our enemies (and our friends, for that matter) to be able to keep their secrets from our nation's foreign intelligence snoops. That's the theory, anyway. The truth is that DES is widely available overseas. The export restriction is relevant only if you happen to be setting up shop overseas or plan to take your secret decoder ring that uses DES when you go on vacation to EuroDisney in France next year.

Not for Business

Using DES, or some other secret-key scheme exclusively, doesn't make much sense in electronic commerce. Here's why: If your online company proposed to transact business with lots of customers over the Internet, you would have to assign each of those customers a unique key. Also, you would have to find some way to securely transmit each key to each customer or risk the key being intercepted and used by an impostor.

Sleep Peacefully

Although DES has not been cracked, some crypto experts think that it's only a matter of time before it is. Theoretically, one could construct a supercomputer to crack DES using what cryptanalysts call a brute force attack. Worrying about DES being cracked is not something that should keep many people awake at night. If you use it to encrypt files on your hard disk or if DES is used as part of a password protection scheme, there's not a lot to worry about.

You don't need to be James Bond to use DES, by the way. Quite a few commercial and shareware computer security programs use DES encryption.

Cracking DES Crypto

See Table 3-1 for some cryptanalysts' calculations about how long it takes to crack a 56-bit key.

Type of Attacker	Budget	Time to Crack 56-bit key
Pedestrian hacker	$400	38 years
Small business	$10,000	556 days
Corporate department	$300,000	3 hours
Big company	$10 million	6 minutes
Intelligence agency	$300 million	12 seconds

Table 3-1: Cracking a 56-bit key.

Ironically, the banking industry—currently the biggest user of DES—does not want the federal government to walk away from DES as a federal information processing standard. In a recent policy statement, the American Bankers Association says it hopes to rely on DES to protect it for at least 10 more years. It's concerned that changing to another crypto scheme will be too costly (and you know how those bankers are about spending their own money) and will hinder its ability to compete for retail and multinational retail funds transfer business.

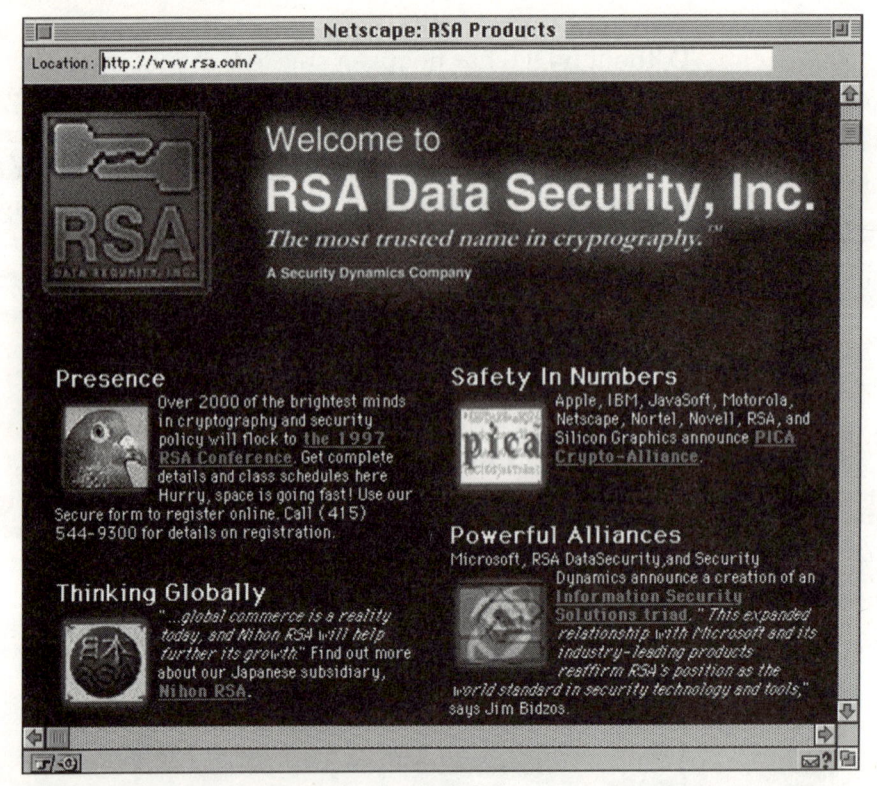

RSA Data Security, Inc.

RSA

RSA Data Security, Inc., based in Redwood City, California, markets a public-key crypto scheme called RSA, which is rapidly becoming a standard for encrypting information traveling over the Internet. The company is named after Ron Rivest, Adi Shamir, and Leonard Adleman—three professors at the Massachusetts Institute of Technology—who in 1977 came up with the algorithm used in RSA.

RSA's cryptography system is not the only public-key scheme available. I'll also discuss another highly popular public-key encryption scheme later in this chapter. What's significant about RSA Data Security is that it has signed pacts with virtually everybody who is anybody in the computer and financial banking industries. Its roster of licensees includes such companies as IBM, Digital Equipment, Lotus Development, MasterCard, Microsoft, Netscape, and Visa.

RSA does two things that DES can't: (1) It gives you a way to come up with a key to scramble messages without having to meet each other face-to-face or risk sending the key through the mail, over a network, or any other way that would render it vulnerable to interception. (2) It can be used to create digital signatures, which are fast becoming a key component of electronic commerce.

RSA uses DES for part of the encryption job. Messages are encrypted using the DES key, and RSA is used to encrypt the DES key. Both keys are sent in what RSA calls an RSA digital envelope.

Why not just use RSA and forget about DES? You could, but RSA does not encrypt and decrypt as fast as DES, so you might not want to use it by itself for long messages. RSA readily admits that DES, when used in software, is generally at least 100 times as fast as RSA and 1,000 to 10,000 times as fast in hardware. The company says that, although it probably will narrow the gap, RSA will never match the performance of DES.

RSA for Networks

RSA is best used in situations in which several people are at work. One of its key benefits is that you and I can swap keys across a network with little fear that someone will crack the key codes even if they succeed in intercepting them.

Let's say Bonnie and Clyde are still busy with their bank-robbing plans. When Bonnie wants to send Clyde a message, here's how it works using RSA: First, Bonnie encrypts the message with DES, using a key chosen at random. Next, she uses Clyde's public key to scramble the DES key. The two keys and the message are sent to Clyde over a network. Clyde unscrambles the DES key using his private key and then uses the DES key to unscramble the message.

In Their Prime

RSA crypto strength is based on the difficulty of factoring prime numbers, a concept that only Pythagoras, Bernoulli, and other mathematicians can understand. Here is how RSA explained it in a press release:

Prime numbers are those numbers that are divisible by only themselves and 1. Any non-prime number can be always represented as the product of its prime factors. For example, the number 113549 can be represented as the product of its prime factors 271 and 419. Finding the prime factors of a given number is known as factoring it. The larger the number, the harder it is to factor. The largest number to be factored thus far is the 128 digit number. Each RSA user has a unique key of around 150 digits so, even if you were able to factor the number, you would have a single user's key.

RSA is widely used in many products, but it's not something you can buy and use off the shelf as a stand-alone product. As I mentioned, the company has been very aggressive in signing licensing agreements with several of the major computer industry companies. For example, RSA is used in products made by Apple, IBM, Lotus, Microsoft, Netscape, and Novell. Although it's not an official standard, it's heading that way. If you use a product that features encryption, knowing what kind is helpful not only for peace of mind but also for ensuring compatibility with other programs.

Pretty Good Privacy

I mentioned earlier that there are public-key crypto schemes other than RSA. If all you really want is to scramble messages (even messages containing credit card numbers), you can use something like Pretty Good Privacy (PGP), a public-key encryption program that's fast becoming the crypto package of choice for many PC users. In addition to its industrial-strength protection, it's free. The program was developed by Phil Zimmerman, who thinks everyone should have the right to privacy. In fact, Zimmerman calls PGP "guerrilla freeware."

More Than Pretty Good

PGP is more than pretty good; it's so good that the U.S. government would rather you don't use it. (You can, however, as long as you don't ship it overseas.)

PGP uses the International Data Encryption Algorithm (IDEA) and RSA algorithm.

IDEA, invented in 1991, is being touted as a possible successor to DES. The key is twice as long as that of DES and even longer than that of triple DES. Yet IDEA is similar enough to DES that it could be used as a replacement.

There are DOS, Apple Macintosh, Commodore Amiga, Atari ST, UNIX, and other versions of PGP. It also comes in two DOS flavors: PGP, which is free but not licensed, and MIT PGP, which also is free but is licensed for noncommercial use only in the United States. It is not compatible with earlier versions. There is, however, a modified version called PGP with UI (unofficial international) in the version number that Zimmerman has not approved. There's also a version called ViaCrypt, which is licensed for commercial use in the United States and Canada.

Harold Highland, a famous security expert, doesn't think much of PGP. He worries that it hasn't been thoroughly tested and that someone may try to hack PGP, putting in a hidden loophole and then posting that version in as many places as possible. Those are certainly legitimate concerns. As long as you're not swapping messages with the Central Intelligence Agency, you don't have much to worry about—yet.

Get It Online

You can get the program from a wide variety of sites, including commercial online services such as America Online and Prodigy, as well as by anonymous File Transfer Protocol (FTP) and bulletin board services (BBSes).

If you're Internet-savvy and have a program like Archie, you can search Archie servers to find out where the file is stored and then download it. Search for prog pgp26a.zip for the PC version and pgp2.6 for the Macintosh version.

PC users can use Telnet and Mac users can use Fetch to get the program from several sites offering anonymous FTP. While getting a copy of PGP, you also can get the *PGP Guide for PC* for PC users or *How to MacPGP* for Mac users. Both freebie guides provide handy information on how PGP works and how to set it up. If you're a Windows user, also get pgpwin.zip, a freeware Windows front end for PGP. There's also a shareware version called winpgp.zip that costs $45, but I'm not sure why you would want it, given that the freebie version does the job quite adequately.

If you're unable to run FTP but have e-mail access, have PGP sent to you by sending an e-mail message to ftpmail@decwrl.dec.com; include your return e-mail address, and leave the subject line blank. In the body of the message, type **help**. In a couple of hours or less, you'll get instructions on how to use the service.

Setting Up PGP

To quickly set up PGP, the process is the same for the PC and Mac version. I won't go through the steps here, because the documents that come with PGP as well as the guides I mentioned earlier are very good. If you're using pgpwin for a Windows or Mac front end, it's pretty intuitive. There are a few things that you should know about the setup that the documentation really doesn't cover, so that's what I'll cover here.

Everything in Its Place

Create a directory or folder for PGP. Unzip or unstuff PGP if you haven't done it already, and store the files in your PGP directory or folder.

If you're a PC user, you'll also need to use the SET command twice in your AUTOEXEC.BAT. Set the path name for the directory where you unzipped PGP by entering **SET PGPPATH= C:\PGP**. Next, set the time zone for your system by entering **SET TZ=** and your time zone, as indicated in the PGP documents. For example, if you're on the East Coast, you would enter: **SET TZ=EST5EDT**.

Generate Keys

Start PGP. First, generate your private and public keys. If you're looking at a graphical user interface, double-click on the Generate keys object. If you're in DOS, type **pgp -kg**. After that, follow the instructions that appear onscreen.

PGP gives you a choice of four key sizes: 384, 512, 1,024, or a user-selected number of bits. The larger the key, the more secure the RSA portion of the encryption. Select 1,024. It takes longer to generate a key of that size, but key size will not have an impact on the speed at which you can encrypt and decrypt messages.

Enter User Name
Next, you'll be asked to enter a user name. Enter your name, followed by your e-mail address in angle brackets, as shown in the online example.

Create a Pass Phrase
Next, you'll be asked to enter a pass phrase.

PGP encrypts your secret key with this pass phrase to ensure that only you can use it. That and your secret key are what protect you from the Vandals, Visigoths, and other barbaric hordes, so you'll need a secure pass phrase. It must be long enough that it cannot be guessed easily, yet memorable enough so you're not tempted to write it down. It also should contain a mix of numbers and uppercase and lowercase characters. If your pass phrase is a single word, a computer can try all the words in the dictionary and eventually find your password.

Your phrase probably should be made up of at least eight characters (more are even better), which is why it's much better than a password. Here is an example of a pass phrase: i8an8BAll4diNner@meLs.

Enter Random Keystrokes
Next, you'll be asked to enter a bunch of random keystrokes. Timing the keystrokes, PGP generates the random numbers used to create the keys. You'll hear a beep when you've entered enough, after which PGP starts generating the keys. Depending on your machine speed, it should take only about a minute or two to make the keys.

That's it. You're set.

Key Rings Are for Keys
Your keys are stored on key rings. There's a private-key ring and a public-key ring. The private-key ring has your private key on it. The only thing protecting the key is your pass phrase, so you can see why it was so important to choose carefully.

Public-key Rings

The public-key ring is where you'll keep your public key. Public keys also are stored on a public-key ring in a key server. To add yours to the key ring, send an e-mail message to -public-keys@pgp.mit.edu. Include your return e-mail address, and enter **ADD** in the subject line. Enter your public key as the body of message.

You'll also have a public-key ring of your own keys as well as the keys of friends, colleagues, and others with whom you communicate.

You can retrieve the PGP key of a single user or of all the users on the server, as well as perform other key-related tricks, using the same setup. The PGP documentation explains how to use INDEX, GET, and other commands.

You'll probably want to maintain a short key ring consisting of the public keys of people with whom you frequently communicate and a long one for everyone else. Why? PGP must search through the key ring to find the right one. If the key ring is short, encrypting and decrypting is relatively fast. If the key ring is long, the process can take a very long time.

Deleted But Not Gone

Once you've scrambled your message, get rid of the original plaintext message and any temporary files that your word processor might have created. Deleting the file is not final, however. Any number of recovery utilities on the market can be used to retrieve those files.

To prevent deleted files from being resurrected, overwrite the plaintext file. You can do this using the PGP -w (wipe) option. You can also use one of several utilities to permanently shred a file. After that, there's little if any way to get those files back.

If someone steals your key ring or pass phrase, you need to create a key-revocation certificate and send that to one of the public servers. The certificate basically alerts everyone that they can no longer trust the public key. The problem is that, if you lose either the secret key or the pass phrase, you can't create the certificate.

There's a solution to this catch-22, however: Create a key-revocation certificate at the same time you generate your key pair. Extract the revoked key to another ASCII file using the -kxa option again. Finally, delete the revoked key from your public-key ring using the -kr option and place your nonrevoked version back in the ring using the -ka option. Save the revocation certificate on a floppy disk. Store the secret key on a backup disk, and put the two disks in a safe place (a safe or bank deposit box).

More Digital John Hancocks

PGP, like RSA, is a public-key crypto program and so can be used to create digital John Hancocks or to attach a digital signature to a message without encrypting it. You might use that feature if you want to post a message that anyone can read while assuring them that the message actually comes from you. The digital signature prevents anyone from changing the message, at least not in such a way that the change would not be spotted.

For example, giving the command PGP -sat <filename> will only sign a message; it will not encrypt it. Even though the output looks as if is encrypted, it really isn't. Anybody could recover the original text.

ViaCrypt

There's a commercial version of PGP available called ViaCrypt PGP, which is marketed by ViaCrypt for about $100. Zimmerman, PGP's author, licensed the company to sell the program, which is virtually identical to PGP 2.3. Why spend $100 when you can get it free? The commercial version has fewer bugs than PGP, and the company now has licenses from RSA and others whose technologies are used in PGP. In addition, it is presently available only for MS-DOS and UNIX. ViaCrypt PGP was developed in-house after the company acquired a license for the algorithm from PKPartners. The private-key crypto algorithm is IDEA, for which ViaCrypt has also obtained a license.

A Few More Code Systems

There are other crypto schemes, such as Kerberos and RIPEM. They're not in widespread use like DES, RSA, and PGP, but I'll quickly summarize the three you might have encountered on the Net.

RIPEM

You can use this public-key program to securely send messages across the Internet. Based partly on Privacy-Enhanced Mail (a method for sending Internet e-mail), it features encryption and digital signatures using RSA and DES algorithms. Shareware versions for Mac, MS-DOS, and UNIX machines are available also.

Kerberos

Kerberos, named after the fearsome three-headed watchdog in Greek mythology that guards the gates of Hades, is an encryption scheme that enables computer users to use the applications on UNIX networks. It is a secret-key network authentication system developed at MIT in 1979, which uses DES for encryption and authentication.

Kerberos Server

In a Kerberos system, a designated Kerberos server handles key management and other tasks. The server database contains the secret keys of all users, generates session keys for users, and authenticates the identity of a user who wants to use certain network services.

When you first log in to a networked computer, you enter your login ID and password. Your login ID goes to a Kerberos database containing the IDs and passwords of every authorized user and compares that to your password; your password remains at the workstation, where there is little chance of it being intercepted.

To use applications that are on the network, you must first authenticate yourself (that is, prove you are who you say you are). To do that, you request a *ticket* from a computer known as the key-distribution center (KDC). The KDC confirms your identity and issues the ticket, which is good for only a certain period of time. You send the ticket along with an *authenticator* that validates the ticket to the application. The application examines both the ticket and the authenticator and lets you in.

Clipper

Although the Clipper Chip is not really a crypto standard you have the option of using, you may have read about it in newspapers or heard it discussed on television and radio. It triggered controversy in 1993 when the federal government proposed it as a national standard for encryption. Under the proposal, the chip would be used in telephones to encrypt conversations so that anyone eavesdropping would not be able to understand what was being said. There also was some talk about using it to scramble data.

Good for Wiretappers

The Clipper Chip proposal went one step further and proposed that law enforcers should have a way to decrypt conversations for court-approved wiretaps. The key that would be used to unscramble the conversations would be held by a trustworthy third party who would release it only when presented with a wiretap court order. As an additional safeguard, the key would be split in two, and each half would be given to different holding agencies.

The Clipper Chip was met with vociferous opposition from a variety of groups, particularly civil libertarians and others concerned about individual privacy. While the Clipper Chip was intended to protect privacy, the rub was that the technology was developed by the National Security Agency (NSA), the federal government's supersecret spy agency. Privacy watchdogs reasoned that the NSA probably would know how to unscramble conversations without having to get the keys, having a ready-made backdoor through which it could eavesdrop. Also, the NSA is unwilling to let anyone get a good look at the formula to scramble conversations, so it is uncertain just how secure the Clipper Chip really is.

It does not seem that Clipper will ever come to pass, but you never know: "Forewarned is forearmed."

Buyer Beware

Products that use DES, RSA, or some of the other mainstream encryption schemes are pretty secure. Even if they can be cracked, it's not likely that your officemate, neighbor, or spouse will be the one to do it. If nothing else, it would take a lot of time and money—probably more than it would pay back. But products that use top-shelf crypto also command higher prices, and thus you may be tempted to use something that is not quite as secure or a product that claims to be "just as good as the best one on the market" but really isn't.

Not all companies want to pay licensing fees to use a particular algorithm (many are patented), so they come up with one of their own.

Keep in mind that if you buy a product that uses encryption based on a proprietary algorithm, you may be buying yourself little more than a false sense of security. There's no way of knowing just how good it really is. In any case, if someone really wants to know how a particular algorithm works, they can figure it out using software that they can get at any Egghead software shop.

It's Good Business

Reputable sellers of encryption products want their algorithms to be closely scrutinized to ensure that they are indeed secure. Not only does that mean the product will stand up under repeated attacks, it's also good business. The algorithm for DES, one of the most widely used encryption standards today, has been tested for more than 20 years. In that time, some of the brightest crypto experts have tried, without success, to crack it.

All that said, encryption products that use proprietary encryption schemes often are good enough to stymie casual spies. If all you want to do is protect a few files on a hard drive, they may be perfectly adequate. It's a trade-off between what you can afford to pay and what you can afford to lose.

A growing number of products such as word processors and databases use encryption to protect passwords and files. These applications use watered-down crypto schemes that can be circumvented easily. Either they use poorly implemented or weak crypto algorithms or someone can circumvent them using a cracking program.

For example, AccessData in Orem, Utah, sells a software program that can unscramble WordPerfect, Lotus 1-2-3, QuattroPro, Microsoft Excel, and Paradox files. It costs $185, which might not be much to someone who is really interested in seeing what's on your machine. The company will send you a free demo disk that will decrypt passwords of 10 or fewer characters (most are, I'd bet).

By the way, the product was originally developed to help computer users get back into their systems and recover files after they had lost their passwords.

Encrypting Electronic Mail

If you're on vacation, and you decide to drop Granny back home a note, you scribble "Wish you were here" on the back of a postcard and drop it in a mail box. If someone at the post office reads it, you don't care much. Suppose you want to send Granny a letter asking for your inheritance a bit early because you need to pay off some gambling debts. You would seal the letter in an envelope before mailing it. That's pretty personal stuff that only Granny and you should know about.

But without proper precautions, sending electronic mail offers about the same level of confidentiality as sending someone a postcard. To protect your message, you need to put it in an electronic envelope and seal it to make sure that a snoop can neither read nor alter your message.

Acting on MIME

Lotus, Microsoft, and other e-mail software vendors are behind an enhancement to the Multipurpose Internet Mail Extensions (MIME) standard, called S/MIME, as Internet security and compatibility concerns grow. S/MIME allows users to send encrypted and digitally signed messages between e-mail programs from disparate vendors if they are S/MIME-compliant. The older Privacy-Enhanced Mail (PEM) standard for text-only Internet e-mail did not become popular because the process of verifying messages was too complex. Even though no S/MIME-based e-mail programs are currently available, vendors such as NCD Software are developing applications. Ilex Systems, Inc., recently debuted its $99 Secure-A-File that encrypts e-mail messages, including MIME attachments such as graphics or software.

In mid-1996, Banyan, ConnectSoft, Frontier Technologies, and Worldtalk announced plans to introduce secure e-mail packages based on news/MIME. Those products were slated to debut later in 1996. In addition to the companies already mentioned, CE Software, FTP Software, ICL, Lotus, Microsoft, Netscape, Qualcomm, RSA, SecureWare, and The Wollongong Group have boarded the S/MIME bus.

S/MIME was proposed late in 1995 as a way to encrypt and authenticate e-mail sent over Simple Mail Transfer Protocol (SMTP) networks. Naturally, e-mail packages that support S/MIME as a standard will be able to exchange messages. At the moment, e-mail packages from Novell, Lotus, and Groupwise can encrypt messages transmitted on internal networks but cannot exchange messages among one another. S/MIME will make it possible for them to do that.

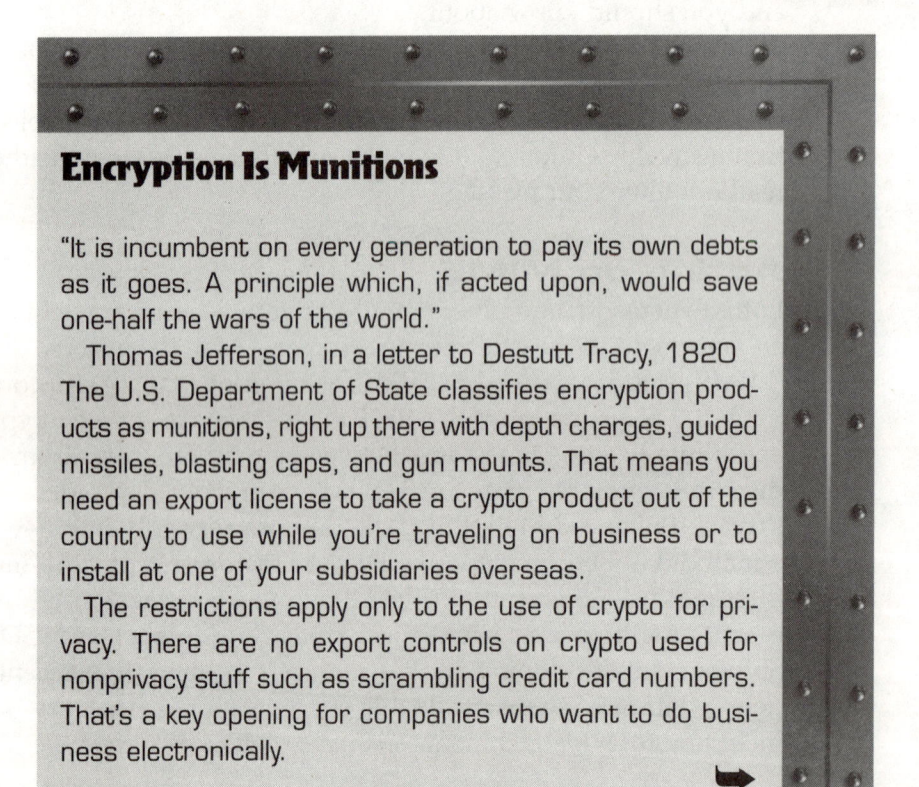

Encryption Is Munitions

"It is incumbent on every generation to pay its own debts as it goes. A principle which, if acted upon, would save one-half the wars of the world."

Thomas Jefferson, in a letter to Destutt Tracy, 1820

The U.S. Department of State classifies encryption products as munitions, right up there with depth charges, guided missiles, blasting caps, and gun mounts. That means you need an export license to take a crypto product out of the country to use while you're traveling on business or to install at one of your subsidiaries overseas.

The restrictions apply only to the use of crypto for privacy. There are no export controls on crypto used for nonprivacy stuff such as scrambling credit card numbers. That's a key opening for companies who want to do business electronically.

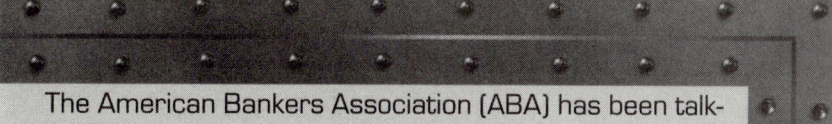

The American Bankers Association (ABA) has been talking to the Department of State and the NSA, among other agencies, about using industrial-strength encryption to scramble 16-digit credit card numbers. Assuming the NSA agrees, the crypto would be used only for credit cards. Such an agreement would cut export approval time from more than a year to a matter of weeks. According to the ABA, the NSA has already approved the plan and is preparing to announce it around the end of 1996.

The bankers want the NSA to approve the use of keys that are 80 bits long, zillions of times harder to crack than the 40-bit keys currently being used. All other information still would be scrambled using significantly weaker crypto keys.

CyberCash, based in Reston, Virginia, already has won NSA approval for a similar encryption proposal.

The U.S. government long has been reluctant to grant export licenses for really good crypto products. The NSA must approve the export licenses, and they're willing to do that only for crypto products they can crack.

The makers of crypto products have been trying to get the government to lighten up on crypto export restrictions. One argument in their favor is that there's no way the Internet will ever be made more secure for commerce until the trade restrictions are lifted and crypto freely used.

Also, many of the restricted products already are widely available overseas because many European companies market crypto products. Restricting exports only stymies competition and gives the edge to the other guys, U.S. makers say.

Exportable versions of U.S. encryption software use 40-bit keys, which many experts feel offers virtually no protection. Even though a longer key is harder to crack, a determined code-cracker could probably punch through a

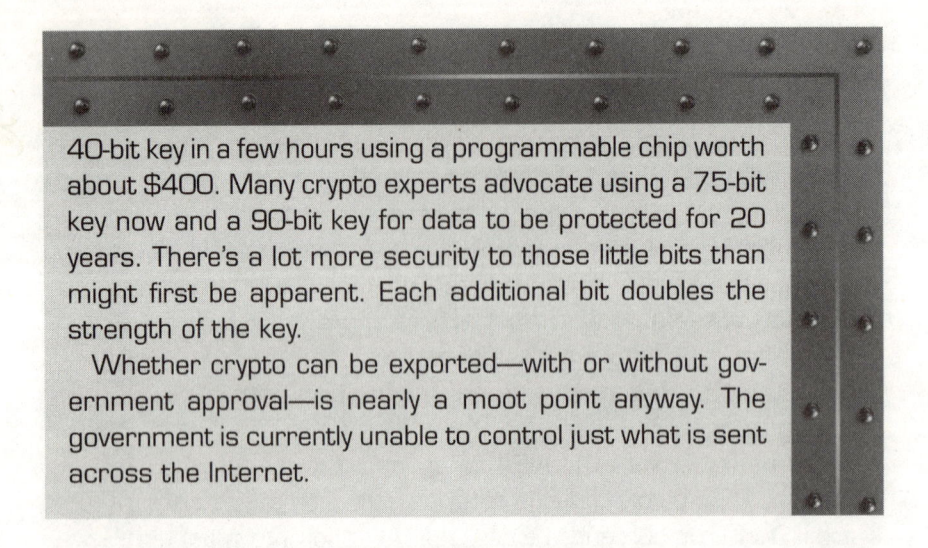

40-bit key in a few hours using a programmable chip worth about $400. Many crypto experts advocate using a 75-bit key now and a 90-bit key for data to be protected for 20 years. There's a lot more security to those little bits than might first be apparent. Each additional bit doubles the strength of the key.

Whether crypto can be exported—with or without government approval—is nearly a moot point anyway. The government is currently unable to control just what is sent across the Internet.

Close, But Not Foolproof

Cryptographers (the code makers) and cryptanalysts (the code breakers) have been locked in a *Mad* magazine-style spy-versus-spy sort of spiral. Codes are becoming increasingly complex, while computers are becoming more capable of performing faster and more complex code-breaking calculations.

Consequently, don't ever make the mistake of thinking, whatever crypto system you elect to use, that it is foolproof. If the prize is worth it, there will be people who will spend the money on technologies and other methods to seize it.

In 1996, cryptanalysts found a number of security loopholes in Netscape Navigator, the popular World Wide Web browser. The export version of Navigator uses an RSA encryption scheme based on a randomly generated 40-bit key. The problem is that the random number was not all that random and could be divined readily using brute computational force. A similar loophole was discovered in Kerberos, which creates its random key from a selection of about a million numbers, a trivial amount for code-breaking computers.

Encrypting proprietary information, credit cards, and other sensitive data before transmitting them over the Internet is only part of the security equation. If the client or server side of the equation is compromised, you essentially have no security.

To prove a point about the vulnerability of encryption schemes, First Virtual Holdings cobbled together an automated program that captures credit card numbers and other sensitive information as they are entered through a computer keyboard (before it can be encrypted).

First Virtual, which has been hawking its own Internet payment system since 1994, wants to punch holes in claims being made by Netscape, CyberCash, Microsoft, and other competing outfits aiming to offer secure credit card transactions across the Net.

Make It a Policy to Protect Yourself

I'm a big advocate of written policies that set standards for the accepted and proper use of a company's information systems. I go into detail about what these policies should cover in another chapter, but right now I want to get you thinking about developing a policy for encryption.

It probably is obvious that you should encrypt credit card numbers, secret sauce recipes, new product development plans, and other proprietary or sensitive information, whether or not you intend to send it over the Internet or other network. But what about information that is sensitive but not necessarily harmful to your business if it is intercepted or falls into the wrong hands?

You have to answer a number of tough questions that probably only you can answer. However, I'll provide some clues along the way, to help get you thinking in the right direction.

Encryption can be costly to implement and use, and it can bring fragile networks to their knees when the processing load is high. You can't encrypt everything—that's neither practical nor desirable. You need to find a balance between what must be encrypted and what can be left in plaintext.

Should everyone in your business be able to encrypt messages? Suppose a disgruntled employee decides to encrypt all of your important information and then walk off without telling anyone the key? If you decide employees must encrypt information, how do you make sure it is actually done, and how do you enforce it?

What about the recipient of the information? Will he or she know how to decode the message?

How strong should the encryption be? Should you use encryption that came with your e-mail program, for example, or should you use something stronger? What type of encryption should you use? Who will be responsible for managing the keys?

You need to develop a company-wide policy that answers these questions and provides guidelines on what should be encrypted, when it should be encrypted, and who should do it.

Moving On

Encryption is what makes electronic commerce and digital money systems work across the Internet and World Wide Web. It is being used to scramble credit card numbers and other sensitive information, to sign documents and provide irrefutable proof of the identity of both parties, and as the cornerstone in a wide variety of digital money transaction systems and protocols.

Without assurance that their transactions will be safe from crooks and snoops, customers will refuse to do business electronically. Even now, many shoppers will not send their credit card numbers to digital merchants for fear that they will be intercepted. It doesn't matter that there is little evidence that credit card crooks are busily snatching numbers as they travel along the Net. It also doesn't matter that, if a credit card number is snatched and used, the rightful owner's liability is limited to $50.

Digital merchants will come to rely on encryption not only to safeguard their transactions with customers but also to protect their own sensitive and proprietary information from unauthorized and disgruntled insiders and outsiders alike.

4 Digital Money

In the real world, when you want to purchase goods and services, you can pay by cash, credit card, or check. Most traditional forms of payment, which are based on the seller and buyer interacting face-to-face, also feature built-in protective mechanisms to ensure that goods and services are delivered as promised and payment (or a refund) is made. For example, you can withhold payment until the goods arrive or obtain a refund if the goods are less than satisfactory.

But how can merchants conduct business over the Internet or World Wide Web and get paid for it?

There are currently two basic ways to make payments electronically over the Internet: credit cards and debit cards. The Gartner Group, a top technology consulting company based in Stamford, Connecticut, states that, while little business is transacted on the Internet today, probably 80 percent of those transactions are based on credit cards and 20 percent on debit cards. That's not likely to change much over the next five years or so, according to Gartner's analysts.

Various forms of digital money or electronic cash also are being developed, using software to emulate cash, checks, and other payment forms. Because few other systems combine attributes of real and virtual money, we'll take a look at some of the ways money is going digital.

No Credit Card Safeguards in Cyberspace

Several safeguards mitigate credit card fraud in the real world today. For example, when you buy something in person, you hand the clerk your credit card. He or she may ask for additional identification before running the card through an electronic reader. The reader transmits the credit card data and sales amount and asks the acquiring bank for authorization for the sale. The acquiring bank processes the transaction and routes the authorization request to the bank that issued the card. If you have sufficient credit in your account to cover the sale, the issuing bank generates an authorization code. The code is sent back to the acquiring bank, which in turn sends the approval or denial code to the point-of-sale electronic reader. The clerk asks you to sign the sales draft, which obligates you to reimburse the card-issuing bank for the amount of the sale.

Lots of steps in the process ensure that the transaction took place, that it was an authorized transaction, and that those involved were able to engage in this particular transaction.

To thwart thieves who otherwise might steal credit cards from mailboxes, credit card issuers now require that a consumer first activate a new card by dialing an 800 number and providing information that only the customer is likely to know, such as his or her mother's maiden name. Even if someone does get hold of your card number, credit card companies are making it harder for thieves to use stolen numbers. Many companies require that you provide the four-digit code printed (not embossed) on the card, which verifies the user has possession of the card. In addition, consumers are liable for only $50 if a card is used by someone else.

There are safeguards even for over-the-phone purchases. As a result, consumers can feel reasonably secure that the phone call is private, the person on the other end is indeed an employee of the merchant company, and the goods will be shipped as promised. And merchants are bound by "card-not-present" rules the credit card issuer has established. Merchants should understand this, but.... There are guidelines for accepting credit cards when the buyer is not making the purchase face-to-face, as is the case when a consumer makes a mail-order purchase.

Once you hand over your credit card to pay for a meal, what prevents the server from using it to buy a VCR or a color TV? A level of trust, backed by the probability that the waitperson won't get away with such behavior for long.

In cyberspace, few of these same safeguards apply. The seller can't always confirm the identity of the buyer, and there are no "card-not-present" rules for Internet-based transactions. The guidelines for taking a credit card for a mail-order purchase are not applicable for transactions over the Internet.

Many digital money companies strive for credit card-based systems that offer the same protection consumers and merchants now enjoy.

Credit Where Credit Is Due

Although practices vary for conducting secure business transactions using credit cards over the Internet, they share at least four common objectives:

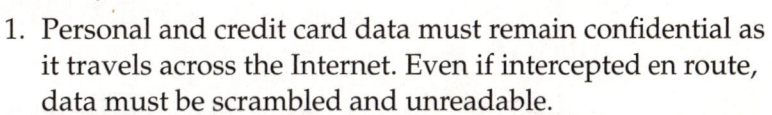

1. Personal and credit card data must remain confidential as it travels across the Internet. Even if intercepted en route, data must be scrambled and unreadable.

2. Personal information, credit card data, order information, payment instructions, and the like should be made secure (incapable of being altered). The concern here is not only fraud but also the reliability of the transaction, which should not be processed if someone has tampered with critical information.

3. Merchants must be able to verify that the person using a credit card is the rightful user of the card and card account.

4. Consumers must have assurance that the merchant is legitimate and has authorization from a financial institution to accept credit cards.

Cashing In on Credit Cards

Although there's been much talk lately about securely processing credit card transactions over the Internet, that part of Internet commerce is a done deal. It can be done right now by encrypting the credit card number with Pretty Good Privacy (PGP) or some other encryption scheme and sending it to the seller as an e-mail message.

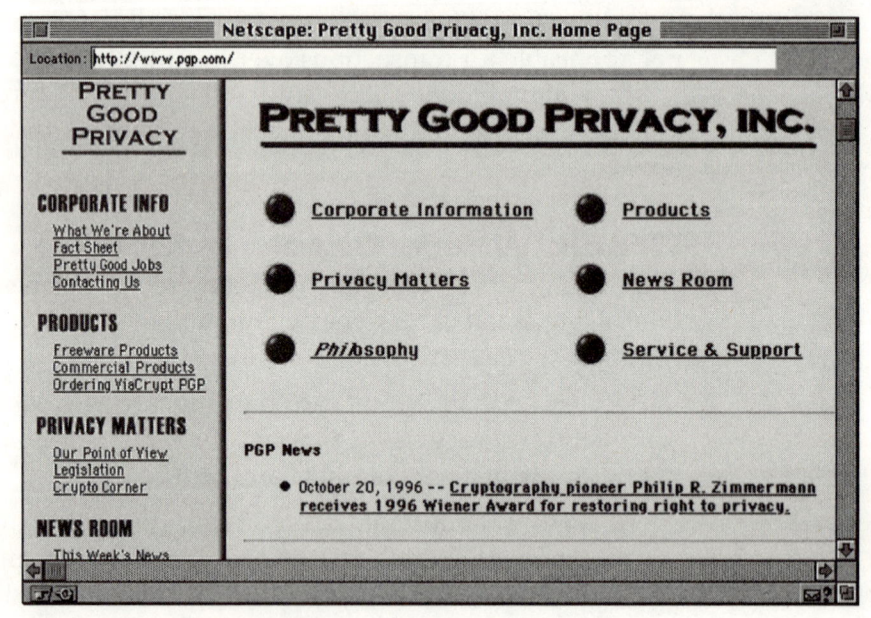

Pretty Good Privacy, Inc.

That's not enough, however. Digital merchants also must concern themselves with factors such as the speed at which transactions are carried out, the ability to perform transactions spontaneously, the privacy of seller and buyer, and the need to establish that the seller and buyer are exactly who they claim to be. That identity issue is critical; what's needed is a way to ensure that, after the fact, neither buyer nor seller can deny having engaged in the transaction. In security-speak, that assurance is called *nonrefutability*.

Although credit card data can be transmitted securely, if consumers don't trust the systems, they won't use them. Assuring consumers that online transactions are protected and private is one way digital merchants can distinguish themselves from competitors.

Much attention has been focused on theft of individual credit cards as they are transmitted from buyer to seller. While the chances that a crook will snag credit card account numbers as they travel the Internet are relatively small, the odds increase as more and more credit card transactions are processed on the Internet. Hackers can readily use filters to automatically extract credit card and account information from e-mail messages. If even a fraction of the expected millions of credit card transactions per day are intercepted, the losses easily could reach significant amounts.

But the real vulnerability of credit cards may be elsewhere on the Internet. Smart crooks will target servers operated by digital merchants and payment processors, seeking only those files in which hundreds and even thousands of credit card numbers are likely to be stored.

Better Business in Cyberspace

What's to protect consumers from being bamboozled by con artists who masquerade as legitimate business owners? It's easy to set up a Web site solely to harvest credit card numbers or sell merchandise that the operator has no intention of delivering. Should the law investigate, con artists can pack up and be back in business at another site quickly.

Consider too that setting up a scam on this level requires very little money and little talent beyond being able to create Web pages. You'll hear more and more about such crimes because of the rapid growth and use of the Internet around the world. There is no reason to think that there will be fewer crimes in cyberspace than in the real world.

The possibility that a scam outfit might set up a Web site to gather credit card information and then ring up purchases prompted the Council of Better Business Bureaus (CBBB) to set up a Web site that will, in its words, "provide a safe harbor in the uncharted waters of Internet commerce."

In mid-1996, the Better Business Bureau (BBB) announced plans to open a Web site aimed at keeping tabs on online businesses the same way it monitors traditional businesses. The BBB also says it is keeping an eye out for Web sites operated by thieves and others bent on fraudulent activities. The service is called BBBOnLine and is slated to be operational early in 1997 (www.bbbonline.com).

Participating companies that commit to meeting BBB standards will be licensed to display an encrypted BBBOnLine seal in their online advertising, and the nation's 137 Better Business Bureaus will monitor their online performance. The seal will be withdrawn immediately from any business that fails to answer consumer complaints or otherwise refuses to comply with BBBOnLine standards.

When a consumer locates an online advertiser displaying the BBBOnLine CARE seal, he or she will be able to link to the BBBOnLine home page, which will show the standards met by the advertiser and allow the consumer to return directly to that company's Web site or to obtain a BBB reliability report on the company. A BBB reliability report includes information on the company's management, length of time in business, goods and services, complaint experience, and other evidence of marketplace behavior, as well as the BBB's conclusions regarding the company's marketplace record. The BBB reliability report will then link back to the company's Web site, if the consumer chooses, or allow intermediate movement to the BBB's home page to find other consumer information.

The site is being sponsored and funded by AT&T, Eastman Kodak Co., Netscape Communications, and other companies, and the project has been endorsed by the Federal Trade Commission.

Setting Standards for Security

A number of organizations and companies—notably MasterCard and Visa—are attempting to establish standards that would provide authentication of cardholders, merchants, and banking institutions and protect the confidentiality and integrity of payment data.

Initially, it seemed as though digital merchants would be faced with having to choose between at least two different standards for payment processing using credit card and other bank card products over the Internet:

- Secure Electronic Payment Protocol (SEPP), a proposed standard created by IBM, Netscape, GTE, CyberCash, and MasterCard

- Secure Transactions Technology (STT), a proposed standard created by Microsoft and Visa to handle secure payment with credit cards over the Internet

Fortunately, reason prevailed. After months of squabbling, early in 1996 both groups agreed on an electronic commerce specification called Secure Electronic Transaction (SET). Lacking a unified approach to this problem would have been akin to requiring retailers to operate one credit card reader for Visa and an entirely different one for MasterCard. A complete copy of the specifications can be retrieved from www.mastercard.com/set/set.htm.

Secure Electronic Transactions

The participants developing the SET protocol are still hammering out the details but, not surprisingly, SET already has lots of support from GTE, IBM, Microsoft, Netscape, SAIC, Terisa, VeriSign, and many other top industry players.

According to its proponents, SET satisfies a number of business requirements for example, it:

- Provides confidentiality of payment information and enables confidentiality of order information transmitted along with the payment information

- Ensures integrity of all transmitted data
- Provides authentication that a cardholder is a legitimate user of a branded payment card account
- Provides authentication that a merchant can accept branded payment card transactions through its relationship with an acquiring financial institution
- Ensures the use of the best security practices and system design techniques to protect all legitimate parties in an electronic commerce transaction
- Ensures the creation of a protocol that neither depends on transport security mechanisms, nor prevents their use
- Facilitates and encourages interoperability across software and network providers

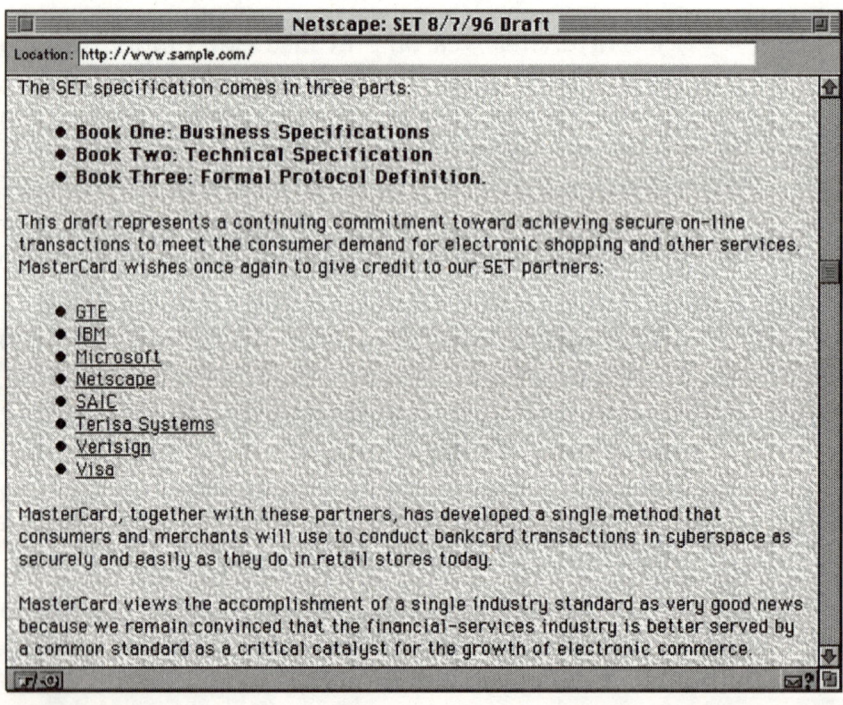

SET specifications.

Like most other secure credit cards schemes being developed these days, SET relies on public-key cryptography to scramble credit card numbers and other sensitive data. What distinguishes SET from other emerging standards is that it also uses symmetric or single-key crypto.

The way it works makes me think of one of those wooden dolls that have successively smaller dolls within. Credit card data or other messages are first encrypted with a randomly generated symmetric encryption key. This key in turn is encrypted using the message recipient's public key. This creates a digital envelope for the message that is sent to the recipient along with the encrypted message itself. After receiving the digital envelope, the recipient decrypts it using his or her private key, retrieves the randomly generated symmetric key, and uses that key to unlock the original message.

SET also relies on public-key crypto to create digital signatures, which means that a participant using SET has two asymmetric key pairs: A *key-exchange pair* is used to encrypt and decrypt, and a *signature pair* to create and verify digital signatures. As I mentioned previously in the chapter on encryption, public-key crypto works in two directions: The private key is used to encrypt and sign a message, while the public key is used to decrypt and verify a signature, and vice versa.

New Ways to Sign

SET introduces a new wrinkle in digital signatures, called *dual signatures*. Here's how it works, according to MasterCard's initial SET specifications.

Bob wants to send Alice an offer to purchase a piece of property and an authorization to his bank to transfer the money if Alice accepts the offer. However, Bob doesn't want the bank to see the terms of the offer, nor does he want Alice to see his account information. Further, Bob wants to link the offer to the transfer so that the money is transferred only if Alice accepts his offer. He accomplishes all of this by digitally signing both messages with a single signature operation that creates a dual signature.

A dual signature is generated by creating the message digest of both messages, concatenating the two digests, computing the message digest of the result, and encrypting this digest with the signer's private signature key. The signer must include the message digest of the other message for the recipient to verify the dual signature. A recipient of either message can check its authenticity by generating the message digest on its copy of the message, concatenating it with the message digest of the other message (as provided by the sender), and computing the message digest of the result. If the newly generated digest matches the decrypted dual signature, the recipient can trust the authenticity of the message.

If Alice accepts Bob's offer, she can send a message to the bank indicating her acceptance and including the message digest of the offer. The bank can verify the authenticity of Bob's transfer authorization and ensure that the acceptance is for the same offer by using its digest of the authorization and the message digest presented by Alice of the offer to validate the dual signature. So the bank can check the authenticity of the offer against the dual signature, but the bank cannot see the terms of the offer.

Within SET, dual signatures are used to link an order message sent to the merchant with the payment instructions containing account information sent to the acquirer (the credit card company). When the seller sends an authorization request to the acquirer, it includes the payment instructions sent to it by the cardholder and the message digest of the order information. The acquirer uses the message digest from the merchant and computes the message digest of the payment instructions to check the dual signature.

Setting Up Certificates

I also previously explained that public-key cryptography requires third-party verification of each person using private- and public-key pairs to safeguard against impostors intercepting or tampering with the transaction process.

That third party is a certificate authority (CA), an organization that verifies the identity of each person involved in a particular public-key crypto scheme. It's similar to two people obtaining birth certificates from the town hall in order to get a marriage license, which they must present to the justice of the peace or cleric so they can be married.

The CA creates a message containing the first person's name, personal information, and public key. This message, called a *certificate,* is signed digitally by the CA. The process is repeated for the second person.

Because SET participants have two key pairs, they also have two certificates. Both certificates are created and signed at the same time by the CA.

Although Visa and MasterCard are cooperatively promoting SET, the two credit card companies plan to handle digital certificate services differently and have selected digital certificate service providers with which they had prior business relationships.

Visa International has chosen VeriSign to operate its digital certificate service for member financial institutions that want to provide customers with secure credit card transactions. MasterCard International has signed on with GTE Corp., through GTE's CyberTrust unit in Needham, Massachusetts. CyberTrust markets network security products to the federal government, including the world's largest public-key management system, which is used by the Department of Defense.

MasterCard and Visa expect that products based on SET can be shipped overseas despite the federal government's limits on exporting encryption. The federal government allows products using encryption to be exported if they meet the following conditions:

- Data being encrypted are of a financial nature.
- Data content is well defined.
- Data length is limited.
- The cryptography cannot easily be used for other purposes.

Presumably, as long as the SET protocol is limited to the financial side and the cryptography used for SET cannot easily be put to other purposes, software vendors should be able to obtain import and export licenses.

Getting Set to Use SET

Before they can receive SET payments from credit card users or process SET transactions, merchants must do two things: The first is to set up a relationship with a credit card institution that processes SET transactions. The second is to register with a CA such as VeriSign or GTE's CyberTrust.

The process is automated, using merchant registration software the credit card issuer or the merchant's bank supplied to the merchant. To start the merchant registration process, the merchant sends a request to the CA, asking for a registration form and a copy of the CA's key-exchange certificate, which contains the CA's public key.

The registration form is one that has been supplied to the CA by the merchant's financial services company. The CA sends the appropriate form—which the CA digitally signs—and a copy of its key-exchange certificate to the merchant.

The merchant must have two public- and private-key pairs to use SET—one pair for the key exchange between the CA and the merchant and the other for digital signatures. Merchant registration software generates the necessary keys.

The merchant completes the form, filling in information such as the merchant's name and address. The merchant's registration software digitally signs the registration. Next, it generates a symmetric key used to encrypt the registration. That key is in turn encrypted into the digital envelope using the CA's public key. Finally, the merchant software transmits the registration form back to the CA.

On the receiving end, this process is reversed: The CA decrypts the digital envelope and retrieves the symmetric encryption key. That key is used to decrypt the registration form and its contents. The CA then uses the signature key in the form to verify that the request was signed digitally, using the corresponding private key. Assuming the signature can be verified, the registration's contents then are verified against information the merchant supplied. Finally, the CA creates and digitally signs the merchant certificates, which it then encrypts, using a newly generated symmetric key (itself encrypted using the merchant's public key), and sends back to the merchant.

When the merchant's software receives the encrypted certificates, it decrypts the digital envelope and retrieves the symmetric key, which it uses to decrypt the registration response containing the merchant certificates. Once the certificates are verified, they're stored on the merchant's server for use in transactions.

SET's primary advantages and disadvantages are as follows:

Advantages

- SET permits direct interaction between buyer and seller, without resorting to third parties or intermediaries. That in turn should mean lower credit card transaction fees.

- SET employs powerful encryption using single- and public-key crypto.

- Consumers' credit card numbers are never seen by the merchant.

- Transactions are credited to the merchant's account right away.

- SET has the support of leading computer and credit card companies.

Disadvantages

- Special software will be needed by buyers, merchants, and others to process SET transactions.

- SET is still under development.

- Merchants must have a relationship with a bank or card issuer that accepts SET transactions.

- SET is designed to process MasterCard and Visa cards only.

VeriFone Internet Commerce.

Ready, SET, Go

VeriFone Inc., which sets up systems that link retailers, banks, and credit card companies, is among the first to announce products based on the SET specification.

The products include vGATE Internet gateway software and vPOS merchant software. At a press conference in June 1996 to unveil the two products, VeriFone's marketing executives showed how the system operated by ordering products from a demonstration Web site.

The transaction flowed from the Web site through the vPOS software to the vGATE software residing on a server owned and maintained by VeriFone in Menlo Park, California. In actual use, the vPOS software will reside on a Web server at the merchant's site, and the vGATE software will sit on an Internet gateway machine operated by a bank to handle credit card transactions.

VeriFone's vGATE Internet gateway software enables financial institutions to handle credit card transactions from digital merchants over the bank's own secure networks.

The vPOS point-of-sale software, priced at $1,500 per license, sits on the merchant's Web server.

Wells Fargo already has installed vGATE in a bank in San Francisco, and it plans to sell and distribute vPOS software for merchants. The Royal Bank of Canada, Novus Services (Discover Card), and Hitechniaga MBf Group, an Asian financial services provider, also say they have signed on to use VeriFone's software.

VeriFone dominates the in-store credit card authorization terminal business: The company claims to have terminals in 75 percent of all U.S. stores and 65 percent of the global market. VeriFone already has announced plans to offer in 1997 vWALLET software designed to enable consumers to securely transmit credit card numbers and other personal information over the Internet.

Two Other Credit Card Crypto Standards

SET goes a long way toward establishing standards for the use of credit cards over the Internet, but it is not the sole standard to emerge by any means.

Two other technologies—Secure Sockets Layer (SSL) and Secure HyperText Transfer Protocol (S-HTTP)—already are well on their way to becoming standards for securing data, and not just credit card data, either.

SSL was developed by Netscape Communications Corp., the Mountain View, California, developer of Netscape Navigator and Netsite Commerce Server, one of the first secure Web servers. Netscape has made SSL publicly available for noncommercial use and is licensing it for commercial use. The two standards often have been pitted against each other, but observers say they provide different forms of security.

S-HTTP was developed by Terisa Systems, a joint venture between security software developer RSA Data Security and Enterprise Integration Technologies, and is being worked on by the Internet Engineering Task Force and promulgated by the World Wide Web Consortium.

Secure Sockets Layer

In October 1994, Netscape published the specification for SSL on the Internet. Recently, the company also published the source code to the reference implementation, called SSLRef, on the Net. SSLRef is free for noncommercial use and is available for flat-fee licensing by companies that want to use it in commercial products.

Several top companies and organizations in the high-tech industry are backing the SSL protocol for Internet security. Its proponents include Apple Computer, Bank of America, Digital Equipment Corporation, IBM, MarketNet, MasterCard International Inc., MCI Communications Corp., Microsoft Corporation, Novell, Inc., Sun Microsystems, Inc., Visa International, and Wells Fargo. These companies are either licensing SSL source code or providing SSL-enabled products, creating online payment systems incorporating the SSL protocol. According to Netscape, more than three million people already are using SSL-enabled products, which have been available since December 1994.

SSL initially was developed to secure communications between browsers and servers on the World Wide Web, but it now can be used with an Internet application.

SSL is layered beneath application protocols such as the HyperText Transfer Protocol (HTTP), Telnet, the File Transfer Protocol (FTP), Gopher, and (NNTP) Network News Transport Protocol and layered above the Transmission Control Protocol/Internet Protocol (TCP/IP). This strategy allows SSL to operate independent of the Internet application protocols. With SSL implemented on both the client and server, your Internet communications are transmitted in encrypted form, ensuring privacy.

It is based on a crypto algorithm marketed by RSA Data Security and features a straightforward way of securing the content of messages as they travel along networks; authentication, which uses certificates and digital signatures to verify the identity of parties in information exchanges and transactions; and message integrity, which ensures that messages cannot be altered en route.

SSL Security Holes

Not long after Netscape went public in August 1995, the SSL encryption in Netscape Navigator 2.0 was cracked from two different angles.

Netscape, the premier browser for navigating the WWW, comes in two versions: one with industrial-strength security features for use in the United States and another with watered-down security features designed for use everywhere else in the world.

Netscape Navigator's export version of SSL uses a 40-bit key size for the RC4 stream-encryption algorithm. According to Netscape, a message encrypted with 40-bit RC4 takes, on average, 64 MIPS-years to break. That means a 64-MIPS computer needs a year of dedicated processor time to break the message's encryption. In comparison, the U.S. version of Navigator uses a 128-bit key that is vastly more secure (and probably unbeatable).

Why would Netscape create two versions of its fabulously popular browser? Uncle Sam made them do it. The federal government has decided that the widespread use of strong encryption overseas would make it difficult for U.S. intelligence agencies to snoop on foes and friends, hinder law enforcement, and threaten national security. They also maintain, with some justification, that drug dealers, terrorists, child pornographers, and many other bad elements would use encryption to hide their tracks and evade punishment. As a result, the feds have set restrictions on the importation of products that use encryption and have placed limits on the length of the keys—the formula—used to scramble data.

To test the strength of Netscape's exportable version, a group of computer science students here and overseas set out to crack it and, at the same time, thumb their collective noses at Uncle Sam. Damien Doligex, a 27-year-old computer scientist working for a French computer lab, cracked the code in only a few days.

Doligex used what in security-speak is known as a brute-force attack to hammer repeatedly on a bit of encrypted text until he was able to decipher it. Doligex used the computer power of more than a hundred workstations, during times the machines were not being used in the computer lab. It took him eight days.

It was a significant technical feat, although it should be noted that a different key is used each time to encode messages, so that it would be impractical to use the same attack repeatedly to harvest credit card numbers. In fact, there are considerably easier and faster ways to commit credit card fraud. But the attack proves that encryption is far from foolproof.

A few weeks later, in September 1995, two graduate students at the University of California at Berkeley discovered yet another, more serious flaw in Netscape. They found that the random-number generator used to scramble messages and data was, in fact, not random at all.

The students realized that the randomness of the keys was linked to a computer system's clock time and so learned it was possible to guess what keys might be used. Linking the random-key generator to the system clock is something that only amateurs would do, not crypto experts. Once they discovered the flaw, the students were able to crack Netscape's encryption scheme in a matter of hours.

Netscape quickly closed both loopholes, as well as one other related to the way Netscape handles Java applets, in a new release of its browser. Even so, there are a couple of lessons here:

- All new programs are susceptible to security loopholes, and digital merchants should wait until the programs have been proven trustworthy in everyday use or tested by security researchers to see whether they contain serious flaws before acquiring new technology or upgrading to the latest release.

- Complete security goes beyond merely using encryption: It extends from the start to the end of any route over which transactions must travel.

A number of other security flaws—some quite serious—have been discovered in Netscape Navigator (as well as in Microsoft's Internet Explorer browser) by researchers at the Safe Internet Programming project at Princeton University. More on that in the chapter on WWW security.

What are SSL's primary advantages and disadvantages?

Advantages

- SSL has broad industry support.
- It is widely used in many products.
- The domestic version features probably unbeatable security based on 128-bit keys.

Disadvantage

- The international version may not be secure enough.

Secure HyperText Transfer Protocol

S-HTTP was developed by Terisa Systems, a joint venture between security software developer RSA Data Security Inc. and Enterprise Integration Technologies. It is an extension of the HyperText Transfer Protocol (HTTP), the standard for communications on the World Wide Web.

S-HTTP was designed to add security to applications on the WWW and provide for encryption, digital signatures, and authentication. The browser and server negotiate between themselves for the best way to transmit messages back and forth in a variety of different ways. For example, browsers that incorporate S-HTTP are able to communicate with HTTP-only servers and S-HTTP servers are able to respond to requests for HTTP-only browsers. These sorts of transactions would not have S-HTTP security, however.

That flexibility means a variety of public-key crypto standards can be incorporated into S-HTTP clients and servers, like Public Key Cryptography Services (PKCS), Privacy-Enhanced Mail (PEM), and Pretty Good Privacy (PGP).

S-HTTP would not require an electronic shopper to have a public key or register with a certificate authority. That is particularly significant to digital merchants, because it means that transactions could occur spontaneously without requiring the shopper to have an established public key.

SSL or S-HTTP?

SSL and S-HTTP are sometimes compared to each other, but in fact, the two are complementary. S-HTTP provides security at the document level, using public- and private-key encryption to create digital signatures. SSL was developed to provide security to the network link itself.

Allan M. Schiffman, one of the codevelopers of S-HTTP, uses the following analogy to explain the differences between the two protocols and show how they work together. SSL can be viewed as the locked postal truck transporting mail between two different locations, while S-HTTP is the individual envelope or package that prevents people from seeing the mail contents.

S-HTTP's primary advantages and disadvantages are as follows:

Advantages

- S-HTTP has the flexibility to use any encryption scheme or combination of schemes.

- Unprotected transmissions are possible for participants without public or private keys.

Disadvantage

- S-HTTP is not ready yet. Approval is pending from the World Wide Web Consortium and the Internet Engineering Task Force.

Checking Out the Web

What about paying by check over the Internet? Isn't that something that consumers and merchants would like to do? Sure, but not as much as they would like to use their credit cards. Electronic payment schemes that would permit secure transfer of electronic checks are not well developed . . . yet. Fortunately, sending a check securely need not be complicated. Conceivably, a consumer could send an encrypted e-mail message to a merchant with authorization to withdraw funds from the consumer's bank account. The use of public-key crypto and digital signatures would make it almost foolproof.

CheckFree, the University of Southern California/Information Sciences Institute's NetCheque, and NetChex offer check processing over the Internet by means of the Automated Clearing House. I'll provide more details on what these and other companies offer in electronic payment systems in the next chapter.

Gimme Digital Money (That's What I Want)

While it may be comforting to have a wad of cash stuffed into one's wallet, those greenbacks are starting to wear out their welcome in most places. Just to handle the green stuff costs money handlers more than sixty billion dollars a year in the United States alone. Money is a burden when you have to collect, deliver it to a bank, store it in a vault and guard it from thieves. And when such new technology as scanners and high-quality color copies make it easier for counterfeiters to roll their own bank notes, money can be more bother than it's worth.

Digital cash can replace cold cash in Internet transactions, as well as in restaurants, movie theaters, stores, or anywhere else consumers spend money. Digital merchants also can transact business with suppliers and vendors using electronic money for supplies or payroll, eliminating the need for checks or conventional banking.

If money could be digitized—making it more adaptable—you could use it for purchases worth a fraction of a cent, for example. Every digital cent could efficiently and securely be accounted for and tracked from start to finish. If money is the root of all evil, then digital money would be the end of all crime, and more, according to David R. Warwick in his article, "The Cashless Society" (*The Futurist*, November 1992):

> The immediate benefits [of digital money] would be profound and fundamental. Theft of cash would become impossible. Bank robberies and cash-register robberies would simply cease to occur. Attacks on shopkeepers, taxi drivers, and cashiers would all end. Urban streets would become

safer. Security costs and insurance rates would fall. Property values would rise. Sales of illegal drugs, along with the concomitant violent crime, should diminish. Hospital emergency rooms would become less crowded. A change from cash to recorded electronic money would be accompanied by a flow of previously unpaid income-tax revenues running in the tens of billions of dollars. As a result, income-tax rates could be lowered and the national debt reduced.

While no one knows what the future will bring, it's clear that the best alternative to cash on the Internet today is digital cash.

Let's take a look at how an electronic money system might work: My weekly paycheck of $500 is electronically deposited into my bank account. When I want to make an electronic purchase, using software my bank or a digital money mint company provides, I first create a randomly generated, 100-digit number that represents $100. Next, I encrypt the 100-digit number using the private- or secret-key component of a public-key crypto system. That creates my digital signature, and I send it to the bank. My e-cash software, with a friendly user interface, permits me to create the keys that I need to withdraw the electronic funds that I require. It's as easy as withdrawing spending money for a Saturday night on the town from an automatic teller machine.

The bank uses my public key to decode the number, establishing that I indeed sent the number. When my bank learns that I want $100, it takes the funds out of my account. Next the bank encrypts my 100-digit number with its private key (digitally signing the number for the second time) and sends the number back to me. The digital dollars—now in the form of an encrypted number—are stored on my PC's hard drive just as though I had stuffed the bills into my wallet.

Next, I hop on the WWW and navigate to L.L. Bean's Web site. (L.L. Bean does maintain a Web site though they don't take digital cash yet.) I peruse their catalog, find a soft, brushed-fleece plaid shirt for $49 and a sturdy pair of rugged canvas pants for $34. I place my order by entering into a form the catalog numbers of the items that I wish to purchase, a brief description, my clothing sizes, the address where I want the items shipped, and so on.

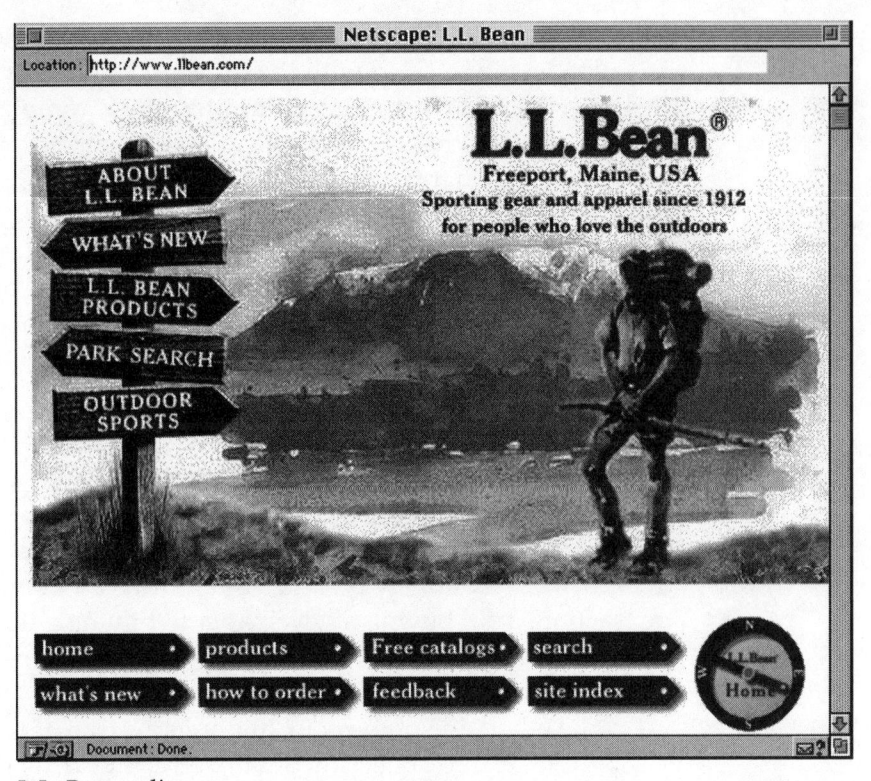

L.L. Bean online.

Next, I open my cyberwallet, enter the amount that I wish to subtract and click on the Pay button. The number representing $100 (which equals my purchase amount plus overnight shipping) is transferred to L.L. Bean's electronic cash register. If I were to change my mind suddenly, I could hit the Cancel key and stop payment on the order.

L.L. Bean's bank uses my bank's public key to decrypt the 100-digit number, verifies that the number has been digitally signed by my bank and that the digital dollars are legitimate, credits L.L. Bean's account for $100, and sends them a digitally signed deposit slip.

Meanwhile, back at the ranch, whenever I want to take a look at my withdrawals, payments, deposits, and all of the other usual bank account functions, I run the software, punch a couple of keys, and take a look at my statement. The bank no longer sends me a statement every month—there's no need to—and saves itself millions of dollars per year.

Suppose while I'm visiting various sites on the Internet, I download a file infected with the dreaded Muncher virus, which replicates crazily, crashes my computer, and scrambles my data. What happens to my electronic cash and the record of my transactions? Nothing that I can't readily retrieve using the digital cash software's recovery function. I reconnect to the bank, restore my account information, and replace my lost money with the same digitally signed digital dollars. Since every cent can be accounted for, the bank can readily verify whether those digital dollars have been used already. Try that after leaving your wallet or purse in the back of a taxicab!

Conspicuous Consumers?

Because digital money is based on public-key crypto and digital signatures, every digital cent you download and spend can be tracked. The technology behind digital cash can monitor every transaction, from buying a newspaper to buying a house. Public concern about this lack of privacy is the reason many companies accept digital cash but don't publicize it.

On the other side of the coin, anonymous transfers of digital cash would lead to abuses by organized crime, drug dealers, tax evaders, blackmailers, money launderers, and a host of other rogues. If money cannot be traced, even ordinary citizens can secret their funds—a system no government is likely to accept.

A system of two distinct kinds of e-money—one that can be identified and tracked and another that can be used anonymously like real cash—may provide a solution. There is a technique called *"blind signatures"* that was developed by DigiCash, an Amsterdam-based company involved in setting up e-cash systems. I'll explain how that works in the next chapter when I talk about DigiCash and some of the other digital money companies.

One of the other key concerns about digital money is what's to prevent someone from counterfeiting digital money merely by copying it? In e-cash parlance, that's known as *double spending*, and is fairly simple to counteract: The bank issuing digital cash maintains a database of all of the digital dollars that it has issued and that have been spent. If you, as the merchant, receive an order that the customer wishes to pay for with digital money, all you have to do is check with the bank to see if it is viable—very much the way you'd check with a credit card issuer to verify that a customer has enough credit to cover a planned purchase.

It also would be possible for a bank to always know just how much e-cash an account holder had on hand. If the amount inexplicably hits a certain threshold, the authorities could be alerted to the possibility that fraud is underway. Or a limit could be placed on how much e-cash can be withdrawn per transaction. Low transaction limits would make e-cash impractical for money laundering or drug dealing.

One Micropayment at a Time

Digital money is software, so it can be adapted to transactions in which real money would never work. One of the exciting possibilities for digital cash is to use it to make micropayments ranging from fractions of a cent to ten or twenty dollars.

Micropayments would make it possible for electronic publishers, for example, to sell information a page at a time for a cent or less. Researchers at Carnegie Mellon University are working on a project called NetBill that would sell technical journals, comics, and local newspapers that way. Mellon Bank provides the banking services for the pilot, and Visa International handles the data processing links needed to connect point-of-sale terminals to Mellon Bank.

NetBill acts as go-between, handling authentication, account management, transaction processing, billing, and reporting services for publishers and customers. It also maintains the accounts for merchants and customers through a server that is linked to the bank, Visa, and other financial institutions.

NetBill transfers the information from merchant to buyer and at the same time debits the buyer's account and credits the merchant's account for the amount of the purchase. Later, NetBill can transfer the funds in the NetBill account to the merchant's bank account or replenish funds in the buyer's account, using the buyer's bank or credit card.

NetBill also ensures that both the consumer and merchant are protected. The consumer is guaranteed of the certified delivery of goods before payment is processed, and the merchant is guaranteed that the consumer cannot access the goods until payment has been received.

Rocket Science, an online video game company, and Games CyberCash, one of a growing number of digital cash companies, are working on electronic coin services that would give consumers the ability to play video games and pay for them over the Internet. Game players using Rocket Science's Internet game engine would download game environments, characters, and other essentials and pay as they play in denominations of 25 cents or less.

E-wallets

I'm an enthusiastic supporter of smart cards, so I can't understand why they aren't more popular here in the United States. The typical smart card is the same size as an ordinary credit card and about twice as thick. Embedded in the card is a microprocessor that can do a variety of neat things, depending on how you program it.

When used to store digital cash, they're called *stored-value cards, electronic wallets,* or *electronic purses.* Smart cards also can store anything from personnel records to health records that a patient brings to the doctor when it's time for an annual checkup.

The cards can be inserted into a terminal to buy goods and services in a store or into a home PC to pay for goods and services across the Internet. Personal information, login IDs, credit card data, and the like can be encrypted automatically and sent securely, reliably, and quickly across the Internet.

With a smart card as an electronic wallet, consumers would no longer need to carry real money in their wallets or fumble for exact change when purchasing small-ticket items. It would replace not only the cash in your wallet but also the wallet.

You can personalize the cards, which can be used efficiently by both sophisticated and naive consumers, by handicapped people who can't use automatic teller machines, and by those who dislike using ATMs. Banks will cash your out-of-town personal check if you have cash in your electronic wallet, and you can replenish it over the Internet or from an ATM no matter where you are when it runs out. The card could be password-protected and its contents encrypted against loss or theft; it would become unusable automatically the first time someone else tried to use it.

Digital merchants also benefit: They wouldn't have to handle as much cash as before. The chance that a crook could pass off a stolen or phony smart card is almost nil. Transactions could be handled automatically and efficiently, reducing the credit card and bank fees merchants now pay. Best of all, merchants would have instant access to cash as soon as a transaction is completed.

Mondex

Smart cards have been popular overseas, especially in Europe, for many years. Mondex, a consortium of telecommunications companies and banks, has been testing an electronic wallet-smart card in Swindon, England, for more than a year. Amsterdam-based DigiCash, one of the leading promoters of digital cash, has been testing a product that it calls DyniCash, which enables Japanese motorists to pay road tolls while zipping along instead of funneling through a series of tollbooths. The smart card is inserted in a battery-powered reader mounted on the dashboard. E-cash is transferred from the dashboard reader to roadside toll collection booths via microwaves.

In the United States, a number of companies ranging from AT&T to Visa are developing smart cards that can be used in a variety of ways. Although they are far from popular now, that may change over the next few years. The Smart Card Forum, an industry trade group, predicts that by the year 2000 smart cards will be in use in 25 percent of U.S. households.

The 1996 Summer Olympics was the largest and most visible U.S. test of smart cards. Visa Cash, working with three banks—W, First Union, and Nations Bank—distributed a half-million disposable cards for the event. The cards were used at vending machines, subway stations, and some fifteen hundred businesses in the Atlanta area.

Chase Manhattan Bank, Citibank, MasterCard, and Visa are introducing smart cards in New York City in a pilot program that started late in 1996. It is the first test of chip-based, stored-value products in that market. MasterCard and Visa have independently developed stored-value products called MasterCard Cash and Visa Cash, respectively. This pilot will allow merchants to accept cards with chips from either brand in a single merchant terminal, just as they do with traditional credit cards. The cards, which double as ordinary credit cards, can be loaded with digital dollars at ATMs and other terminals. They're designed to be used for payments under $20 at places like newsstands, fast food restaurants, pay phones, and gas stations.

Chase Manhattan Bank and Citibank will issue about fifty thousand of the new chip cards, giving consumers a quick and convenient alternative to using cash. The cards will be accepted by approximately five hundred merchants in one area of Manhattan. The merchants offer a wide variety of goods and services, and many of them accepted only cash in the past. Pilot participants say their objective is to test the dynamics of consumers and merchant acceptance of the new cards.

E-cash Obstacles

Despite all of the perceived benefits of digitized cash, there are as many obstacles blocking its entry into commerce.

Consumers will require a lengthy education before they come to accept and use digital cash as a substitute for cash or credit cards. Mixed results from the Mondex trial in England indicate consumers may not be ready to give up cash. They are reluctant to pay for electronic purses and it's not handy to transfer small sums from one consumer to another. Debit cards are more convenient and easier to use.

Digital cash is a brand new way of transacting business, and as a consequence, there are few rules or regulations. Digital cash also requires an entirely new infrastructure: Merchants will need new software and perhaps hardware. Someone—financial institution, merchant, consumer, or all three—must pay for the smart cards, which are not inexpensive.

And there are regulatory issues that are far from being resolved. Digital money does not fit neatly into an existing category for banking regulation. At least four federal agencies—the Federal Reserve Bank, the Department of the Treasury, the Comptroller of the Currency, and the Department of Justice—have regulatory powers over some aspect of e-cash.

Sorting out the regulatory and legal issues across national borders is probably impossible. What is permissible in one country may not be in another. Many nations regulate or even prohibit the use of encryption, for example.

The security and reliability of nearly all digital money schemes rest on encryption. It would be foolish to think that any encryption scheme cannot be cracked; the possibility may be small, but it exists. For example, a system may be compromised by insiders who get control of encryption keys that permit them to tamper with or divert funds.

Consumers who abuse their credit cards often say they forget that the card represents real money that must be repaid at some point. They tend to lose sight of the intrinsic value of money. That problem is bound to recur with digital money stored in smart cards or transacted online.

Another complaint may come from consumers without PCs who won't have equal access to credit and financial services.

What's Needed for Digital Money to Work?

Digital cash must offer everything that real money provides and more. Thanks to encryption and digital signatures, it is fairly certain that digital money can be created and used securely, with less worry about theft, counterfeiting, and so on than with real cash.

There are no federal laws yet that prohibit anyone from creating their own digital currency, although privately minted money technically is not legal tender. Any person or institution that sets up a digital cash payment plan also would have to establish that it is trustworthy and able to manage the digital mint and its related services properly.

Consumers, merchants, and everyone else who handles money must perceive that digital cash has value, just as cold hard cash, bank checks, and other payment forms have value.

It must be easy to use and readily accessible at any time and from any place. Obviously, merchants and customers want to get their "money" as readily as they can the real thing. Consumers must be able to make spontaneous purchases, to download their money wherever they are and send it off to anyone they choose whenever they wish. That means consumers also must have the option of storing their electronic money on their PCs and in an electronic wallet.

Perhaps, the biggest hurdle to electronic commerce is lack of agreement on a single electronic payment system. CommerceNet of Menlo Park, California, and World Wide Web Consortium of Cambridge, Massachusetts, are collaborating on what the two groups call the Joint Electronic Payments Initiative. JEPI does not expect that a single standard will emerge but rather is exploring ways to make credit cards, e-checks, and e-cash and those systems compatible with one another.

Privacy Concerns

Consumers also must be able to use digital cash like real cash, with at least some degree of anonymity. No one should have to worry that every purchase they make could come under scrutiny by private industry, government, or others. The federal government, on the other hand, must be able to track the flow of money to prevent tax evaders, organized criminals, and others from trying to beat the system. The criminal justice system will want to ensure records of digital cash transactions are available.

That will require at least two kinds of digital money, perhaps anonymous e-cash for small amounts and identifiable e-cash for large amounts. The threshold between a small and large amount could possibly be as little as a thousand dollars.

Regulating E-money

The current federal regulatory structure simply is not prepared to cope with the advent of digital money. For one thing, banking laws are based on geography; computer networks make geography irrelevant. The federal government is sure to seek to regulate companies that issue electronic money much as it now regulates banks. Simply put, new products and services will require new laws.

States also are beginning to recognize the need to address emerging digital cash issues. In early 1996, the Minnesota Department of Commerce issued a public notice seeking information to help draw up rules relating to electronic funds transfer terminals. Meanwhile, Utah has passed the first state-level digital signature law. It provides for the creation of certificate authorities who will verify the identity of a digital signature user and will be liable for making a bad identification, thus assuming some of the risk from sellers and financial institutions. In turn, users will have to be more careful with their private-encryption key and can be held liable for forgeries, says Christopher Sandberg, an attorney with the Minneapolis law firm of Schatz Paquin Lockridge Grindal & Holstein P.L.L.P.

The Electronic Funds Transfer Act (EFTA) provides most of the consumer protection presently in place for electronic fund use. Regulation E of the Federal Reserve System implements the EFTA and controls the use of electronic signatures for consumer debit transactions. Regulation E pertains to banks and their customers for electronic transfers in and out of consumer accounts, including ATM cards and point-of-sale transactions.

Still unanswered is how these regulations can and should be adapted to wholly Net-based digital cash models. One way would be to expand the definition of *access device* to cover software tools and automatically generated security protocols, Sandberg says. This coverage will be particularly important as nonbank entities develop on the Internet.

Moving On

The traditional ways of paying for goods and services, such as cash, credit, and check, require the buyer and sellers to be face to face or have other built-in security features. If the goods or services are not what they are presented to be, the buyer has the option of stopping payment on a check or obtaining a refund.

Doing business over the Internet does not have the same safeguards. Obviously, the buyer and seller are interacting across computer networks, often over distances of thousands of miles.

Much of the talk about doing business over the Internet has revolved around how to safely use credit cards so that both consumers and merchants are protected. There are a number of security initiatives being promulgated by the computer industry, credit card companies, and other financial institutions. They include the Secure Electronic Transactions (SET), Secure Sockets Layer (SSL), and Secure Hyper Text Transport Protocol (S-HTTP). The one thing these three emerging standards have in common is that they are all based on powerful encryption mechanisms to protect the confidentiality of the transaction. The three protocols feature ways of securing the content of messages as they travel along networks; authentication, which uses certificates and digital signatures to verify the identity of parties in information exchanges and transactions; and message integrity, which ensures that messages cannot be altered en route.

Encryption is also the underpinning of a variety of digital cash schemes that are currently being developed and test piloted in the United States and Europe. Digital cash, based on the concept of public-cryptography, can be minted electronically in any amount, including fractions of a cent. Now downloads and every cent of digital cash can be accounted for, which means that it cannot be stolen, counterfeited, or lost.

That is alarming to consumers who worry about a lack of privacy but comforting to law enforcers who say that it would help curtail money laundering, tax evasion, and other crimes.

In addition to the privacy issue, there are a number of other obstacles that must be overcome before consumers, digital merchants, banks, and other financial institutions will want to use digital cash.

Consumers, merchants, and everyone else who handles money must perceive that digital cash has value. Consumers must be able to make spontaneous purchases, to download their money wherever they are and send it off to anyone they choose whenever they wish. That means consumers also must have the option of storing their electronic money on their PCs and in an electronic wallet.

Perhaps, the biggest hurdle to electronic commerce is lack of agreement on a single electronic payment system. CommerceNet and World Wide Web Consortium are collaborating on what the two groups call the Joint Electronic Payments Initiative and are exploring ways to make credit cards, e-checks, and e-cash and those systems compatible with one another.

Chapter 5 examines the leading companies in the digital cash business and compares and contrasts their respective technologies.

5 Digital Money Makers

Several organizations—ranging from university computer labs to major banking institutions—are vying for position in the new world of e-commerce. Each has its own strategy for securely transferring cash, credit cards, or checks across the Net.

For example, in October 1996, VeriFone introduced a low-cost smart card reader and writer called the Personal ATM (P-ATM) that is small enough to fit in the palm of the hand. The P-ATM connects to a standard telephone line and allows consumers to download digital cash from their bank accounts into a smart card electronic wallet, transfer funds between accounts, and purchase goods and services over the Internet and telephone lines.

Several companies, including American Express, MasterCard International, Mondex International Ltd., and Wells Fargo say they will provide products and services that will allow consumers to use their smart cards in a variety of home-oriented devices such as personal computers, Web television sets, and telephones.

VeriFone says that it will sell the P-ATM to financial institutions, which will lease them to consumers for $3 to $5 a month.

Three viable companies, each with a unique approach to electronic money handling, have emerged. They are CyberCash (and companies such as CheckFree that license CyberCash technology),

DigiCash, and First Virtual Holdings. By "viable," I mean companies that are actually in the business of providing electronic payment services. I'll describe these three in detail and then provide a quick overview of some of the others that have a good chance of succeeding.

Cybercash, a new spin on shopping.

CyberCash

CyberCash Inc., based in Reston, Virginia, is one of the first companies to plant a stake in the electronic money handling business over the Internet with a real-time, secure credit card authentication service. Its digital signature security technology is based on the industrial-strength encryption of RSA Data Security, Inc., which uses a 128-bit key that could be unbreakable. Best yet, the company has won approval from the federal government to export its products based on RSA's technology.

Its main products include the CyberWallet, from which consumers make secure purchases with their credit cards, and the Merchant Cash Register, which merchants use to handle their transactions with consumers. CyberWallet and Merchant Cash Register are free. CyberCash says it has distributed some seven hundred thousand wallets and is processing ten thousand credit card transactions a day.

CyberCoin, the fast, easy, and secure way to shop on the Internet.

CyberCash launched in October 1996 a service called CyberCoins, an electronic cash scheme allowing buyers to anonymously make Internet payments of 25 cents to $10. CyberCash gives consumers software for their PCs called Internet Payment Wallet, which allows them to download up to $20 worth of CyberCoins over the Internet. CyberCash has licensed the software to America Online and CompuServe, which will offer the electronic wallet to their subscribers. CyberCash also hopes that it will be able to convince several banks to offer the software to their customers. At CyberCoin's launch, consumers could only obtain the digital coins from NationsBank, a merchant bank, and First Data Corp. Card Services Group, a top credit card processing company. Consumers use Internet Payment Wallet software to download up to $20 worth of "electronic pocket change" and can spend their CyberCoins at sites operated by participating merchants. At launch time, CyberCash had managed to sign up about three dozen merchants, including the *Los Angeles Times* who plans to sell articles from its archives. Consumers pay for their goods or services by clicking on a CyberCoin icon at the digital merchant's Web site. After the purchased items are delivered to the buyer, the participating bank automatically transfers the digital coins from the consumer's account to the merchant account, again at a participating bank. Consumers and merchants must set up a CyberCoin account at a participating bank but are not required to maintain their regular bank accounts with the same institution. Participating banks charge digital merchants a transaction fee (CyberCash has not said exactly what the fee will be) that is shared between the bank and CyberCash. It also plans to offer electronic checks that can be used to move funds between accounts over the Internet but has not announced a launch date.

If it is any measure of acceptance, the company has working partnerships with several banks and financial services institutions, including Wells Fargo Bank, San Francisco, California; Boatmen's Credit Card Bank, St. Louis, Missouri; Norwest Card Services, Des Moines, Iowa; Cardservice International, Agoura Hills, California; CheckFree Corp., Columbus, Ohio; and First Data Merchant Services, Palo Alto, California.

Merchants who accept CyberCash Secure Payments include Farallon, Novell, and Oracle in the computer industry; Daily Bread Company and Virtual Vineyards in the food business; and a diverse group of merchandisers ranging from the CigarSnob to Kids-N-Motion.

Being first is no guarantee that CyberCash will win the electronic payments race, however. The company has yet to turn a profit since its 1994 founding, according to the Gartner Group, a technology and market research firm based in Stamford, Connecticut. Gartner predicts CyberCash will lose some $44 million before finally turning the corner in 1997.

Also, CyberCash must contend with mounting competition from companies like Citicorp and VeriFone as well as DigiCash, First Virtual Holdings, and others touting digital cash and credit transaction processes. Ironically, VeriFone was founded by Bill Melton, CyberCash cofounder and investor.

For Consumers Considering CyberCash

Here's how CyberCash's Secure Payment plan works from the consumer side:

1. Consumers first visit the CyberCash home page (www.cybercash.com) and download a copy of CyberWallet. After the program is launched, would-be cybershoppers must enter personal information (name, address, and so on) as well as credit card information. The program generates a digital signature, automatically used to encrypt and sign transactions. All encryption is at the message level and is therefore independent of the Web browser technology that the shopper uses.

2. Next, a shopper visits a site and finds something he or she wishes to purchase, tells the merchant what the item is, where it is to be shipped, and so on. The Merchant Cash Register server responds by sending a summary of the item, its price, and related information.

3. With confirmation in hand, the consumer opens his or her CyberWallet, chooses a credit card with which to pay, and clicks OK to forward the order and encrypted payment information to the merchant.

4. The merchant receives the packet, strips off the order information, and forwards the encrypted payment information to the CyberCash server. The merchant cannot see the consumer's credit card information. Before sending the payment information, the merchant digitally signs and encrypts it with a private key.

5. A CyberCash server receives the packet, takes the transaction off the Internet, unwraps the data within a hardware-based crypto box—like the ones banks use to handle personal identification numbers (PINs) as they are shipped from ATM network to ATM network—reformats the transaction, and forwards it to the merchant's bank over a dedicated network.

6. The merchant's bank then forwards the authorization request to the issuing bank via the card association or American Express or Discover, which do not participate in the card association. The approval or denial code then is sent back to CyberCash.

7. CyberCash then returns the approval or denial code to the merchant, and the merchant passes it on to the consumer.

8. The entire process should not take any more than 15-20 seconds.

Shop Setup With CyberCash

Here's how digital merchants can set up shop using CyberCash:

1. The merchant fills out a merchant registration form, an application that asks for contact information, name of company, address, type of organization, name of bank or financial service bureau with which it does credit card business, the sorts of products to be sold, and other information. CyberCash then sends the merchant a software license to complete and return.

2. CyberCash issues the merchant a user name and password that allows the merchant to access a restricted area on a CyberCash server and download the free Merchant Cash Register software.

3. The merchant installs the Cash Register software onto its Web server. Cash Register runs under various versions of UNIX (including Linux) and Windows NT. The merchant also must have or open a merchant credit card account at a bank that accepts CyberCash Secure Internet Payments. The merchant indicates on the credit card account application that it intends to accept Internet transactions using CyberCash's Secure Internet Payment Service, submits the application, and waits a week or two for approval.

4. While waiting for approval, the merchant can create or modify its Internet store to use CyberCash. CyberCash will supply—at no charge—the merchant's Web site provider with the requisite software to handle CyberCash transactions.

5. Upon approval, the bank provides CyberCash with merchant and terminal ID numbers, which are used in the system to identify merchants approved by the bank.

Advantages & Disadvantages

CyberCash is an early leader in the digital money marketplace and thus far has little competition. Here are some of the advantages and disadvantages of CyberCash Secure Internet Payments plan:

Advantages

- It offers real-time, secure credit card authentication service.
- Encryption uses keys that are 128 bits long and can be exported.
- It offers partnerships with a wide variety of banks and financial services institutions.

Disadvantages

- Merchants and sellers must use special software.
- Each merchant must have an account with an acquiring bank that accepts CyberCash Secure Internet Payments.

CheckFree, technology for handling credit card transactions over the Net.

CheckFree

CheckFree, based in Columbus, Ohio, has licensed CyberCash's Wallet technology for its own use in handling credit card transactions over the Internet (www.checkfree.com). The company has been processing bill paying by checks and credit cards for more than a dozen years.

CheckFree's Wallet is compatible with CyberCash Wallet as well as with the CompuServe Wallet (another licensee) and operates much like CyberCash's payment-processing scheme. In fact, a merchant that sets up to accept any one of the three can accept the others as well. Like the others, CheckFree's Wallet is free; consumers do not pay any fees to use it.

Several merchants accept CheckFree Wallet with CyberCash, the CompuServe Wallet with CheckFree, and the CyberCash Wallet. These merchants include Iceberg Software, a software company; the Internet Society, an organization promoting internetworking technologies and applications; MediaMart, an online seller of CD-ROMs and videotapes; Oracle, the noted database and software development company; and Virtual Vineyards, a California fine wine merchant.

DigiCash, a great way send cash through the Internet.

DigiCash

Tiny Amsterdam-based DigiCash and its founder David Chaum have been the leading proponents of Ecash—their term for digital cash protected by public-key cryptography.

What makes Ecash different from other digital money schemes is the complete anonymity it provides the digital cash user. In a typical digital cash arrangement, the bank creates the digital dollars by generating a serial number representing a specific amount (let's say a 100-digit number represents $10) and signs them with its digital signature. Later, when the digital dollars are returned to the bank, it could identify who the consumer paid merely by looking at the serial numbers and the identity of the person or business that cashed them. This lack of privacy rightfully worries many people. Suppose the digital dollars were used to purchase prescription drugs, adult videos, certain books, or other items that might prove embarrassing or harmful to the consumer if revealed publicly?

DigiCash uses an extension to digital signatures, which was developed by Chaum, to inhibit the bank's ability to identify the person spending and receiving the digital dollars. Here's how it works:

1. Rather than having the bank mint and issue the digital dollars, the consumer uses a PC to randomly generate a 100-digit number that represents $10.

2. Next the consumer multiplies that number by yet another random number (the larger the better) and signs it using a private key.

3. The consumer transmits to the bank the encrypted number and instructions to debit his or her account for $10. The bank uses the consumer's public key to verify that he or she indeed created the message. That's all the bank can do, however, since the 100-digit number representing $10 remains encrypted.

4. The bank digitally signs the message with its private key, confirms that the number represents $10 in digital dollars, and sends the number back to the consumer.

5. The consumer removes the randomly generated multiplier and is ready to go shopping.

The process is akin to the consumer creating 10 dollar bills, putting them in an envelope, and mailing them to the bank. On the outside of the envelope, the consumer has written "This contains $10." The bank receives the envelope and notes that it contains $10. The bank embosses the envelope and the $10 inside with its seal of approval, debits the consumer's account, and returns the envelope. The consumer receives the envelope, opens it, and takes out the $10. Later, the bank honors the $10 because it is able to recognize the embossed seal that it applied through the envelope.

Later, when the consumer spends the $10, the merchant sends the digital dollars to its bank. The merchant's bank uses the consumer's bank's public key to verify that it is legitimate. The merchant's bank also checks the 100-digit number against a list of numbers representing digital dollars that the consumer already has spent. Assuming that the number is not on the list, the bank credits the merchant's account and adds the new number to its list of already-spent numbers. Maintaining the database of already-spent numbers is the bank's safeguard against this consumer or anyone else double spending—spending the same digital dollars more than once—or counterfeiting.

Digital Dollar Deals

DigiCash has signed agreements with Mark Twain Banks, an American regional bank; Deutsche Bank, a German bank; EUnet, a Dutch Internet service provider; and Merita Bank of Finland. DigiCash also has been involved in a number of other Ecash-related ventures, including Conditional Access for Europe, a European Ecash and smart cards trial, and DyniCash, in which road-toll fees are assessed on moving cars via smart cards.

To use Ecash, merchants and consumers must work with one of the banks with which DigiCash has signed agreements. The only one in the United States is Mark Twain Banks (www.marktwain.com), based in St. Louis and operating in Illinois, Kansas, and Missouri, which began testing Ecash technology in November 1995.

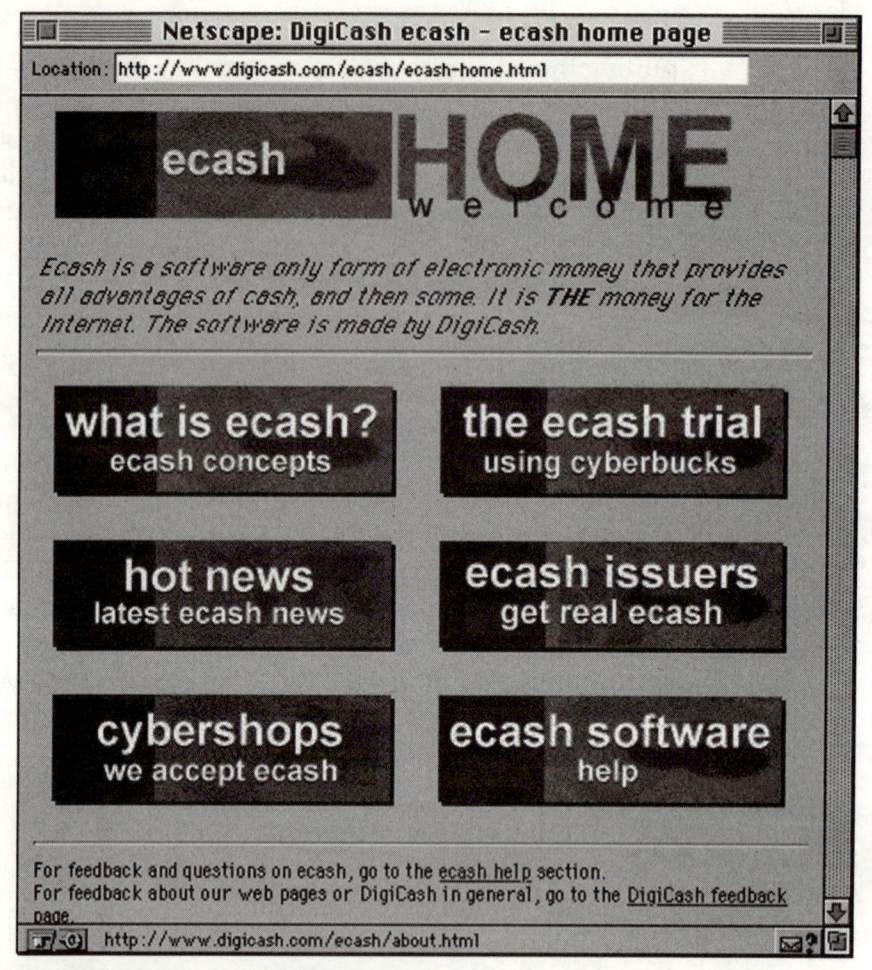

Ecash, the money for the Internet.

U.S. Consumer Accounts

To use DigiCash, a consumer must open a special account with Mark Twain Banks. Called a World Currency Access account, it's a traditional bank account that has no minimum initial deposit requirement and accepts deposits in 25 different currencies.

Consumers also must download and install DigiCash's Ecash software, which enables them to transfer money from the so-called Ecash mint at the bank to their hard drives. To fund the account, consumers send money to Mark Twain Banks by check or wire.

Once the funds are collected, Mark Twain Banks transfers the money (in amounts of $100 or less) to the Ecash mint. Amounts of more than $100 are left in the consumer's account until the consumer asks for it to be transferred. Once the money is moved into the mint, the consumer can retrieve it using the Ecash software.

At this point, the money in the mint is no longer a deposit; it's officially a withdrawal. It can be returned to the bank and left in the account or withdrawn, as with real money.

Consumers pay a one-time setup charge of $11 to $25, plus a monthly fee of $1 to $5, depending on their account balances. There is no per-transaction fee.

Becoming an Ecash Merchant

Becoming an Ecash merchant starts with filling out a merchant account application (www.marktwain.com/digiapp.html). After the bank processes the application, it sends the merchant an account ID and a password.

Next, the merchant downloads the guidelines for setting up the Ecash shop from DigiCash (http://www.digicash.com/Ecash/mt/buildshop.html). The site also includes instructions for UNIX, Windows 95, and Windows NT. You can do it yourself or hire one of a growing number of consultants, who are listed on the Mark Twain Banks and DigiCash Web sites.

Here are the basic requirements:

- If the merchant is using a UNIX machine, the Web server must support the standard cgi-bin interface. The following Web servers have been used and tested successfully: NCSA httpd (1.3 and newer), CERN httpd (3.0 and newer), Apache httpd, Netscape Communications server.

- The merchant's UNIX must be on the list of Ecash-supported platforms.

- The system-wide cgi-bin directory of the Web server must include write access.

- PERL version 4 or 5 must be installed.

- The merchant must be able to create a new UNIX user account or have one available that isn't used for anything else.

Mark Twain Banks' Ecash merchants pay a one-time setup fee of $150 to $500 and a monthly fee of $5 to $25 based on their level of activity. In addition, they pay to move money in and out of their digital accounts—2–3 percent of the first $500 and an additional 2–2.75 percent of the balance. At the time of this writing, Mark Twain Banks offered a 35 percent discount on setup fees and waived all monthly fees for the first three months.

Advantages & Disadvantages

I already covered many of the benefits and drawbacks of digital cash schemes in the previous chapter, so I won't rehash them here. However, here are a few points unique to DigiCash:

Advantages

- Solid encryption guarantees complete anonymity for Ecash users.
- It's the only digital money scheme in actual operation.
- DigiCash promises low per-transaction costs compared to other payment plans.

Disadvantages

- DigiCash has limited support from banks and financial institutions.
- It requires consumers and merchants to work with specific banks.
- It requires consumers and merchants to use specific software.

First Virtual Holdings, Inc.

In February 1996, to prove a point about its Internet payment system compared to those of its competitors, First Virtual Holdings showed off a PC application that looks like a screen saver but actually steals a credit card number as the user types it into the computer.

First Virtual, the first virtual Internet payment system.

You'll remember from Chapter 2, "Risky Business," that a program that appears benign but actually hides another, mischief-causing program is called a Trojan horse. First Virtual Holdings says that it created this Trojan horse to highlight the vulnerabilities of online services that permit consumers to make purchases over the Internet.

If using credit cards over the Internet becomes common, claims First Virtual, a cybercrook could create a password-grabbing program in the guise of a Trojan horse and pass it out to as many unsuspecting users as possible or attach it to a virus in hopes that it will spread from one PC to another. Once activated, the program could capture credit card numbers as they are entered and send them off to the criminal, using the same connection that the computer's legitimate owner uses for Internet commerce.

According to First Virtual, such an attack could undermine the foundations of the economy when millions of credit card users defaulted on their accounts all at once. Who knows whether that would actually happen, but one thing is certain: First Virtual's antics show just how far companies will go to get a head start in the Internet commerce race.

Nothing, Not Even Net

First Virtual's founders, attorney Lee Stein, and computer scientist Einar Stefferud, claim to have launched the world's first Internet payment system in October 1994. However, First Virtual's payment system makes very little use of the Internet. Its approach to safeguarding credit card transactions over the Internet is to not send credit card numbers over the Internet. The company's position is that sending your credit card number over the Internet or entering it into your computer compromises financial security.

Its payment system relies, at least in part, on sending e-mail over the Internet. Instead of sending their credit card numbers to digital merchants when they want to make a purchase, consumers use a VirtualPIN (an alias for credit card numbers). Credit card numbers are never sent over the Internet and never typed into a computer connected to the Internet, thus eliminating the need for encryption and significantly reducing the potential for fraud, says First Virtual.

How it works:

1. A buyer who's ready to make a purchase sends by e-mail a personal VirtualPIN to the digital merchant.
2. The merchant in turn sends by e-mail the VirtualPIN to First Virtual with a request to charge the buyer's credit card for the amount of the purchase.
3. First Virtual sends an e-mail message to the buyer confirming the seller's request for payment.
4. Assuming the buyer confirms this, First Virtual charges the card.

What's a VirtualPIN?

A VirtualPIN is a string of alphanumeric characters that acts as an alias for a consumer's credit card number and other financial information.

Buyers use their VirtualPINs instead of their credit card numbers on the Internet. Digital merchants use VirtualPINs to identify themselves and the bank accounts to which First Virtual deposits merchants' funds. In both cases, the VirtualPIN is tied to financial information that is inaccessible by Internet connection. A crook who succeeds in intercepting an e-mail message containing a VirtualPIN gets only a string of meaningless numbers instead of valuable financial information.

Since its founding in 1994, First Virtual says more than a hundred thousand buyers and sixteen hundred merchants in 144 countries have acquired VirtualPINs.

Getting Set Up to Use First Virtual

To participate in First Virtual's payment program, a consumer must have a private Internet e-mail account and a Visa or MasterCard credit card. Digital merchants also must have private Internet e-mail accounts, plus bank accounts that accept direct deposits from the U.S. Automated Clearinghouse System.

Merchants with direct Internet connections can set up a storefront on their own server. Those without direct access or a server can sell information products through InfoHaus, First Virtual's online mall. (More about that shortly.)

Digital merchants and consumers follow these steps to get VirtualPINs and start using First Virtual's service:

1. Send name, address, and other basic information on the company's enrollment form (http: www.fv.com/newacct). Or request an application by e-mail message to apply@card.com or telnet.card.com. Then follow the onscreen instructions.

2. First Virtual should respond by e-mail within an hour or so. The reply will contain a 12-digit application number, telephone number, and instructions for activating the VirtualPIN.

3. To activate a VirtualPIN for selling, digital merchants must register their bank account information with First Virtual by regular mail (yes, the real postal system). Consumers can register their credit card numbers by telephone.

4. The company will send the activated VirtualPINs in e-mail messages in about 10 business days for merchants and within a couple of hours for shoppers.

The cost of activating a merchant account is $10. The fee is 29 cents per transaction, plus 2 percent of the selling price. First Virtual says this 2 percent transaction fee is based on what the company pays Visa and MasterCard to use their credit card system. There's also a $1 processing fee when First Virtual deposits the proceeds from the merchants' sales into the merchant's bank accounts. The fees are based on the cost of processing the merchants' transactions on the Internet, storing and accumulating them off the Internet, depositing credits into the merchants' bank accounts, and answering customer service e-mail.

Shoppers pay $2 when they sign up for their VirtualPINs and also any time they need to update their credit card information—such as when a card expires and the consumer registers the new expiration date.

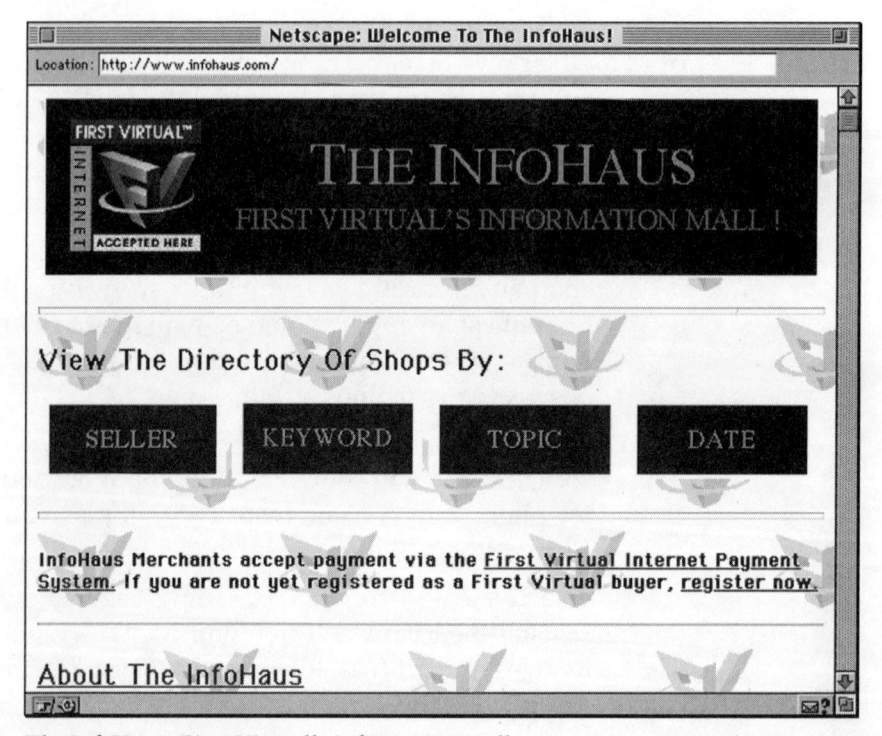

The InfoHaus, First Virtual's information mall.

Shop Basics

Merchants that wish to sell through First Virtual can set up an electronic storefront using their own server and software provided by First Virtual. Merchants who don't want the cost or fuss of maintaining their own servers can sell information products—software, text, and graphics they can download—through the First Virtual InfoHaus online mall. You can visit the site at http://www.infohaus.com or by FTP at ftp://ftp.infohaus.com.

Advantages & Disadvantages

First Virtual claims more than a hundred thousand buyers and sixteen hundred merchants in 144 countries have obtained VirtualPINs. That broad support is a significant advantage for the company. Among its other advantages are:

Advantages

- Processing fees are modest compared to credit card processing fees.
- No special software is needed to use the system.
- Buyers are protected from fraud because charges cannot be made against their accounts without their assent.
- Buyers are anonymous because they use VirtualPINs and because First Virtual does not give the merchants their names.
- Any merchant can sign up to become a First Virtual merchant.
- The merchant needs but an ordinary checking account and is not required to set up any special business accounts with a bank.

Disadvantages

- The merchant assumes all risks.
- There is a lengthy waiting period to become a First Virtual merchant.

- The system rests entirely on e-mail, which isn't always reliable, available, or fast enough.
- There is a long waiting period between the sale and deposit of payment to the merchant's account.

Could-Be Contenders

There are several other companies and university projects developing electronic transaction payment schemes. I'll cover some that are fairly well developed or seem to have potential.

Citibank's Electronic Monetary System

Digital money travels outside traditional banking channels, and online merchants can deal directly with customers without ever going through a bank. That naturally worries banks, which are realizing that the world needs banking but does not necessarily need banks.

Since 1991 Citibank has been developing a digital cash system called Electronic Monetary System (EMS), which should be ready in 1998. The system lets consumers and merchants transact business without using a third party such as Citibank.

EMS was devised by Sholom Rosen, Citibank's vice president of emerging technologies, who said, "EMS is a serious attempt to build a comprehensive electronic money system that reflects the interests of the regulatory authorities, the banking system as it exists today, and the rapid manner in which technology will continue to change." (Cato Institute 14th Annual Monetary Conference, May 23, 1996, Washington, D.C.)

EMS Basics

- Issuing banks generate electronic notes (money) on demand to customers; there can be any number from one to many.
- Correspondent banks accept and distribute the electronic money.
- Clearing banks clear issuing bank notes and settle accounts.

- Subscribers (buyers and sellers) use Money Modules (essentially a secure processing environment) for storing their electronic money, performing online transactions with a bank, or exchanging electronic money with other Money Modules.

EMS notes can be created on demand in any currency. The notes can be withdrawn as cash from a demand deposit account or used to draw down an approved line of credit. Each note carries a complete electronic audit trail and is reconciled by the issuing bank. EMS cash notes circulate and can be redeemed at the bank or transferred to another subscriber. And like cash, the value of each note is guaranteed by a bank.

With the potential for fraudulent use of electronic money systems, EMS was designed to deal with the three basic principles of security: prevention, detection, and containment. EMS addresses prevention through the use of cryptographic protocols and physical protection of the Money Modules. Each communication session is authenticated and secured, and a security server authenticates each Money Module by periodically validating its electronic certificate. A special protective coating makes the Money Module hardware itself tamperproof, thus physically protecting the sensitive software it contains.

To help identify duplicate or counterfeit notes, EMS (invisibly to the user) regularly sweeps electronic notes into the bank for validation and control before returning new notes to the Money Module. The system also reconciles notes cleared to notes issued.

EMS contains suspected fraudulent use in several ways:

- Electronic notes carry an expiration date that limits the window of opportunity for transfers. The value of the notes does not expire; the ability to move them does. EMS also can block both further use of Money Modules that are known to be corrupted and future circulation of fraudulent notes. The system also can cause a Money Module certificate to expire, thereby putting the Money Module out of commission.

- EMS strikes a balance between the needs for system security and customer privacy, addressing those critical issues in a way that guarantees every transaction can be traced without the need to know the identity of the customer.

- EMS provides an infrastructure for applications such as simple retail point-of-sale, electronic payments between corporations, interbank payments, and party-to-party foreign exchange.

Citibank attributed the slow growth of electronic commerce over open networks, such as the Internet, to the poor security across the network and the absence of adequate protection for the buyer and seller as they attempt to conduct business without any face-to-face contact.

One basic risk of doing business over open networks, for example, is that of reneging: The buyer can pull the plug upon receipt of the goods but before paying, or the seller can pull the plug upon receipt of payment but before shipping the goods. In cyberspace, the secure receipt of both payment and electronic goods must be redefined.

A companion technology known as Trusted Agent was designed along with EMS to guarantee payment for and delivery of electronic goods and services purchased over the Internet or any other open network. Through the use of secure transaction umbrellas, EMS and Trusted Agent together ensure that both the customer and the merchant are safe, because payment and delivery are locked and synchronized. Payments are released to the merchant and electronic goods released to the buyer only upon the successful fulfillment of both sides of the transaction.

Trusted Agent not only integrates information with the movement of money but also verifies that the cybermerchant is actually who it purports to be. Trusted Agent also carries information explaining the nature of a payment—such as an invoice number required by businesses when posting payments—and creates and delivers a secure receipt at the end of a transaction.

Trusted Agent is not limited to electronic money applications but can use credit or debit cards as the payment medium over an electronic network.

NetCash & NetCheque

NetCash and NetCheque are payment systems being developed at the Information Sciences Institute (ISI) of the University of Southern California (USC). As you might expect, NetCash is a scheme for digital cash; NetCheque is a scheme for electronic checks. Both are based on encryption and digital signatures. NetCheque is not being offered by anyone, although ISI is seeking a partner to provide commercial NetCheque services.

Online Pocket Change

NetCash is similar to DigiCash's Ecash: Digital money consists of a sequence of numbers that are encrypted and digitally signed by the digital money mint or issuing bank. In this case, NetCash is being handled through the NetBank Payment System (NetBank), operated by Software Agents Inc., Germantown, Maryland. Address e-mail to netbank-info@agents.com for more information.

Here is an example of a NetCash $10 bill:

```
NetCash US$ 10.00 A123456B789012C
```

NetCash, again like DigiCash's Ecash, provides for anonymity, although not to the same degree. The NetCash user's identity can be traced if all participants in a transaction are in collusion; with DigiCash, the Ecash user's identity remains hidden even if all transaction participants work together to identify the e-money user. NetCash's developers contend that unconditional or complete anonymity is not needed because banks, electronic money mints, and the like have no need or even incentive to monitor what consumers do with their digital dollars.

NetBank issues NetCash in amounts up to $100 (in denominations of 25 cents to $100) and is best suited for making purchases in the $10-$20 range. It can be used to buy pages of a newsletter for 25 cents each or shareware software, for example.

Consumers purchase NetCash from NetBank by sending payments to software agents via e-mail, fax, or mail. They pay for their digital dollars using credit cards or checks. There is a conversion fee equal to 2 percent of the amount of NetCash purchased, with a minimum fee of one dollar.

NetCash/NetBank Merchants

Only a handful of online merchants accept NetCash. They include publications (*Boardwatch Magazine* and *The Internet Informer*), shareware software companies (Peter N. Lewis, Kagi Engineering, and DTV Engineering), and bulletin board and online service providers (The PhoeniX Rising, SGIR, The Sprawl, The Wahrsaga, and PEI Crafts).

How to Become a NetCash/NetBank Merchant

To sign up, merchants must complete a service agreement that includes information such as name, address, tax ID, description of product or service, and estimated monthly sales volume. A one-time fee of $19.95 must be submitted with the service agreement. When NetBank receives the form, it creates a merchant account, and notifies the merchant by e-mail.

A merchant that receives NetCash requests reimbursement by depositing the NetCash into their NetBank merchant account. The merchant pays a conversion fee equal to 2 percent of the amount of NetCash being reimbursed, with a minimum fee of $4.

The NetCheque System

A NetCheque account works much like an ordinary checking account. The electronic check writer creates the check by filling in all the information you would expect to see on a real check: name of payer, name of financial institution, account number, name of person to whom the check is being written, and amount. As with a regular check, the payer must sign and the payee must endorse the NetCheque. It's done electronically using the encryption technology called Kerberos that I discussed in Chapter 3, "Encryption & Digital John Hancocks."

The check writer retrieves a so-called ticket containing a secret key that has been encrypted twice, once with the check writer's password and the second with the bank's password. The check writer signs the check electronically with the ticket. The check goes to the bank by e-mail, where it is decrypted. Since the ticket could have come only from the Kerberos server or the writer of the check, the bank knows the check is legitimate.

To use NetCheque, a user must set up an account with a NetCheque accounting server (none was in operation at the time of this writing) and obtain a NetCheque software release. This software can be downloaded from USC/ISI at ftp://prospero.isi.edu/pub/netcheque/distribution.

Set up an account with NetChex.

NetChex

NetChex, based in Phoenix, offers what it calls a virtual checking account, which is an extension of a customer's existing checking account (http://www.netchex.com/netchex.html). Checks that are paid to merchants are encrypted and signed digitally.

To become a NetChex member, a consumer or merchant first must complete an enrollment application and return it by fax or mail. The consumer then downloads NetChex Client software, which is used to generate NetChex transactions, cancel transactions, generate signature keys, maintain the account, and reconcile account statements. The consumer receives by telephone an unlock code that is necessary to install and set up the NetChex Client software. The software is unique to each PC and cannot be copied from one machine to another. It generates a signature key that is used to encrypt the transaction data before it is sent to NetChex for processing. NetChex Client software also makes use of what the system calls a check code, which represents the number of checks that each consumer can use. The consumer must prepay checks in increments of 10 at 50 cents each, plus a $2 service charge. The customer replenishes checks by updating the check code by phone.

Meanwhile, the merchant receives a so-called merchant code, a 32-character ID that is used to identify the merchant's name, address, phone number, and other relevant information. When consumers make purchases using their electronic checks, they receive from the merchant a reference code of up to 48 characters, which the merchant uses to link the customer and the transaction.

Once NetChex receives the electronic check, it sends confirmations to the consumer and the merchant. The actual check is generated, made payable to the merchant, and sent to its bank for deposit within 24 hours. Merchants pay 3 to 5 percent of the face value or $1 per check, whichever is greater. There is also a monthly service charge of $10.

Moving On

Companies such as CyberCash and DigiCash had little chance of succeeding without partners in banking, computers, and telecommunications. Now, several companies in these crucial fields are working on electronic commerce plans based on digital money, electronic purses, and related technologies.

CyberCash, for example, has agreements with Wells Fargo Bank, Norwest Card Services, Cardservice International, and several other leading companies. The support of highly visible companies in the financial industry will help legitimize the notion of electronic commerce using digital money. CyberCoins, an electronic cash plan that allows consumers to make payments of

25 cents to $10 over the Internet, is the first Internet payment program that is widely supported by the key participants in electronic commerce, especially banks and merchants.

CyberCoins's future is promising because it is a low-risk opportunity for consumers to experiment with digital money and presumably boost their confidence in electronic commerce.

VeriFone's plan to put personal automatic teller machines into homes also is significant because it promises to boost consumer awareness of smart card technology as well as digital money.

Net Security: Your Digital Doberman

6 Safe Shopkeeping on the WWW

Thousands of companies are scrambling to set up shop on the World Wide Web (WWW) and sell their wares virtually to anyone, anywhere, anytime. They're gambling that Web shoppers will buy goods and services at the click of a mouse button instead of hopping in cars and driving over to a real mall. Maybe you're thinking about setting up your own Web site and joining this latest gold rush. Hold that thought for just a minute.

Not surprisingly, outlaw hackers also have discovered the Web. Gangs with monikers like the Chaos Merchants and the Internet Liberation Front are regularly attacking WWW sites, altering information and causing mischief in other ways:

- In 1995, a couple of weeks before the debut of the MGM-United Artists film *Hackers*, digital vandals claiming to be members of the Internet Liberation Front hacked a site maintained by the film's promoters. They defaced the site's home page with computer crayon scribbling and altered text to read ". . . this is going to be a lame, cheesy promotional site for a movie . . . click here for a big waste of bandwidth . . ."

- Even comedian Rodney Dangerfield's Web site has been broken into by a group of hackers known as the Chaos Merchants. They stole his home page and left a picture of a naked woman. Chaos Merchants is known in cyberspace as a rebel group with a dislike for the Microsoft and IBM empires, as well as a distaste for all commercial ventures.

- A hacker who apparently opposes Net censorship and gun control attacked the Department of Justice's Web site in August 1996. The DOJ's pages were replaced with pages bearing Nazi swastikas, pictures of Adolf Hitler, sexually explicit material, and a picture of George Washington with the caption "Move my grave to a free country! This rolling is making me an insomniac." The doctored pages also had links to other Web sites that were unflattering to President Clinton, Bob Dole, and Pat Buchanan.

- The following month, the Swedish Hackers Association decided to protest the treatment of five of their members, who were on trial for a variety of computer-related crimes, by trashing the Central Intelligence Agency's Web site. They changed the CIA's logo to the Central Stupidity Agency, and posted "Stop lying, Bo Skarinder" in English and Swedish. Skarinder is the trial prosecutor. They also changed the CIA's links to connect to Playboy's site as well as other sites frequented by members of the computer underground.

Attacks like these are easy to dismiss as the pranks of youthful hackers who have too much time on their hands. But the problem is far more serious than anyone might have contemplated previously. Some hackers alter prices, product descriptions, and other critical information on Web pages. No one yet knows what a Web site's liability is in such cases, but clearly it could have negative financial impact.

The fabulously successful World Wide Web is electronic commerce's equivalent of a "killer application," that is, an application that makes a technology skyrocket. The Web has been in existence for only a few years, yet is the fastest growing segment of the Internet.

The WWW has developed into an international bazaar where consumers anywhere in the world can shop for goods and services at any time. But as shopping on the WWW becomes more popular, it will no doubt attract more thieves, because as bank robber Willie Sutton once observed, "That's where the money is."

This chapter details the primary ways that thieves and others can attack the systems of both sellers and buyers.

Attack Modes

WWW attacks are focused in three primary areas:

- Network infrastructure supporting the WWW.
- Web servers, which house electronic storefronts and other business activities.
- Web browsers, which are used by Web shoppers to view and retrieve information and make purchases.

Web servers rely on Transmission Control Protocol/Internet Protocol (TCP/IP), the same protocol that governs all Internet communication. They're susceptible to the same sorts of attacks aimed at firewalls and other parts of networked systems. Attacks against Web servers may include denial-of-service attacks, such as the *synflooding*, which overwhelms a computer with packets of data until it shuts down; intercepting transmissions to eavesdrop on confidential information or to break into a site; and forging IP addresses to masquerade as someone trustworthy.

These attacks have been described in Chapters 1 and 7, so I won't rehash them here. In this chapter, I'll detail how outlaw hackers, cybercrooks, and other rogues can exploit Web servers and browsers, and what digital merchants and consumers can do to protect themselves.

Web Server Security

When you set up your own Web site, you hope the world will beat a path to your door. The problem is that along with the paying customers come the shoplifters, vandals, and many others you'd rather not attract. You're accessible not only to window shoppers but also to those who want to break the window and loot the display.

Web sites are among the easiest to attack and plunder, mainly because Webmasters, the people responsible for setting up and maintaining Web servers, as well as the site administrators, pay little if any attention to Web security. Web sites are designed for easy access and typically offer such features as online forms and electronic mail, which can be exploited readily.

It's easier and easier to set up a Web server these days, easy enough that Webmasters are just as likely to be creative types as technical experts. Also, many departments within companies are setting up their own Web sites, often without the help, sometimes without even the knowledge, of information systems administrators and managers.

Says Fred Cohen, a top consultant on WWW security who is credited with creating the first computer virus in 1983:

> [Web sites are] being implemented in the most hostile of environments with a completely untrained and unaware user base as a basis for a global system for distributed computation and electronic commerce. It has inadequate protection for integrity, availability, and confidentiality.... It may introduce large liabilities to both providers and users.... [The browsers, servers, and networks have] fundamental design flaws that make it inherently difficult to protect..., and it is being implemented on an unprecedented scale in a very short time frame almost entirely by people who do not understand the protection issues.

Do It Yourself, or Not

You have two basic choices when setting up a Web site: Rent space through an Internet service provider (ISP) or set up a Web site on your own. If you lack sufficient in-house technical expertise or resources, renting space on a server operated by an ISP is your only option. On the plus side, it could be the most secure approach, because someone else also has a vested interest in protecting the site. However, the downside is that you won't have a high level of integration between the Web server for selling goods and services and your internal systems used for processing and shipping orders.

If you create your own Web site, you have complete control over the Web marketing and order processing sides of the business. One drawback is that you also are responsible for security, not only for the server but also for all the internal information systems to which your organization connects.

Web server software is complex and, like any other sophisticated software, is bound to have bugs, some of which can be used to circumvent security. The more sophisticated a server, the more likely it will have security holes.

Most Web servers run on UNIX. As I mentioned earlier, UNIX is not easy to secure, even for UNIX gurus. From the start, UNIX was meant to be accessed by remote users. UNIX's large number of built-in servers, services, scripting languages, and interpreters means there are many entry portals for hackers to exploit. Over the years, hackers and others have probed UNIX's defenses and exposed numerous loopholes originally intended to facilitate remote access. UNIX software is often free and widely available, giving hackers a chance to pore over the source code to find loopholes. And tools for cracking UNIX are widely available.

Hackers and others in search of security loopholes regularly probe popular Web server software such as the National Center for Supercomputing Application's (NCSA's) Apache in search of security loopholes. One such loophole permitted hackers to take over NCSA UNIX Web servers, find passwords and other critical files, and execute programs. NCSA has issued a patch for this loophole, but assuming it's now hacker-proof would be foolish.

Mac Web servers are not as vulnerable to hacking as their UNIX counterparts. The Mac's operating system was not designed with remote access in mind. As a result, it is more difficult for hackers to exploit. Also, Mac applications are somewhat self-contained in that they do not interact a great deal with one another. They're generally easier to set up and administer than are UNIX applications, reducing the likelihood that security will be compromised. Mac source code isn't as readily available and so not as susceptible to being scrutinized for configuration errors, bugs, and other potential security loopholes.

Storefronts in a Box

A number of companies market "storefronts in a box" that permit digital merchants to set up an outlet safe from electronic shoplifters, pickpockets, and others who might steal their dollars and wares. IBM Corp., Microsoft Corp., Netscape Communications Corp., and Open Market Inc.—to name but a handful of companies—offer these "instant" secure storefronts.

A common feature of these all-in-one secure Web servers is support for authentication using digital signatures or IDs as well as for the leading security protocols such as Secure Sockets Layer (SSL) and Secure Electronic Transactions (SET) credit card encryption protocols, Secure HyperText Transfer Protocol (S-HTTP), and Private Communication Technology (PCT).

These are in addition to the basic security features provided by Web servers. Webmasters can restrict access to the server based on the prospective site visitor's domain name and IP address. They also can set up a variety of user groups based on domain name and IP address and then restrict access of each group to specific directories and files.

Other common features include:

- Tools for setting up the site, automatically loading and updating Web pages, linking front- and back-end operations, and other critical site-operation activities.

- An electronic shopping basket that consumers fill with their purchases.

- Transaction history that tracks the shopper's buying habits and makes it possible for digital merchants to customize their Web sites for individual shoppers.

Microsoft Merchant System

I've arbitrarily decided to describe Microsoft's Merchant System to give you a glimpse at how a storefront in a box might work. Its selection is not an endorsement of this product, which I've never used, and is not meant to imply that this system is better than what is offered by Netscape, Open Market, or anyone else. Buyer beware: Much of the information I present here came directly from Microsoft.

The Microsoft Merchant System can be used to run a single storefront or to host multiple storefronts in an Internet mall environment. It can be operated by a single merchant or by a third-party host, such as an ISP.

With the Microsoft Merchant System, merchants can build storefronts using "starter stores," which are sample store configurations that can be tailored to a merchant's needs.

Merchant System supports SSL and SET credit card encryption protocols. As I mentioned in an earlier chapter, Microsoft was a principal architect of the SET specifications proposed by Visa and MasterCard as an industry standard for secure processing of credit card payments over the Internet.

Microsoft Merchant System includes VeriFone's virtual point-of-sale (vPOS) and vGATE, the first Internet payment products to implement the SET protocol. The two products provide for the authentication of consumers and digital merchants and ensure that merchants can safely route financial transaction information directly to the card issuer.

Microsoft Merchant has three components:

- Merchant Workbench
- Merchant Server
- Shopping client

Merchant Workbench and Server run on Windows NT-based servers, and the shopping client runs on desktops running Windows, Windows 95, Windows NT, Apple Macintosh, or UNIX.

Merchant Workbench Features

Merchant Workbench is a set of tools for setting up and managing electronic storefronts. These include tools that do the following:

- Configure and administer software for tax calculation, shipping, and handling.
- Develop and test Web pages, which includes layout products and categories used in an online store; create product pages from information in a product database; test new store configurations before going live.
- View orders.
- Set up logos and accepted payment methods unique to each merchant and establish security limits for each type of customer.
- Report on consumer browsing and buying behavior on the merchant Web site.

Merchant Server Features

The Merchant Server is a set of services used throughout the Merchant System for electronic retailing—ranging from product browsing on the client side to order processing and financial transactions on the server side:

- Presale services for content publishing and creation of orders.

- Sale services related to order processing (with taxing, shipping and handling, and pricing calculations), order routing, and so on.

- Postsale services such as confirming orders and responding to client-generated requests for order status.

- General services consisting of a merchant information service that provides merchant names and addresses, logos, the merchant's accepted payment types, and so on.

Shopping Client

This component runs on consumers' computers to allow them to place products or services they want to buy in an electronic shopping basket. It handles encryption, storage of credit card information, and shopping history on the consumer's machine.

The shopping client must be used with a Web browser. It is compatible with any popular browser, not just Microsoft's Internet Explorer. Its features include:

- Shopping Basket manages and displays the items selected for purchase and provides View Basket, Add to Basket, Delete from Basket, and Pay Now functions.

- Persistent storage enables consumers to interrupt the shopping process and store items for an extended length of time without having to reselect the items when they resume shopping.

- Management of address and payment information includes such items as default shipping addresses and payment types.

- Order History tracks purchases made from the shopping client, as well as the merchant's name, description of the item, purchase amount, and order status information.

Shopping Cycle

According to Microsoft, here's how the typical shopping cycle works:

1. Using the Merchant Workbench, the merchant sets up an online store on the merchant's Web server. If the merchant uses an ISP or other service to host the merchant's site in an online mall, the ISP handles store setup.

2. The merchant registers with the acquiring bank and gets a SET certificate for each payment method that is accepted—Visa and American Express cards, for example.

3. The customer downloads the client-side shopper from the merchant Web site or from the Microsoft Web site.

4. The customer registers each credit card and gets a SET certificate for each card that is accepted with the issuing bank's server.

5. Using a Web browser, the customer views the merchant's Web pages and places items in the Shopping Basket. If the consumer's connection to the merchant Web site is lost prior to placing the order, the shopping client retains the state of shopping at the time, meaning it keeps a record of items collected in the basket and stores related data so the consumer can easily complete the purchase transaction when the connection is restored.

6. The customer clicks the Ready to Pay button, which creates a combined order description and payment instruction, which is sent to the merchant's server.

7. The payment instruction goes to the acquirer for authorization and approval through the existing card-brand network.

8. The Merchant Server sends to the shopping application a confirmation of the order with an assigned tracking number.

9. The Merchant Server also forwards the order description to the appropriate legacy systems for payment and order processing.

Cracking Web Sites

Web servers are vulnerable to attacks that permit hackers and assorted thieves to harvest passwords, seize the keys used to encrypt confidential messages, intercept credit card numbers, use a breached system as a springboard to attack other systems, and commit similar acts—all with dire consequences for any business.

Here are some of the ways that attackers may breach Web server security:

- Planting password *crackering programs,* Trojan horses, and other programs designed to gather information useful for breaking into the site, stealing proprietary information, and intercepting credit card numbers and other sensitive information.

- Exploiting bugs or other security loopholes that allow attackers to execute commands on the server's host machine and modify or damage the system.

- Overflowing input buffers, causing programs to overwrite data or programs with data or programs provided by attackers.

- Flooding the machine with so many requests or other commands that consume memory and other resources that the machine is brought to its knees.

- Gathering information about the Web site and other systems that are connected to it, which can be used to expand the attack or use the Web site as a springboard for attacking other sites (For example, they can seize control of the Web server long enough to grab the system's password file and use that to further penetrate the organization's systems or other sites.)

- Altering or defacing the site's Web pages, a fairly common attack strategy that has serious consequences for the organization's business.

Common Gateway Interface Scripts

Exciting Web sites—the sort most merchants probably want to maintain—provide much more than static information. For example, they may allow a customer to search a catalog simply by entering a keyword, update timely information like stock market and news reports in real time, or display marketing messages with special effects, fluttering like banners or marching across the screen.

The more dazzling features and information are fed to the Web server from other systems using *gateways*, which take information from a non-Web source and turn it into dynamic Web documents without missing a beat. Grabbing the information from one place, turning it into Web fodder, and displaying it on a Web page is done using a program known as a *common gateway interface* (CGI).

With CGI scripts, online merchants can provide Web window shoppers with products or services tailored to their unique needs, handle credit card information and pass it along to an in-house accounting system, send a catalog order to another server for processing—nearly anything the imagination can come up with.

These scripts can be written in any programming language that can run on a UNIX server, including PERL—the most popular language for writing CGI scripts—C and shell scripts.

Alas, CGI scripts are the source of many attacks that can potentially kill a business. In fact, the Computer Emergency Response Team (CERT) addressed the issue in one of its regular advisories about the tools and techniques used to compromise computer systems. CERT said it had been receiving reports "at least weekly, and often daily" of intruders who have managed to seize a Web server's password file by exploiting a flaw in a default CGI script. This is a script that is provided by the developer of the Web server software for demonstration.

Two Ways to Exploit

There are two basic ways CGI scripts can be exploited. First, scripts themselves can give attackers such information as addresses of other internal systems that are useful for cracking the site. Second, the scripts can be changed to execute commands the author never intended. This second way has far greater ramifications. This vulnerability is based on the scripts being designed originally to act upon information provided by an outsider, such as processing information entered into a form or as keywords in a search.

Often, demo scripts provided by Web server makers contain trapdoors into your Web site. Needless to say, those scripts should be removed. An attacker could alter the CGI scripts and grab crypto keys used for authentication, steal credit card numbers, create fake purchase orders, redirect shipments of goods purchased by legitimate customers, alter online catalog information, or cause mischief in other ways.

Although the CGI is inherently secure, CGI scripts should be written with care. It isn't a task for nontechnical Web authors or recent computer science graduates with limited experience.

Keep in mind that the more complex the script, the more likely it will contain bugs. Be wary of scripts that read files on the Web server, because they may violate access restrictions. Scripts that write files can overwrite key files or permit attackers to introduce programs they can use to penetrate the system.

There are many more considerations that savvy Webmasters should be aware of when writing CGI scripts. Your responsibility as the head of the electronic enterprise is to make sure that you have the right person doing the job.

Security Precautions

For Web servers running on UNIX systems, here are some general security precautions to take, but you really need a guru to do the job properly.

Many organizations allow employees to create Web pages and post them with little or no preview. This is not good policy! Employees can post sensitive information, set up links to sites that your organization would rather not be associated with, violate copyright law, and write CGI scripts that contain security flaws.

Only trusted employees should have permission to change files. You should limit access to directories in which key files are kept, such as configuration files, to a handful of employees responsible for maintaining the Web server. To be sure permissions are set correctly on a system, run the COPS program available at ftp://ftp.cert.org/pub/tools/cops.

Most servers let you place restrictions on who can access your server, what directories and files they can read and write to, and more. Make sure you have the appropriate level of rights and privileges for each employee. Obviously, not everyone needs access to every file. You can further limit access to remote users (both inside and outside of the organization) based on their IP address, subnet, or domain. To make sure that people with login privileges choose good passwords, run Crack, available from ftp://ftp.cert.org/pub/tools/crack.

These sorts of restrictions will not stop the more wily hackers, who are able to spoof the server by concealing their real IP addresses, which makes it appear they're connecting from trusted addresses. As an additional safeguard, you should require that remote users have a login ID and a password. Further, the passwords must be well chosen, consisting of a combination of at least six alphanumeric characters. The passwords can be intercepted in transit between the browser and server, so they should be encrypted and stored in encrypted form.

If you don't need them, remove services such as File Transfer Protocol (FTP), Sendmail, shells, and interpreters such as PERL.

To stay alert to break-in attempts and similarly suspicious activity, run Tripwire, available from ftp://coast.cs.purdue.edu/pub/COAST/Tripwire.

Use the Internet to stay informed about developments such as software flaws and attack techniques. Appendix A lists resources such as mailing lists, Web sites, and security-related organizations to further help you.

Keep current on new software updates and patches, and apply them as soon as they're released. Don't count on your vendors to alert you when security holes have been uncovered in their products.

Regularly analyze your Web traffic for signs of suspicious activity such as files uploaded to your site whose content or purpose is not apparent.

Install only those programs and files you need and eliminate all others. Be wary of demo CGI scripts that are provided by the vendor. Some of these scripts have proven vulnerable to exploitation by outsiders.

Counsel employees on sensible system management techniques and tools. Use access control. Limit access to files and directories to only those who really need this access. Run Tripwire, COPS, and similar security programs designed to probe for security weaknesses.

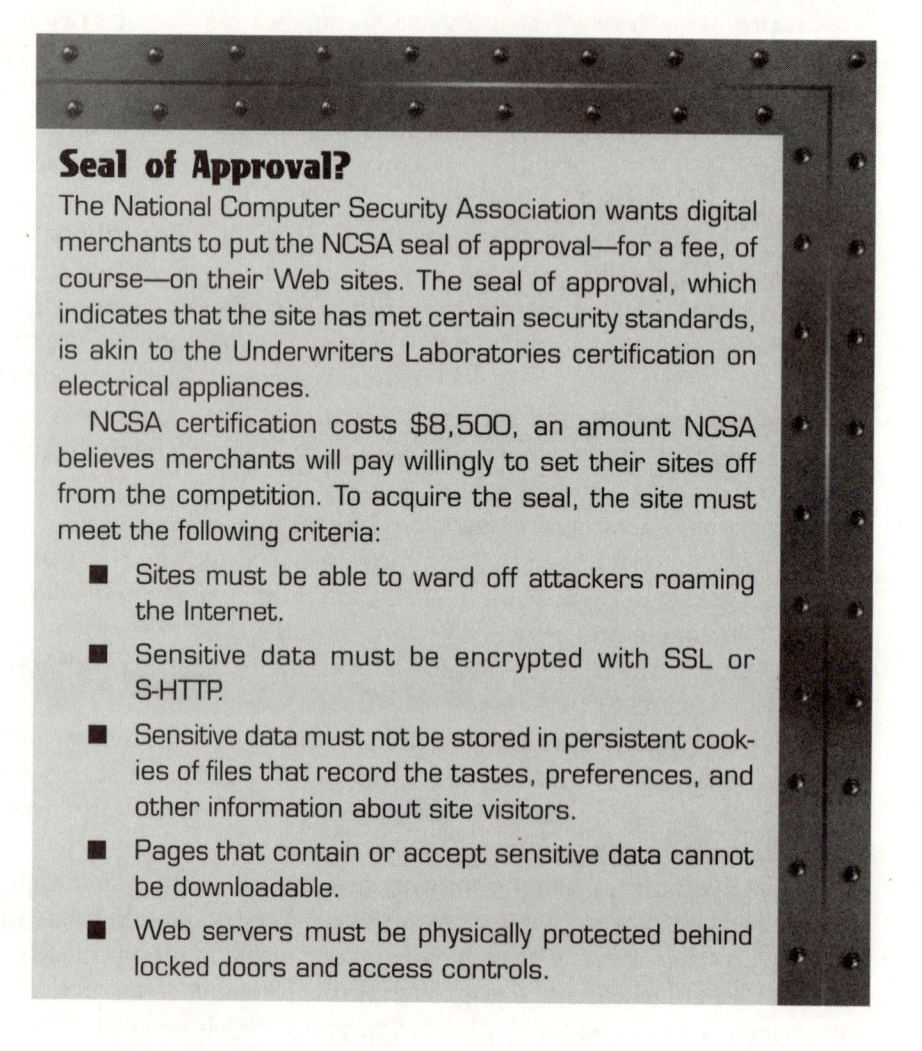

Seal of Approval?

The National Computer Security Association wants digital merchants to put the NCSA seal of approval—for a fee, of course—on their Web sites. The seal of approval, which indicates that the site has met certain security standards, is akin to the Underwriters Laboratories certification on electrical appliances.

NCSA certification costs $8,500, an amount NCSA believes merchants will pay willingly to set their sites off from the competition. To acquire the seal, the site must meet the following criteria:

- Sites must be able to ward off attackers roaming the Internet.
- Sensitive data must be encrypted with SSL or S-HTTP.
- Sensitive data must not be stored in persistent cookies of files that record the tastes, preferences, and other information about site visitors.
- Pages that contain or accept sensitive data cannot be downloadable.
- Web servers must be physically protected behind locked doors and access controls.

Sacrificial Lamb

If you want to make the server available to the rest of the world, you'll need to place it somewhere outside the firewall. This is called a *sacrificial lamb* configuration. The server is at risk of being broken into, but if that happens the attacker still could not penetrate the security of the inner network.

You don't want to run the WWW server on the firewall machine. If the server is compromised, the firewall will go down with it because the attackers will circumvent firewall security next. If the firewall is configured to prevent outsiders from using FTP, it might not recognize an FTP request that has been converted to HTTP by a Web server placed in front of the firewall.

Narrow World Webs

Many companies are setting up WWW servers with no intention of ever connecting them to the Internet. Many *intranets* are being set up to provide employees with easy access to a wide array of information—ranging from personnel benefits enrollment forms to proprietary marketing plans.

As you probably know by now, employees are far more likely than outsiders to commit computer crimes. They are more highly motivated to launch attacks, have greater access to sensitive information, and are more knowledgeable about the organization's inner technology.

Intranets obviously are vulnerable to attack by insiders, as is any other corporate system. Using many of the same security precautions you'd use to protect a system from outside attacks also should help guard against inside attacks.

In addition, some firewall makers are offering products that provide defenses against attacks from within. Firewalls for intranets support a variety of protocols used on internal networks, such as IPX, NetBEUI, DECnet, SNA, and AppleTalk, in addition to IP.

These firewalls are designed to close potential vulnerabilities. For example, Windows NT's NetBEUI protocol has a backdoor intended for remote administration by a technician, but any insider could exploit it to circumvent security.

Outsiders in

Some companies are opening their intranets to suppliers, valued customers, and others they regularly do business with. Chicago's Blue Cross/Blue Shield of Illinois, for example, has given health care providers access to its intranets. It wants to allow doctors and hospitals to transmit medical forms and other documents to the intranet.

Based in El Monte, California, the $1.2 billion electronic components company Marshall Industries has opened its intranet to some 150 suppliers and several thousand manufacturers' representatives. The reps can dial in and obtain price quotes, sales reports, product information, and the like.

If this is something you're contemplating, you'll need strong identification and authentication—using one-time passwords, for example—and encryption. No matter how robust your security measures, don't put sensitive or proprietary information on an intranet where unscrupulous insiders or outsiders may access it.

Security in Browsing

Microsoft Internet Explorer and Netscape Navigator have a wide variety of features, ranging from the ability to send and receive e-mail to the ability to download small applications that run on the user's desktop. They've also been enhanced with many security features, such as alerting you when you are submitting information to a Web site that has not been encrypted and warning you that a file you are about to download could harbor a virus.

Both browsers support SSL for starters. Microsoft and Netscape have pacts with VeriSign Inc., under which the users of these two popular browsers get free digital IDs. Web sites automatically read the digital IDs, providing authentication for site visitors. In addition, Explorer features Authenticode, which is based on using digital certificates to affix a seal of approval on software; CryptoAPI, an ActiveX encryption capability; and PCT, a secure TCP/IP protocol. Navigator features encryption based on 128-bit keys (domestic version).

The main security concern with browsers of all kinds is that they are able to download documents, images, Java applets, and many other media types and execute them on the desktop, often using helper applications such as Microsoft Word. Therefore, if a browser user, for instance, downloads a Word document, he or she risks receiving a document infected with a macrovirus or a PostScript file containing code that will trigger an unwanted action such as deleting important files.

The biggest concern is that with these browsers you can download Sun's Java and Microsoft's ActiveX software components (Java for Explorer and Navigator and ActiveX for Explorer). These self-contained applications can cause all sorts of mischief once they are executed on the desktop—Sun's and Microsoft's claims to the contrary notwithstanding.

Some firewall vendors, such as Trusted Information Systems and Checkpoint Technologies, have added to their products the ability to block Java applets from entering the organization. TIS gives administrators the option of preventing or allowing applets through the firewall. Checkpoint features a limited amount of screening that gives administrators some ability to selectively block Java applets from entering.

Java

Web technology continues to evolve, and many digital merchants are exploring ways to add moving images, virtual reality, audio, and other multimedia-rich formats to their sites. One of the most exciting ways to do that is with Sun Microsystems's Java, a programming language that provides Web sites with features such as scrolling marquees, rotating 3D figures, stock market quotes that are updated in real time, and other razzle-dazzle effects.

These special effects are done with applets—small programs written in Java—which are embedded into Web pages. When Web surfers click on a Java applet, it is downloaded to their computers and executed. All of the processing happens on the PC instead of the Web server, which means that the performance of the applets is not limited by modem speed, bandwidth, or other such factors.

You're probably thinking that if you download applets and run them on your PC, what's to prevent them from doing weird and evil things? For example, what's to prevent some scoundrel from creating a Java applet that steals information or permanently scrambles the data on your hard drive?

Java's developers built in a number of security checks and balances they say mitigate against such things happening. These safety valves include a set of security rules built into the language itself, a verifier, and a class loader.

Java's Own Security

Java is an object-oriented program, and those objects are organized into classes. Each class has its own set of rules as to what the objects in that class can and cannot do. For example, these rules prevent one object from masquerading as another object, which in the past has been a potential security vulnerability in other object-oriented programs. Java's compiler checks the source code to ensure that objects do not violate the security rules placed on them.

In addition, Java programs must pass through a number of other security checkpoints such as when the program is compiled, after the program is sent to the Web browser, and when the program loads and executes on the desktop. At each of these checkpoints, the program's code is checked to verify that it conforms to the rules of behavior established by the programmer. The program would not run if a hacker were to embed a virus into it before sending the program to the Web browser, for example.

Play in the Sandbox

Java-enabled browsers, such as the latest versions of Microsoft Internet Explorer and Netscape Navigator, include the Applet Security Manager. All applets must conform to and cannot extend or modify this in any way. Here are some of the operations the security manager does not permit applets to do:

- Read or write files on a PC's hard disk.
- Establish network connections other than to the server that the applet came from.
- Dynamically load libraries.
- Obtain sensitive or personal information like the name of the person using the browser.
- Launch other programs stored on the PC.

Refer to Sun's Applet Security Frequently Asked Questions (FAQ) site at http://java.sun.com/sfaq for a complete set of things applets can and cannot do. Sun calls this restricted area (where applets are allowed to execute) the *applet sandbox*. The Applet Security Manager ensures that applets "play" only in the sandbox.

Says Sun: "If code downloaded over the net damages data on your hard disk due to a bug, rather than due to malicious intent, in some sense, you don't care—you only care that your data was damaged. The sandbox protects you against buggy code as well as against malicious code."

Sun plans to strengthen the applet sandbox in future releases with digital signing of applets so you can determine an applet's origins and keep out applets that appear untrustworthy.

Java's Security Flaws

Despite Sun's many assurances to the contrary, computer scientists in the United States and in Europe have found numerous flaws—more than a dozen over a period of 18 months—in Microsoft's Internet Explorer 3.0, Netscape's Navigator 2.0, and Sun's Java and JavaScript.

Some of the flaws have been quite serious, as was the one found by Ed Felten, Drew Dean, Dan Wallach, and Tom Cargill at Princeton in August 1996. The computer research team uncovered a bug affecting the Microsoft Internet Explorer 3.0, beta 2 and earlier. The applet exploited this bug to obtain full file system and network access, among other things. Why didn't the Applet Security Manager prevent this from happening? The bug was the result of a mismatch between a piece of code in the security manager and the code written by Microsoft that used it. This mismatch could be interpreted as a bug in either piece of code, or it could be interpreted as a miscommunication between the two programmers, the researchers said.

That was only one of three bugs the researchers uncovered that month. In a Java program, the types of objects—characters, numbers, and arrays, for example—must be defined. The researchers found that, under certain circumstances, an applet could redefine one of Java's array types. This was enough to break Java's type system and completely circumvent all security mechanisms, researchers said. The end result was an applet that could read and write files when it was supposedly unable to.

In June 1996, David Hopwood, a computer scientist at Oxford University, discovered a bug in Java security that affects Netscape Navigator 2.02 and Netscape Navigator 3.0. beta 4, that could launch programs. Again, Java supposedly doesn't permit this to happen in Sun's applet sandbox security model. Applets purportedly are unable to create and use class loaders to define classes. However, an applet that has its own class loader can use it to define and execute classes that Java would normally prohibit it from running.

About the same time that *Datamation*, a computer industry magazine, was touting the virtues of Java's security features in its March 15, 1996, issue in an article entitled, "Yes, Java's Secure. Here's Why," the Princeton University researchers found yet another Java security flaw in Netscape's Navigator. The Princeton researchers said they had found a way for a downloaded Java applet to be able to contact other computers on a company network, sometimes including those behind a firewall.

Researchers also uncovered other Java security bugs affecting the verifier and the class loader, which Sun says are critical security clamps on Java applets. Netscape, Microsoft, and Sun have fixed the bugs in the releases of their products or have issued patches.

Hostile Applets

Java has come under close scrutiny by researchers and code crackers, who worry that Java applets can be used both for good and for mischief. They are concerned that rogue developers will create "hostile applets" capable of shredding security barriers or causing trouble in other ways after being downloaded.

I previously mentioned that Princeton researchers uncovered a bug in Java that permitted an attacker to run applets that circumvent security barriers designed to limit access to a system by outsiders. They also found another bug that would permit a hostile applet to read, modify, and delete files.

Hostile applets up to now have been mainly developed as academic exercises. You can see a collection of these applets on the Hostile Applets Home Page maintained by Mark LaDue, a doctoral candidate in applied math at Georgia Tech and a consulting engineer working at BellSouth's mobility unit in Atlanta. For more information, point your browser to http://www.math.gatech.edu/~mladue/HostileApplets.html.

The collection includes applets (all written by LaDue) that can do the following:

- Annoy you with a very noisy bear who refuses to be quiet.
- Bring your browser to a grinding halt.
- Make your browser start barking and then exit.
- Attack your workstation with big windows, wasteful calculations, and more noise, effectively excluding you from the console.
- Cause an applet window to open asking for logon and password without warning you that the information can be intercepted.
- Kill all other applets.
- Forge electronic mail.
- Obtain your user name.
- Exploit your workstation to run someone else's program and report the results.

For the most part, these applets are designed to run on UNIX workstations, PCs running Windows 95, and Macintoshes running System 7. Not all of the applets run on all of the machines.

You'll notice that many of these applets are capable of doing the sorts of things that Sun says applets should not be capable of doing. I can't personally vouch that these applets function as LaDue claims, however. I don't want to find out the hard way, frankly. LaDue says that he has tested them thoroughly, and a number of researchers support his claims.

There are other examples (again, purely academic) of hostile applets at the computer science department at the Web site of the University of California, Berkeley (http://whenever.CS.berkeley.edu/graffiti).

JavaScript

In addition to Java, Web navigators have JavaScript to worry about. The two are similar in name but really are different. Java is a programming language, with features similar to other sophisticated languages such as C++. JavaScript is a scripting language, with features similar to other simple scripting languages such as HyperText Markup Language (HTML), which you can use to create Web pages. JavaScript is a series of extensions to HTML.

Like those in Java, JavaScript's security vulnerabilities are only now being discovered. In 1996, John Robert LoVerso at the OSF Research Institute in Cambridge, Massachusetts, uncovered three JavaScript security holes in Netscape Navigator 2.01. You can see a description of these bugs at http://www.osf.org/~loverso/javascript.

Here's what the bugs that permit JavaScript scripts to execute are capable of:

- Uploading a password file stored on a hard disk on a PC or on a network.

- Obtaining directory listings stored on a hard disk on a PC or on a network.

- Monitoring all pages the user visits during a session, capturing the URLs, and transmitting them to a machine designated by the attacker.

These attacks require the unwitting participation of a Netscape Navigator 2.01 user, who is tricked into clicking on a button on a Web page without being warned that the click will upload a file. The remedy? Simply turn off JavaScript in Netscape 2.01 or upgrade to Netscape 3.0, which has been corrected. Of course, there are no guarantees that other holes don't exist.

Active Software Components

The same computer researchers here and abroad who have uncovered numerous security loopholes in Java and JavaScripts say they expect to find Microsoft's ActiveX to be similarly flawed. Building a secure mechanism for embedding executable programs in Web pages is an extremely difficult task, they point out.

ActiveX Controls, formerly called Object Linking & Embedding (OLE), is Microsoft's approach to embedding a wide variety of software components, such as sound bites, graphics viewers, animation sequences, and credit card transaction processing applications into Web pages. Java applets can coexist with ActiveX controls on an HTML page.

Active scripts, including those you can create in Visual Basic, Scripting Edition, or JavaScript-compatible scripts, can be used to link these building components to create dynamic Web-based applications.

ActiveX controls can be built into applications residing on PCs, letting them perform more efficiently and faster than with Java applets. For example, developers can use a feature of ActiveX called CryptoAPI to embed basic crypto services into their applications to generate and manage keys, encrypt and decrypt files, create digital signatures, and so on. An application that lacks encryption can borrow another application's encryption mechanism.

ActiveX controls work with a variety of programming languages from Microsoft and third parties including the Microsoft Visual C++ development system set, Borland Delphi, the Microsoft Visual Basic programming system, and, in the future, Microsoft's development tool for the Java language code named Jakarta.

Although it's still too early to know what security loopholes are present in ActiveX, it's a safe bet that they do exist. Digital merchants should be wary of deploying the technology on their Web sites before more is known. One key security concern is that ActiveX transmits controls in machine code—meaning that, if a virus or program with malicious intent is inserted into the control object, it will have direct access to the hard drive where it is stored.

Microsoft plans to have the control sender attach a digital signature to the object so that the recipient knows the code has been verified and certified as clean. Code-signing authentication is useful for ensuring an object has not been tampered with during transmission; it does not mean that the object was not designed to cause harm before being transmitted, however.

Last But Not Least

The Princeton team found one other significant browser loophole in Microsoft Internet Explorer 3.0 in August 1996—this one unrelated to Java—that would let an unscrupulous Web page creator attack any visitor to the site. The attacker could exploit the flaw to run any DOS command on the machine of an Explorer user who visits the attacker's page. For example, the attacker could read, modify, or delete the victim's files or insert a virus or backdoor entrance into the victim's machine.

The attacker could upload a Microsoft Word template containing a macro—a miniature program that acts as a shortcut for a series of commands—that executes, for example, the format DOS command intended to erase all of the data on a PC's hard disk.

Typically, Explorer asks users if they want to download a potentially dangerous file that might harbor a virus. However, the researchers devised a technique that allows an attacker to deliver a document without triggering a warning message to the user. Merely visiting a Web page containing the attack is enough to expose you to it, they add.

Microsoft has issued a patch for the bug, which you can download from http://www.microsoft.com.

SSL, the encryption mechanism used in Netscape's export version of Navigator, also has been proven vulnerable, as I recounted in Chapter 4.

Moving On

Setting up shop on the WWW is filled with peril. Web servers are particularly attractive to hackers, thieves, and other high-tech tamperers because sites often are poorly maintained and easy to penetrate. As more businesses set up shop, the WWW will become even more attractive to thieves. There are many ways to protect Web sites, however. Secure servers employ credit card encryption technology and other security protocols as the first line of defense, followed by firewalls and sensible system administration.

7 Airbags & Seat Belts for the I-way

When you connect your organization's Web server and the rest of its computer systems, the world may very well beat a path to your doorstep, but not always with the best of intentions. Clearly, you need to protect your corporate connection to the World Wide Web (WWW) and the Internet from people with malicious intent while still providing your employees, customers, and others the access they require.

According to prevailing wisdom, the way to do that is with a *firewall*—a collection of routers, computers, and specialized software. A firewall is similar to the security guard in the lobby of your building. The guard greets visitors and employees, checks employee badges, issues visitor passes, asks visitors to sign the guest register, and so on. If security is particularly tight, the security guard prohibits employees and visitors from bringing notebook computers, cameras, recording devices, and similar equipment into the building. And when employees and visitors leave the building, the security guard goes through a similar procedure but in reverse and ensures people are not leaving the building with company valuables.

Much of *Net Security* is devoted to discussing who is apt to break into computer systems connected to the Internet and WWW and how they are likely to go about it. In this chapter, I'll describe the best defenses available to online entrepreneurs: firewalls, attack simulators, intrusion detection programs, and access control devices such as smart cards.

Cyberguardian at the Gates

A firewall is the same sort of vigilant sentry at the point at which your organization's Web server and computer systems connect to the Internet. Each of these cyberguards is instructed to keep logs on all who pass into and out of the firewall, verify their Internet addresses, monitor what Internet services they use, examine packets of data as they flow in and out, and more.

In particular, you want to set up firewalls to block unwanted traffic while allowing certain traffic to pass. Some firewalls allow only e-mail traffic. Others allow upload but not download of e-mail and files. Still others block everything that is not specifically allowed by default.

Firewalls filter out traffic based on restrictions that you impose. They can be set up to allow connections only from certain Internet Protocol (IP) addresses, and they can filter out traffic based on the port number to which they have been directed. For example, if you want to prevent employees from browsing the WWW, you can have the firewall block traffic to port 80, which typically is used for Web traffic.

Firewalls support mainstream IP services including File Transfer Protocol (FTP), Simple Mail Transfer Protocol (SMTP), Archie, and Telnet, among others. Few support Secure HyperText Transfer Protocol (S-HTTP), which is a consideration when you set up a Web server behind a firewall. Companies whose firewalls support S-HTTP include Milkyway Networks Corp., Technologic Inc., and V-One (also known as Virtual Open Network Environment).

Today, nearly all firewall products are based on UNIX, mainly because UNIX is a highly flexible, multitasking system with built-in security and networking. However, an increasing number of vendors—such as Raptor Systems, Inc., of Waltham, Massachusetts—are offering firewall products based on Windows NT.

Firewalls haven't been around all that long—about five years. The International Data Corp. (IDC), a market research firm based in Framingham, Massachusetts, calculates some forty-two thousand security-minded companies purchased firewalls in 1996. Come the end of the millennium, says IDC, 1.5 million companies will buy firewalls in the year 2000. As you might expect, the popularity of firewalls has been in sync with the growth of the Internet.

Input, a market research firm based in Mountain View, California, figures that U.S. companies spent $820 million on firewall software and services in 1995. Input predicts that U.S. companies will spend $8.1 billion on firewall software and services in the year 2000. That's a whopping compound annual growth of 58 percent. It would seem that the companies getting rich on the Internet are not the shopkeepers but the shop builders!

The Objectives of Firewalls

Before hiring your firewall security guard, you need to create a list of objectives that you expect to accomplish with an Internet connection and then balance those needs against what you perceive the risks to be. You can then determine how much access you require.

Someone in your organization—the CEO or security administrator—must decide just what traffic will be allowed and what traffic won't. At one extreme, you can choose to deny all services except those necessary for connecting to the WWW; at the other, you can choose to provide employees with all Internet services and use the firewall merely to control and track what comes in and out.

These often are political rather than technical decisions. You need to determine which employees should have access and precisely what services they should be able to access. Some decisions might be obvious: For example, you want customer service representatives or support personnel to be able to respond to e-mail messages. But do you also want these same employees to be able to frequent newsgroups?

You must settle such policy decisions before you can set up the firewall. Because your cybersentry can do only what you tell it to do, your instructions must be precise or you risk leaving your internal systems open to attack or mischief by insiders and outsiders alike.

Firewall Basics

Because firewalls haven't been around long, no industry standard applies to them, how they should be configured and so on. In fact, firewall makers don't even agree on the terms they should use to describe the various ways firewalls can be set up.

Firewalls serve two essential functions: to filter traffic based on rules you set, and to act as a gateway for routing packets of information to other destinations or another computer that acts as a surrogate or gateway proxy. These two functions can be combined into a single computer or spread over three or four interconnected computers.

Filtering Out Packets

Most networked companies already have a router or two handling connections between their local area networks (LANs) or between their in-house networks and the Internet. Once you have the router, all you need is to program into it instructions on how it is to handle the Internet traffic flowing in and out of the company. This is a basic firewall, the *packet-filtering router*. Such firewalls are popular because many companies already have invested in a router.

You can set up the router to either:

- Permit all connections (except those you designate) to pass through or

- Prevent all connections (except those you designate) from passing through

The first policy is less restrictive than the second but is also less secure. The second policy is more difficult to accomplish but, if you can implement it correctly, it is the more secure of the two.

Put It on a Table

Programming the router to cover all of the possible variations is a feat in itself. You might want some users to have access to all I-way services, some who can access only some I-way services, and still others who can receive outside e-mail but who have no access to any other I-way services. You should detail all permissions and restrictions in a policy, which is then used to set up the router's filtering tables.

That's a lot easier said than done, as you can imagine. It requires considerable understanding of Internet protocols, for one thing. It's also easy to overlook some of the possible variations and leave holes through which intruders can slip.

Block to Protect

You can protect yourself by making sure that employees have access only to the Internet services—such as e-mail, WWW, and anonymous FTP—that you specify. You can further specify that they access these services only from designated systems. It's a common approach, one that allows the administrator to permit connections from computers that are in turn isolated from more important systems. This approach also prevents employees from setting up, behind the firewall, their own FTP or Web servers that might have security holes in them.

Another common technique is to block access to User Datagram Protocol (UDP) ports. UDP is used to identify the processes that travel back and forth between sending and receiving computer systems. UDP ensures that the right machines and the right applications on those machines are in sync when talking to each other, by assigning a unique protocol port to the sending and receiving machines.

By blocking the ports, you can prevent specific services that you don't want employees to use or that you know are vulnerable to attack from passing through the firewall. For example, e-mail travels through port 25. Many administrators block port 25 because Sendmail, the UNIX mail program, has a number of security flaws that hackers regularly try to exploit.

Hackers also will attempt to exploit the Network File System (NFS) to access network disks and files stored on them. You can stymie such attacks by blocking UDP ports 111 and 2049. UDP ports for services such as FTP (port 69), Finger (port 79), Post Office Protocol (port 110), and the UNIX-to-UNIX copy program (port 540) are among those routinely blocked to thwart hackers.

You also can set up firewalls to refuse connections from IP addresses for any reason. Suppose someone has been hammering repeatedly on your firewall, looking for ways to get in. The first thing you would do is block all connections that originate from the hammerer's IP address.

None of these methods is foolproof. Attackers can install backdoors to get around blocked ports and can fake their IP address to make it appear as though they can be trusted. A particularly savvy hacker can still get into the router, no matter how many pathways you shut down. Since the function of a router is to route packets, it does not provide any auditing or monitoring of unauthorized activity or attempts to subvert security measures.

All in all, a packet-filtering router won't give you top-shelf security, but using a router might be all that you need. It depends in part on what you have to lose. It's certainly the least expensive option.

Several different kinds of gateways are used in building firewalls, but they generally fall into one of two categories: the circuit-level gateway and the application-level gateway.

A *circuit-level gateway* performs all of the packet-filtering duties a router can and then some. The primary enhancement is that it also requires outsiders to identify and authenticate themselves before they can gain access to the in-house network—namely, they must prove they are who they say they are by providing a login ID and a password. More about this process later in this chapter.

The *application-level gateway* is even more specialized. It oversees the security of individual applications, such as electronic mail and file-transferring programs. When users dial in, they are authenticated first by the application-level firewall. Once they get the go-ahead, they are passed to the specific application they are using.

Another advantage is that application-level firewalls can be used to mask network addresses, so that an outsider would not have any immediate clue just how many systems are beyond the firewall. Traffic from an inside system goes in one side of the firewall, passes through an application that hides the connection's origins, and then goes out the other side of the firewall.

With each new day, it is harder to tell the two levels of gateways apart because of the many new variations being introduced. For example, there is a variation of the application-level gateway called a *dual-homed gateway*, a variation of the dual-homed gateway called the *screened-host firewall*, and a variation of the dual-homed gateway and the screened-host firewall called the *screened-subnet firewall*.

Deciding on the right firewall setup is a matter of balancing flexibility and security. Some application gateways have two network interfaces so computers on each side of the firewall can talk to the gateway, but directing traffic between the two networks is impossible. If a service on one side of the firewall does not have a proxy counterpart on the other side, it cannot get through—a highly secure but not particularly flexible arrangement. Other firewalls consist of a packet-filtering router with an application gateway. The router screens out unwanted protocols, preventing them from ever reaching the gateway. Protocols considered trustworthy are filtered and passed around the gateway, direct to their internal destinations. This setup is more flexible but not as secure.

Proxies With Moxie

Whether circuit-level or application-level, gateways primarily forward requests for e-mail, file transfer, and other Internet services to surrogate machines or proxies. They function as go-betweens, taking requests from the outside and relaying them to the inside and vice versa. That slows things down a bit but shields in-house systems from a direct attack.

Proxies are needed for each application. Because they also must interact with specific applications, security can be tweaked to suit each protocol. For example, a proxy for file transfers could be set up to allow files to be downloaded but not uploaded through the gateway. The drawback: Your administrator will be confronted with a need for specialized servers for each client/server application that must pass through the firewall, which is likely to require extensive customization and modification of applications software.

SOCKS

A package of proxying tools called SOCKS helps customize desktop Internet applications so they will work properly with their proxies on the other side of the firewall. In a sense, it is a universal translator, able to speak the same language as a variety of desktop applications and their proxy counterparts. It consists of SOCKS desktop applications and a SOCKS server. The desktop applications are available in UNIX, Windows, and Macintosh versions; the server is UNIX. The desktop versions of FTP, Telnet, and other Transmission Control Protocol (TCP) applications talk to the SOCKS server, which in turn talks to the servers running FTP and so on.

SOCKS takes requests from desktop applications and sends them to the SOCKS server, which authenticates and authorizes the requests, establishes a proxy connection, and passes data back and forth.

SOCKS is free, which is one reason it's so popular. Plus, many free and commercial Internet applications like FTP and Telnet are available with SOCKS capability.

Firewalls Aren't Cure-alls

Some security experts believe that using firewalls as a primary defense shield against the Internet is overrated because sophisticated attackers can circumvent firewalls.

According to the Computer Security Institute's "1995 Internet Security Survey," one out of every five sites participating in its survey had been the victim of a security breach. The trade group, based in San Francisco, says 30 percent of the victimized sites had firewalls.

There's no telling just how many of those sites had improperly configured firewalls, which is almost as bad as having no firewall at all. Firewalls are not easy to set up and maintain. Most firewalls are based on UNIX, which offers a high degree of flexibility but is difficult to master, even for gurus. Also, a company that opts to standardize on Microsoft NT or an operating system other than UNIX will find it has limited firewall options.

Maginot Line of Defense

In the years before World War II, the French built a series of fortifications called the Maginot Line along its border with Germany. When the Germans finally invaded France, rather than attack the Maginot Line, they swept around it, invading France through Belgium.

Similarly, not all attacks on corporate systems involve breaking through the firewall; instead, attackers exploit weak points in the application layer—mailers, word processors, and the like. This type of attack has occurred many times already against various versions of Sendmail and GhostScript, a freely available PostScript viewer.

The current concern is that an attacker will develop Java applets that can come into the organization when an employee or some other insider uses a browser. Once behind the firewall, the hostile Java applet could go secretly about its business.

An increasing number of state-of-the-art firewall product vendors are adding features to prevent Java applets from reaching internal systems. Some vendors let administrators decide whether to allow Java applets; others simply refuse to permit Java applets to enter under any circumstance.

Inside Out

A firewall can't protect your organization against insiders with a grudge or those out to sell the company's secrets to the highest bidder. The American Society of Industrial Security says that 40 percent of attacks can be attributed to outsiders acting on their own; the other 60 percent can be attributed to insiders acting on their own or with a cohort on the outside.

Firewalls must be a part of a consistent overall organizational security architecture. Information comes into and flows out of your organization in a variety of ways, including the telephone, fax machine, laptop computer, floppy disk, and so on. Given a choice, outsiders would rather resort to low-tech methods such as social engineering (socializing with your employees after work, for example) than to hacking computer systems.

Too, information that you cannot risk losing to outsiders should not be on a system accessible by the outside world, even behind the world's most secure firewall. Classified military secrets are not stored in systems with any network connection. Although that level of security might not be necessary in your organization, it's worth thinking about.

Firewalls & Viruses

Firewalls offer little protection against viruses. A lot of data travels in a compressed form today, and virus scanners aren't very effective at scanning compressed files. Thorough searches also are next to impossible due to the sheer numbers of viruses and ways binary files are encoded for transfer over networks.

Traditional virus scanners cannot detect viruses that are attached to e-mail messages once the two enter an organization. E-mail systems encrypt e-mail and attachments, preventing them from being scanned for the identifying bits of code that are unique to each virus. An infected file can be scanned only after it has been opened and saved to a hard disk. By the time that happens, the virus may have traveled widely throughout the organization.

The prank macro virus, for example, easily can ride in on a Word document and then execute behind the firewall. Consider the prospects of what might happen if instead of the prank macro, which causes documents to be saved as templates, it was a Trojan horse that slipped undetected through the corporate security perimeter.

Many companies favor setting a buffer zone in the form of a proxy server that processes files passed along by the firewall and then scans them before handing them off to the internal e-mail system.

Keep in mind that trying to block viruses at the firewall is really a Band-Aid solution. The vast majority of viruses are brought into the office on floppy disks.

The Terror of the Unknown

A firewall is configured to defend against known threats, therefore it is unlikely to thwart attacks with unforeseen scenarios. Denial-of-service attacks are a good example of that.

In mid-September 1996, a hacker or hackers launched a denial-of-service attack—using a technique called *synflooding*—against Panix, an Internet service provider (ISP) based in New York. The attack exploited a feature in TCP/IP, which allows an attack to be mounted against a TCP-based network service such as a Web server, FTP server, or mail server. The computer of a user attempts to synchronize communications with a particular service by sending a request in the form of a bit of data called a SYN packet.

The site hosting the service replies with an ACK, short for acknowledgment. The initiating computer is expected to respond in turn with another ACK, completing the connection. If this second ACK is not returned, the site computer will wait up to 75 seconds for it. Sending many SYN packets without the follow-up ACKs causes the site machine to go into a sort of limbo, waiting for acknowledgments that will never come. The site machine runs out of memory or simply stops functioning altogether.

Although the basic concept was familiar to many computer scientists and Internet experts, the first attack was mounted after it was described in *Phrack,* an electronic newsletter, and *2600,* a magazine sold on many newsstands.

Stopping a synflood attack is difficult but not impossible. It takes a properly set up packet-filtering router. The Computer Emergency Response Team (CERT) has details on this attack and how to block it at its site (http://www.cert.org).

Authentication & Identification

It's easy to think of firewalls only in terms of providing employees with a safe way to access the Internet and to keep the bad guys out. But what about allowing trusted outsiders to come in from the Internet? You might have employees around the country or suppliers and customers you regularly communicate with. They'll need a way to identify themselves when they present themselves to the cybersentry in the electronic lobby. Remember this is a pretty secure place you're running: You're going to want your visitors to prove that they are who they say they are.

In security-speak, this process is called *identification and authentication*. The identification part is pretty straightforward. Visitors have a login ID—something like Smith for most people and Deathmaster for computer cowboys. The authentication part is slightly more complicated.

Passwords Are a Factor

There are three ways for your visitors to authenticate themselves—to prove they are who they claim to be:

- Provide something that only they know, such as passwords.
- Use something that only they have, perhaps a card with a magnetic stripe.
- Use something that is unique to them, like a fingerprint.

Using one of these methods is called a *one-factor security system*. Using two is called a two-factor security system and so on. Withdrawing money from your ATM is a two-factor system. You have the card (one factor), and after you insert it into the ATM, you enter a personal identification number (the second factor). Each added factor adds more security.

One, Two Factors

Passwords are the most common way visitors to a computer site authenticate themselves. There are two types of passwords: *reusable* and *one-time*. Reusable passwords are used over and over again for months at a time. One-time passwords are used once and then discarded.

Reusable passwords are not as secure as one-time passwords. Use the same password long enough, and there is a good chance that someone will figure it out, intercept it during a login session, or steal it from a password file. I won't rehash the discussion on obtaining passwords from Chapter 2 here but will cover one-time passwords and how they fit into a firewall strategy.

Smart Passwords

A growing number of companies, including Border Network Technologies, Inc., Harris Computer Systems Corp., and Trusted Information Systems, Inc., market firewalls that support two-factor authentication based on a device called a one-time password generator.

There are two basic types of password devices: tokens and smart cards. They operate similarly in that they generate passwords that are used once and then discarded. If the password, which is a number that is several digits long is intercepted, it cannot be used at another time. They differ in how they work, however.

A typical token resembles a small pocket calculator, complete with a small keypad and a one-line liquid crystal display (LCD). A site visitor logs in to a computer. The computer responds by sending the visitor a challenge in the form of a number consisting of several digits. That visitor keys the number into the token, which in turn generates another number that it displays on its LCD. The visitor enters this new number, which is now his password, into the computer, which returns an entirely different number. That number is sent to the computer.

The smart card more closely resembles a credit card but with a single button and one-line LCD. Pressing the button on the smart card displays a password several digits long, which you can enter into the computer along with a PIN. The smart card displays a different password every 60 seconds. Using one of these passwords makes the smart card a one-time password device and proves the user has access to the smart card at that moment. The firewall accepts the PIN and password as valid by the firewall or authentication server for only for a minute or so.

Tokens and smart cards are not completely foolproof, although they offer greater security than reusable passwords. An attacker still can hijack a session, taking over the connection as soon as the passcode has been entered and the real user authenticated. Or, an attacker who grabs the user's PIN as it is transmitted and then steals the token or card has everything needed to break into the site.

Encryption

Encryption is one of the most potent weapons available to digital merchants who wish to keep private information private. There are two basic approaches: Encrypt data sent between specific applications, or encrypt data sent between sites.

Most of what I've discussed about encryption so far applies only to encrypting at the application level. For example, I suggested using Pretty Good Privacy, or PGP, to encrypt messages sent by e-mail.

If all you and your employees need to do is encrypt e-mail messages, by all means use PGP or some other public-key crypto scheme. But PGP and other application-level crypto methods are unwieldy for more than one or two applications or for sites at which information needing protection is scattered around lots of machines. You also should consider the support issues: issuing and managing keys, installing the appropriate software on a variety of platforms, training employees, ensuring information encrypted by departing employees is accessible, and more.

Encrypting data sent between sites is more complicated and costly to set up but potentially more secure. There are two approaches: *link-level encryption* and *network-level encryption*.

Link-level Encryption

When data sent over a network between two computers are encrypted, that's known as *link-level encryption*. At each end of the link are black boxes—link encryptors or encrypting modems—that scramble and unscramble all information as it is transmitted and received. Information can be transmitted from a notebook computer to a firewall or from one firewall to another. The entire process is transparent to applications and the people involved.

This sort of security is a key selling point for Electronic Data Interchange, a 20-year-old technology that up until now has had only a few customers. EDI is a fast, safe method of sending purchase orders, invoices, shipping notices, and other common business documents between merchants and suppliers. It is also prohibitively expensive for all but the largest corporations.

Whether a system handles birthday greetings or state secrets, the process of encryption and decryption affects network performance and hinders a system administrator's ability to analyze traffic and perform diagnostics on the network. For example, if the packets are encrypted, there is no way the administrator can analyze test packets because they are encrypted and therefore unreadable.

Link-level encryption guards against eavesdropping on a single link at a time. Information traveling over the Internet can traverse many networks and routers before reaching its final destination. Unless you can rely on encryption at each switching station or otherwise secure all links—which is unlikely—you don't have complete security. Even at sites having link encryption, the incoming information must be decrypted and encrypted. An attacker who penetrates the router is able to grab information easily.

Finally, link-level encryption requires that the sending and receiving computers operate in sync—literally. That makes it impossible to use link-level encryption to several sites simultaneously, as you might do with videoconferencing, for example.

Network-level Encryption

Selectively encrypting and decrypting data during transmission between two sites is known as network-level encryption. It's a secure *tunnel* through which information is protected against snooping. Although not a new idea, tunneling is newly popular. It permits companies to create private networks using the public networks that comprise the Internet. Think of it as Electronic Data Interchange without the expense but with many of the same benefits.

Each packet of data is encrypted before it enters the tunnel and is then decoded at the receiving end. There are two basic ways to do this: Encrypt the packet and leave the IP packet headers intact, or encrypt both the packet and the IP header.

Both approaches protect packet contents from prying eyes. With the first approach, however, the firewall can continue to filter packets. However, it also can let an attacker see what machines are communicating and the protocols they're using. The second approach inhibits packet-filtering but protects the entire packet from snoops.

Individual packets can be encrypted so that information that should be kept confidential is encrypted and less-sensitive information is sent in cleartext. That means less work and better performance for the network.

The individual packets also can be sent anywhere on the network without the need to decrypt and encrypt them along the way. As you might suspect, the sending and receiving machines do not have to be in sync.

Well, if this is so great, why isn't everyone doing it? In one word, "interoperability," or rather the lack of it. There are no virtual private network standards assuring that one firewall can talk securely to another firewall or that a desktop machine can talk to a firewall. Also, site administrators still want fully encrypted packets and the ability to filter.

This is changing. RSA Data Security is pushing a Secure Wide Area Network standard (SWAN) based on the Internet protocol security group of the Internet engineering task force. Firewall and router makers already on record as supporting this initiative include Bay Networks Inc., Checkpoint Software Technologies Ltd., Digital Equipment Corp., IBM, and Raptor Systems Inc.

Input, the market research firm, predicts that standards will not emerge until the second half of 1997 or early in 1998.

Comparing Firewall Features

Determining which firewall is right for your organization is a complex process based on variables such as the existing network configuration, personnel, budget, and other critical factors. Evaluating a firewall takes a lot of study and research; this section will review some of the key features you'll want to consider.

Identification & Authentication

Your options are reusable passwords and smart passwords, using either a Security Dynamics smart card or an Enigma Logic token. Some firewalls support smart cards or tokens right out of the box, while others support them if you add software and related options. Firewalls that support both right out of the box include those by Border Network Technologies Inc., Digital Equipment Corp., and Harris Computer Systems Corp.

Encryption

Not all firewalls support link encryption. Some that do include products by ANS CO+RE System Inc., Checkpoint Software Technologies Inc., and Milkyway Networks Corp.

Proxies

As I mentioned, not all firewall architectures are based on using proxies. If this is what you want, find out what proxies a firewall under consideration supports. Some—V-One's SmartWall and SOS's Brimstone, for example—support SMTP, Network News

Transport Protocol, HTTP, Telnet, FTP, Gopher, and S-HTTP, while others may support only three or four of these protocols. (That's not necessarily bad because it limits the number of ways an outsider can break into your site.) Milkyway Networks Corp., SOS Corp., and Technologic Inc. market firewalls that support the gamut.

Address & Machine Name Hiding
Almost all firewalls are capable of hiding the name of machines used for news and mail, as well as internal addresses, to make it more difficult for outsiders to determine what machines are behind the firewall and what services they are running.

Auditing
You can't tell how well your barriers are withstanding attack unless you walk the security perimeter from time to time. That's where auditing comes in. Firewalls allow site administrators to track who logs in, how often they log in, and what services they use. That's important information. Equally important is knowing how many times someone has failed to log in, which could indicate an outsider probing your system for weaknesses. If you suspect this, you can monitor any suspicious activity in real time and receive an alarm.

You also should review the kinds of reports the system generates and how useful that information is. If the reports are unhandy to review, you may avoid them.

Administration
How easy is it to set up and operate a firewall? Does it provide a graphical user interface for setup and configuration? Can it be administered from a remote location? Most important, you want a firewall that is as transparent as possible to employees and demands little from them. Most vendors claim their products do that; make them prove it.

Pricing
Firewalls range in price from free (the Trusted Information Systems (TIS) Firewall Toolkit) to as much as $100,000. Free or inexpensive firewalls include software and little else. For $30,000 or

more, you can buy everything you need, including technical support, in a single package. Digital Equipment Corp., IBM, and Raptor Systems Inc. are among the companies offering one-stop-shopping packages.

The TIS Internet Firewall Toolkit is available from ftp://ftp.tis.com/pub/firewalls/toolkit.

Vendors

Does the vendor of the product you're considering regularly provide updates? Are they likely to inform you whenever there are potential problems and provide security fixes in a timely manner? You don't want to learn about a new security flaw through personal experience.

Personnel

Finding the right firewall for your organization requires considerable technical expertise and skill. It takes a savvy administrator to set up a firewall with a sophisticated level of filtering and to update it whenever the company's network changes.

Firewalls are relatively new, and experienced firewall gurus are few. If you don't have the in-house talent, hire a consultant or buy a turnkey system from a vendor who provides the level of support you require.

Attack Simulators

If you want to find out how secure your TCP/IP network really is, think like a burglar. Prowl your organization's electronic streets to see who's not home during the day and jiggle door handles to see who forgot to lock up.

Breaking and entering can be a full-time job. Fortunately, canvassing your electronic neighborhood for security loopholes has become considerably easier, thanks in part to Security Administrator's Tool for Analyzing Networks (SATAN), the notorious attack simulator released in April 1995. Attack simulators do what burglars do: look for ways to break in.

SATAN was the subject of considerable scrutiny and controversy when it was released as freeware by Dan Farmer and Wietse Venema. The SATAN codevelopers said their tool allowed security and net managers to examine their own networks for security holes. Critics countered that SATAN could be used as readily by hackers to probe for weaknesses through which they could enter and attack sites.

I doubt SATAN is being widely used by hackers to break into computer installations. It requires PER 5, knowledge of C programming in UNIX, and 32 megabytes of random access memory (RAM). Not many hackers have those technical skills or the money for a high-end computer.

In any case, the biggest danger from SATAN may be a false sense of security for security and network managers who use it. SATAN scans for only about a dozen potential loopholes out of the many dozens known to exist.

Internet Security Systems and Qualix Systems Group market commercial TCP/IP scanners that do the same kind of checking SATAN does. What do the commercial scanners have in common? Each claims to look for several dozen known security vulnerabilities, to use hypertext to produce reports, and to use Web browsers to read those reports. The reports also include direct links to sites containing security advisories released by CERT and other Internet security watchdog organizations.

Internet Security Systems' Internet Scanner 3.2 reportedly looks for some 130 known security holes, generates a vulnerability report on every device on the network, and recommends ways to close whatever holes it detects.

Internet Scanner, which runs on HP-UX, AIX, Linux, SunOS, and Sun Solaris, systematically probes each device on a network. These devices include UNIX hosts, firewalls, routers, Web servers, and PCs. The company says it uses the same techniques a hacker would employ in an attempted break-in.

Internet Scanner is the only attack simulator on the market that looks for vulnerabilities beyond UNIX. For example, it can detect the recently discovered file- and print-sharing vulnerability of any TCP/IP network that runs Windows 95, NT, or Windows for Workgroups.

NetProbe from Qualix Systems Group (a division of Qualix Group) scans the local network's address range to find known loopholes and improper configurations that might allow unauthorized remote access from within or outside a firewall. It performs more than 85 tests and is capable of running those tests against a hundred hosts in less than five minutes, the company says. Once the tests are completed, the program generates a report citing the vulnerabilities it has uncovered and offers suggestions on how to close them, including pointers to security advisories. One potential drawback: NetProbe runs only on SunOS and Solaris.

NetProbe also performs security checks on Network Information Service (NIS) domain names, Domain Name System (DNS) entries, and Network File System (NFS) directories. All three can be exploited by outsiders to penetrate a system. For example, NIS parcels out a variety of databases from the server to the desktop computers. One of these databases is the password file, which may be seized by NIS if the administrator does not properly configure it or runs it on a computer that is not protected. DNS is a database that contains information that links the host names of computers with their IP addresses. If a hacker succeeds in grabbing the database, he can use it as a road map to find and attack other machines at the same site. If a hacker subverts NFS, he may be able to alter files and directories, masquerade as someone using a trusted or approved machine, or mount similar attacks.

Neither attack simulator will find all security loopholes (even known ones) nor will these programs automatically fix the loopholes they uncover. They merely report the presence of certain vulnerabilities and suggest ways to close the security gaps. Keep in mind that attack scanners are only one part of the security picture, which should also include backup, disaster recovery, firewalls, and other measures.

Get SATAN

You can obtain a copy of SATAN for your own system from ftp://gatekeeper.dec.com/pub/net/SATAN.

You also can get a paper on Internet security written by the developers of SATAN by sending e-mail to majordomo@wzv.win.tue.nl. In the body of the message write: **Get satan admin-guide-to-cracking.101**. To keep up with the latest SATAN news, access codeveloper Dan Farmer's Web page: http://www.fish.com/satan.

SATAN: Security Administrator's Tool for Analyzing Networks.

Intrusion Detection

The problem with diagnostic tools like attack simulators and sniffers is that the bad guys can use them to break into networks as readily as the good guys can use them to strengthen security barriers. How can security or net managers know when ostensibly good tools are being used against their networks?

There are a number of commercial and free monitoring tools that will signal systems administrators when SATAN is being used to probe their sites. Courtney, developed at Lawrence Livermore National Laboratory, looks for the telltale pattern of requests that SATAN uses to probe a machine as well as keeps an eye out for other suspicious activities that might signal attempts to find weaknesses in your machine. Courtney can be found at http://ciac.llnl.gov/ciac/ToolsUnixNetMon.html.

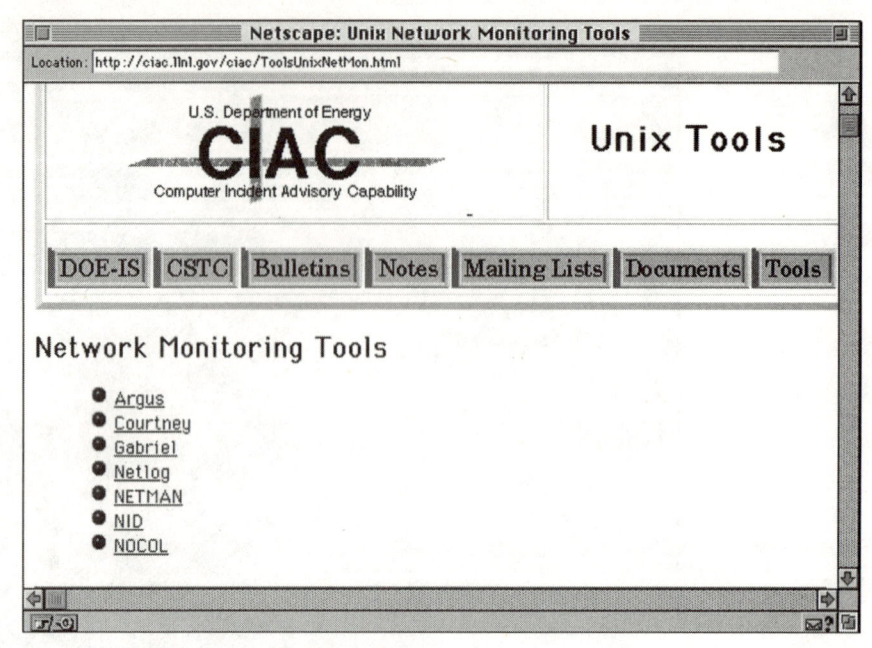

You can find Courtney at CIAC's site.

Another free tool, Gabriel, also logs probes coming from attempts to run SATAN against a site and then sounds an alarm.

Intrusion-detection software from companies such as AXENT Technologies, Bellcore, and Network Systems are known as *rule-based anomaly detectors*, which constantly monitor networks for signs of suspicious activity. The software is configured with rules governing normal activity and then monitors any activity falling outside that. For example, if an employee who normally uses an application at a specific time or place suddenly starts using the application after hours or from a new location, Gabriel triggers an alarm.

AXENT Technologies markets a product called OmniGuard/Intruder Alert (ITA) that is designed to detect suspicious activities on systems, warn of potential intrusions, and alert security administrators. ITA monitors both activity on the internal network and activity coming into the organization from the Internet.

In addition to acting as a virtual watchdog, ITA can perform real-time checks of access control settings, analyze and reduce system logs, monitor applications, and track other security controls such as firewalls.

Netstalker was designed specifically to complement Network Systems' NetSentry firewall, which examines both the header and packet data to filter packets based in the software application being run. Like OmniGuard/ITA, NetStalker acts as a watchdog for a wide variety of hacker attacks and sounds an alarm when intruders attempt to breach the network's security fences.

When NetStalker determines a network is being attacked, it alerts the network manager that a break-in or misuse has occurred and provides a report on the attempted activities.

The net manager receives the alert as an e-mail message or a call to a pager. It audits system use, providing net managers with an audit trail they can examine for signs of suspicious or unauthorized transactions or other activity. Finally, it scans suspicious data packets that the firewall rejects, to see if they contain the telltale signatures of common hacker tools, such as those found in SATAN.

Bellcore's Pingware network security scanner, searches for vulnerabilities in FTP, SMPT, and other services.

Hack Attack Aftermath

You installed a firewall and, despite your best efforts, a hacker broke in and tampered with your company's data. What do you do? Here's what the Federal Bureau of Investigation (FBI) National Computer Crime Squad recommends companies do before and after being victimized by computer criminals:

- Post a No Trespassing sign that warns all intruders who log in to your system that their activities will be monitored.

- Check your audit reports for signs of illegal activity. You need to know exactly when and how the intruder entered your system, where the culprit went, and what he or she did while inside. If it's an insider, you'll also need to know who got in. It's especially important to close the security loophole and check the system for programs or files of suspicious origin. The last thing you need is a password-grabbing Trojan horse, logic bomb, or some other bit of rogue code on your system.

- Contact the appropriate law enforcement agencies. Depending on the extent of the crime and any dollar loss, contact local, state, and federal officials. The first thing they'll want is evidence. You'll also need to substantiate how you calculated the dollar amount for your loss.

- Bolster your case with clear-cut evidence of what happened and why you believe a crime has been committed.

- Familiarize yourself with local, state, and federal computer crime statutes. Check to see if your state has a computer crime law and exactly what sorts of crimes are covered. Not every state expressly prohibits planting a virus in a computer system. Federal law enforcers get involved only if the criminal used a "federal interest computer." A federal interest computer is any computer that can be used to access federal data, which probably means every computer connected by a network. The federal government does not have to own or operate the computer.

- Set a trap. Lock down everything except the few files you want the intruder to find. Then monitor the system for this activity.

- Designate one person to secure potential evidence, such as before-and-after tape backups. Store the evidence in a locked cabinet with only this person having access. The person also should keep a record of resources used to reestablish the system and locate the perpetrator.

- Contact CERT at Carnegie Mellon University's Software Engineering Institute in Pittsburgh, Pennsylvania. In 1994, CERT handled more than two thousand incidents affecting more than forty thousand sites, half in a single attack. They received more than three thousand hotline calls, published 15 security advisories, and received more than twenty-nine thousand e-mail inquiries. The Software Engineering Institute has a WWW home page (http://www.sei.cmu.edu), which carries CERT advisories. These advisories detail how to obtain patches or use workarounds for security problems.

They're also available through anonymous FTP from info.cert.org. To be added to the CERT mailing list, send e-mail to cert-advisory-request@cert.org. System administrators can get CERT contact information through its 24-hour telephone hotline (412-268-7090), by fax (412-268-6989), or by e-mail (cert@cert.org).

No Trespassing

The systems banner that welcomes visitors may provide clues to the operating system being used, which hackers can use to their advantage. The FBI suggests using a banner that warns anyone dialing into a system that it is intended for private use by the company that owns it and that unauthorized users should stay out.

Federal agencies use the following warning banner, which was developed by the Justice Department:

> To protect this system from unauthorized use and to ensure that this system is functioning properly, system administrators monitor the system. This system is for the use of authorized users only. Individuals using this computer system without authority, or in excess of their authority, are subject to having all of their activities on this system monitored and recorded by system personnel. In the course of monitoring individuals who improperly use this system, or in the course of system maintenance, the activities of authorized users may also be monitored. Anyone using this system expressly consents to such monitoring and is advised that if such monitoring reveals possible evidence of criminal activity, system personnel may provide the evidence of such monitoring to law enforcement officials.

The banner is carefully worded. It explicitly states that the activities of anyone—authorized or not—using the system may be monitored. You'll note that the warning banner also doesn't provide any clues about who owns the system.

While this sign might not keep hackers out of the system, it's a much more valuable security tool than you might think. Here's why Let's say you begin to monitor the activities of a hacker who broke into your system. You set up your electronic stakeout, record all illegal activities, perhaps even bait the hacker with phony files, and track the intruder to his or her point of origin. With evidence in hand, you call the computer crime cops, who arrest the hacker. It sounds good, until you learn it's against the law to monitor the hacker's activity on your system without his or her consent. Although it might seem ironic, the hacker could sue you for invasion of privacy!

The Electronics Communications Privacy Act (ECPA) is very specific about who may monitor another's electronic communication and under what circumstances. The ECPA says that owning the system doesn't give you the right to eavesdrop. For that, you need a court-approved wiretap. Think of the telephone company in your area: They own the system, but it's against the law for them to listen in on your conversations.

Tools for Firewall Builders

Some of the free tools that site administrators can use to build and secure firewalls are available direct from the following Web sites: http://ciac.llnl.gov/ciac/SecurityTools.html and ftp://coast.cs.purdue.edu/pub/tools/unix

COPS

The Computer Oracle and Password System (COPS) was developed by Dan Farmer who also helped develop SATAN. COPS checks your system for known security holes. You can find them at http://ciac.llnl.gov/ciac/SecurityTools.html or ftp://coast.cs.purdue.edu/pub/tools/unix.

Crack & Cracklib

Employees who use common passwords such as LOVE and SEX or whose passwords are the same as their login IDs are likely to have their accounts broken into. Crack, developed by Alex Muffett, looks for goofy and otherwise vulnerable passwords and Cracklib bars employees from creating passwords that Crack can guess. Look for them at http://ciac.llnl.gov/ciac/SecurityTools.html and ftp://coast.cs.purdue.edu/pub/tools/unix.

Passwdplus

Passwdplus, by Matt Bishop, is another useful password-checking program that compares passwords being used against those in a dictionary of easily guessed passwords. Find them at http://ciac.llnl.gov/ciac/SecurityTools.html or ftp://coast.cs.purdue.edu/pub/tools/unix.

SATAN

SATAN generated a lot of excitement and heat for Farmer and codeveloper, Wietse Venema, and is now widely used by site administrators and hackers alike to probe for security holes. It is available at ftp://gatekeeper.dec.com/pub/net/SATAN.

SOCKS

Developed by David Kobas and Michelle Koblas, SOCKS eases the burden of customizing applications to permit them to talk to their proxies. It includes a variety of generic system calls such as Rconnect, Raccept, and Rbind that replace standard calls such as connect, accept, and bind. It is available at ftp://ftp.nec.com/pub/security/socks.cstc and http://www.socks.nec.com/.

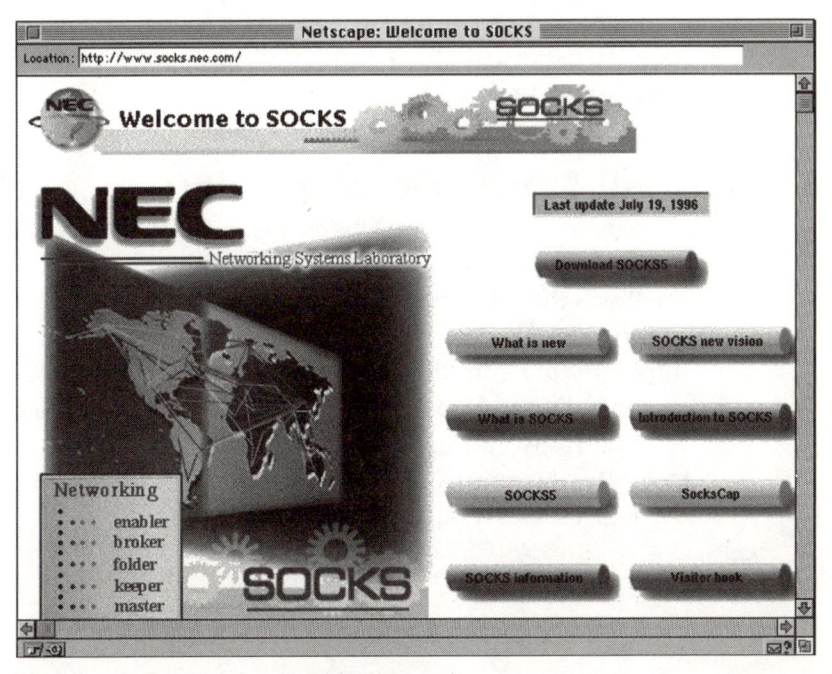

Welcome to SOCKS (www.socks.nec.com).

Tiger

Tiger scans UNIX systems for known security holes. It was developed by Doug Schales at Texas A&M University. You can find it at ftp://net.tamu.edu/pub/security along with several other security tools and information. It's also available through Purdue's COAST project site at ftp://coast.cs.purdue.edu/pub/tools/unix.

TIS Internet Firewall Toolkit

You can find this toolkit at ftp://ftp.tis.com/pub/firewalls/toolkit. You can choose from a variety of its programs. It also contains directions—*configuration practices*—for setting them up. You can use it to authenticate visitors and control access in other ways, set up proxy servers, and protect your system against common attacks. It was codeveloped by firewall guru Marcus Ranum.

Tripwire

Tripwire takes a snapshot of files and directories on your UNIX system and periodically checks this against any changes that have occurred. Files or directories that have been inexplicably altered may signal that a hacker has been at work. Gene H. Kim and Gene Spafford developed Tripwire and are involved with the COAST project at Purdue. These tools can be found at http://ciac.llnl.gov/ciac/SecurityTools.html and ftp://coast.cs.purdue.edu/pub/tools/unix.

Overall Look at Security

No single technology provides absolute security. A solid security defense is created in layers, starting with employee awareness of methods that outsiders and vengeful employees use to compromise information systems security. It also includes various security measures to strengthen operating systems and applications your organization uses, as well as your connections to the outside world.

Your firewall must be part of an overall strategy that includes security awareness, operating system and application security, network security, and transaction security.

Security Awareness

Security is a people problem as much as a technology problem. You must train employees to be on the alert for potential security problems, whether caused by a hacker attacking the organization's computers or an employee shuttling work between home and office on a disk infected by a virus.

In earlier chapters, I described such techniques as creating hacker-proof passwords and spotting viruses. Be sure your employees also are aware of these threats. In addition, bolster such training with employee security policies that spell out precisely what employees may and may not do while using the organization's computer systems. In Chapter 8, I'll provide tips on how to create an effective employee computer security policy.

Operating System Security

Good system administration also can prevent security violations. This means appropriately protecting files and directories, not running unnecessary or dangerous network services, and practicing smart security management.

Although I can't delve into desktop and operating systems security in this book, you also should be alert to potential security flaws when these are announced and take whatever steps are warranted to fix them.

For example, late in 1995 Microsoft scrambled to fix security holes in Windows 95. Early users of Win95 had found a flaw in the file and print services for NetWare that let networked PC users browse other hard drives without permission. Another flaw in file and print services for Microsoft Network let intruders using a UNIX workstation dial into networked PCs running Win95. At about the same time, a group of Finnish hackers uncovered yet another security loophole that made it easy for intruders to crack network and e-mail passwords. Microsoft posted fixes for all of these security problems.

This is not to say that Win95 is less secure than other operating systems but rather to emphasize this point: No matter what security precautions you take, if you don't apply patches and close potential security loopholes in the operating systems and applications you use, your systems remain vulnerable to attack.

Application Security

Encryption is the underpinning of security on the Internet. Not everything that passes through your firewall needs to be encrypted, yet you need to establish policies to explain to employees what information must be encrypted and who may encrypt information. You also must establish a procedure that provides checks and balances. You don't need a disgruntled employee encrypting all of his or her data before leaving the company without your being able to decrypt it.

In earlier chapters, we looked at security approaches such as SecureHTTP and Secure Socket Layer (SSL). Not limited to WWW applications, SSL also can be adapted to any program that uses the TCP/IP socket interface.

Network Security

When purchasing new hardware or software, evaluate products not only for cost, performance, and compatibility but also for security features. Many security loopholes are created when different operating systems and platforms are made to work together.

Company networks—even small ones—consist of a melange of computer platforms, operating systems, protocols, and applications. None of these fit seamlessly together to form a tight security barrier. There are always loopholes, for example, when two different e-mail systems are being used. Often, competitive pressures compel vendors to introduce new applications and digital merchants and others to deploy them before testing has proven they're secure.

Vendors are paying closer attention to security at the operating system level. Microsoft, for example, has recently signed agreements with RSA and its parent Security Dynamics to acquire authentication and encryption technology for Windows NT. If providers build security into the operating system, companies that use it are likely to use the security. One part of the agreements calls for Microsoft to embed RSA's encryption technology into CryptoAPI for encryption and digital signatures. Another part licenses Microsoft to support Security Dynamics' smart card and server authentication in upcoming versions of NT and Internet Information Server.

These and other agreements will let developers create products that provide tighter security across a variety of applications. For example, one application could borrow the encryption and digital signature tools built into another application so that a company can pick and choose the most appropriate crypto scheme.

Moving On

Firewalls are the main way digital merchants can protect their Web sites and other connections to the Internet. But firewalls are not foolproof and must be part of the organization's overall security posture. Before installing a firewall, be sure you have a security policy in place that defines which activities are acceptable and which aren't. Employees must buy into these policies, particularly those who will have Internet accounts. If you can't afford to lose or make public certain information, then don't put it on any system accessible by outsiders, no matter how confident you are in the firewall architecture that you use.

8 The Law Comes to Cyberspace

Doing business in cyberspace is filled with many unique and novel legal issues that merchants on Main Street usually don't need to worry about. Digital merchants operating electronic storefronts, catalog showrooms, and other Web sites, however, have to contend with issues such as copyright infringement, defamation, pornography, privacy, and more.

This chapter provides an overview of some of the legal issues that have an impact on the way you do business in cyberspace. For example, I'll review a few of the proposed changes in copyright law and explain some of the new technologies—such as cryptographic containers—that help make Net sales of copyrighted information a little safer for the copyright holders.

Your employees having Internet access also can create problems rarely encountered in traditional business settings. Because insiders commit most computer crimes, I'll also explain written employee computer security policies—why you should have them and what they should cover.

I'm not a lawyer so I can't give legal advice. I just want to alert you to potential legal issues you might encounter online so that you can discuss them with your attorney (who might not have all of the answers either).

Legal Gray Areas

Congress, state legislatures, and the courts are only now starting to grapple with copyright infringement, privacy, libel, and similarly complex legal issues affected by digital communications. The online world does not require a set of laws that are distinguishable from those that govern the real world, but electronic commerce and online communications add unique legal twists that were not foreseeable when the laws were first crafted. Legislators are just now trying to clear up some of these gray areas, sometimes without a clear understanding of the technologies involved or a real aim in sight.

In mid-1995, Congress passed the Communications Decency Act (CDA), designed to protect children from being exposed to pornography while they are on the Internet. It was signed into law by President Clinton in February 1996. The CDA sets fines and prison time for distributing obscene or indecent material to minors over a network.

When the act was passed, the American Civil Liberties Union, the Electronic Frontier Foundation, and other advocacy groups asserted that the act went too far in limiting the First Amendment rights of individuals and online businesses.

In mid-1996, three federal judges in a Philadelphia court case agreed. The judges said Congress was required to extend the same liberty to free expression in cyberspace as applies now to print materials. They also said the law is unconstitutionally overbroad. The judges said the act has had a "chilling effect" on adult speech. Further, the court said, no technological solutions can protect children consistently from indecency on the Internet. The judges also decided the wording of the law was unacceptably vague. The government plans to appeal the decision to the U.S. Supreme Court.

Libel law as it applies to cyberspace and electronic commerce also is being redefined. Just who is responsible when a libelous message is posted? The person writing the message? The company whose system is used to post the message? Both?

In one recent high-profile case, Prodigy—one of the nation's largest online service providers—was held liable for posting a message that defamed a New York investment bank. In another case, Massachusetts court held Mass Internet, an Internet service provider (ISP), responsible for distributing libelous, obscene messages. The court ordered the ISP to pay $500,000 in damages. Mass Internet had become the target of a lawsuit after a family was deluged with telephone calls because a Mass Internet subscriber had posted a message saying a woman wanted to receive sexually explicit telephone calls day or night. The message, which included the family's telephone number, prompted more than 600 obscene phone calls. When the family asked the ISP to remove the message, it refused, triggering the civil action.

If cases like these are any indication, digital merchants will be found liable for defamatory statements made by employees and other users of the site. Despite the activities of free-speech advocates and others, it seems online companies are to be held to the same standards as newspapers and magazines. If you're planning to set up a Web site, you should set limits on what you will permit on your site.

There also have been calls for changes in copyright law, notably by the Department of Commerce. Those proposals also are likely to be met with resistance by civil libertarians and others who believe such changes would be overly stringent.

Even when the law is clear, it can be nearly impossible to prosecute the people who shoplift from electronic storefronts, violate copyright laws, and commit other crimes, even when they can be identified. Often criminals can use the Internet to conceal their identities and places of origin. And global networks cross not only geographic but also regulatory and jurisdictional boundaries.

What legal recourse is available to a U.S. business operator who has been victimized by a hacker operating from Argentina? The short answer is none. An Argentine hacker cannot be extradited to the United States for computer fraud.

Take the case of Julio Cesar Ardita, 22, of Buenos Aires: U.S. Department of Justice officials would like to get their hands on the young man. They say he used the Internet to invade Harvard University computers and from there break into U.S. government computers containing confidential research on aircraft design, radar technology, and satellite engineering. The case is notable because it is the first time federal authorities obtained a court order to monitor private electronic communications. They eavesdropped on Ardita as he broke into Harvard's computers. Investigators developed a portrait of the attacker and gathered evidence against him. On December 28, 1995, U.S. officials formally charged him with violating provisions of the Computer Fraud and Abuse Act. However, the only way federal authorities can arrest Ardita is if he attempts to enter the United States.

Call Your Attorney

If a consumer accesses your Web site and downloads a Java applet that trashes the information stored on his or her hard drive, what is your corporate liability if you have not taken reasonable precautions against such an event? You should consult your attorney before you set up shop and regularly after that. Your attorney can look at material posted on your Web site to, among other legal questions:

- Be sure that it does not violate someone else's copyright
- Advise you how to word disclaimers of responsibility for what is posted on sites that are linked to yours
- Take a look at your proposed employee security policy to make sure it will hold up in the event you wish to terminate an employee for using the corporate system in an unauthorized manner

Changing Copyright Law

Probably more than most laws, copyright law has not been able to keep pace with technical advances for copying and distributing information made possible by computer technology. If you spend only a few minutes hopping from one Web site to another, you will encounter many copyright violations. Most people know copyrighted material is protected and that they can't simply scan and post on a Web page a Dilbert cartoon or an article from *The New York Times*. Even so, this happens every day.

Setting up a Web site brings various copyright infringement issues into play that are not so readily understood or clearly within the bounds of copyright law. For example, what if you provide a link from your Web site to another without seeking the other Web site operator's permission? It's a copyright violation because you have not given Web navigators permission to download material from your site through the site from which they're linking.

Is it legitimate to copy the HyperText Markup Language (HTML) source code used to format a Web page? Yes. Copyright law applies only to creative content, not to page format. While you can't copyright a single link to a page, you can copyright a list of links, especially if those links are artfully or uniquely arranged in a way that sets them apart from other link lists. Just because you don't see a copyright notice does not mean the work is publicly available. That's probably the most common mistake today.

Copyright law has undergone a number of changes in recent years. The steps creators or authors have to take to ensure ownership of their works have changed considerably. Creators used to be required to put the word *copyright* or the copyright symbol (©), the year, and a statement of ownership on their works.

Now copyright protection applies automatically as soon as works are "fixed in any tangible medium of expression, now . . . known or later developed, from which they can be perceived, reproduced, or otherwise communicated, either directly or with the aid of a machine or device." It makes no difference whether the material is printed or stored on a hard drive.

There's no requirement to register the work with the Copyright Office or provide a copyright notice. However, if you don't want others using the material posted on your Web site, you should register your work and prominently display the standard copyright notices. Your claim to copyright is considerably stronger if you actually file for copyright protection, which is available for a $20 fee. Including the copyright notice may help offset a common copyright infringement defense: that the material was innocently appropriated, an assertion that can minimize the infringer's liability. With copyright protection in place, you also have the right to collect legal fees and statutory damages if you win a copyright violation case.

Without the copyright registration, you must prove that unauthorized use of your material was harmful to your business and provide a price tag for your loss, which can be next to impossible.

If you run your own Web site, you can monitor who is accessing your site and downloading material. If a Web visitor spends a lot of time at your site and downloads page after page of information, you can investigate further or send the offender an e-mail message asserting that you own the material.

If you're serious about protecting your copyright, you can require that visitors register before using your site. You can issue passwords and conceal information on the page that makes it easier to trace.

Copyright Rewrite

The Department of Commerce has released recommendations to rewrite copyright law to make it clear that transmitting a protected work over the Net is a violation of the law. The recommendations also would make it a crime for anyone to circumvent protection schemes that the copyright holder places on the works to prevent them from being used without authorization.

A working group on intellectual property rights was established within the information infrastructure task force to examine the intellectual property implications of the National Information Infrastructure (NII) and make recommendations on any appropriate changes to U.S. intellectual property law and policy.

The report makes a number of specific recommendations:

- Clarify section 106(3) of the Copyright Act, which relates to transmission of phono records over networks, and terms such as *transmit* and *publication*

- Permit libraries to prepare a limited number of digital copies of works to preserve them

- No longer require the use of a copyright notice

- Permit nonprofit organizations to reproduce Braille and other formats of previously published works and distribute them to the visually impaired

- Prohibit the use, manufacture, or importation of devices designed to circumvent technological protections that prevent unauthorized copying
- Bar the dissemination of copyright management information known to be false and the unauthorized removal or alteration of copyright management information
- Support legislation that would make it a criminal offense to willfully infringe on a copyright by reproducing or distributing copies with a retail value of $500,000 or more

Already some industry groups—such as the Consumer Electronics Manufacturers Association and the Institute for Electrical and Electronics Engineers—believe that a bill based on these recommendations would be overly stringent. The bill would make it a crime, for example, for a person to forward an e-mail message (e-mail messages are copyright-protected).

Cryptographic Copyright Containers

The owners of published information, including authors and publishers, would like to be able to protect their hard work from being freely distributed over the Net without authorization. Most information available on the Net today is being passed from one Web site to another and from one PC to another, often without considering the information owner's copyrights and without payment of royalties. This freewheeling attitude is a significant obstacle to the lucrative notion of being able to sell "content" along with CDs and fine wines over the Net.

Technology companies and other organizations have introduced a variety of novel ways to protect copyrighted images, text, audio, video, and other media types displayed on Web sites and to prevent them from either being downloaded or copied in the first place or being distributed without fee in the second.

Protecting copyrighted material also makes it possible to create new ways to make money. Couple that with an electronic payment method, and there is no end to what can be sold. Once information has been tagged with an identifying label or digital watermark and encrypted, it could be sold without fear that the buyer would use the material in ways not intended by the copyright owner.

The payoff for digital merchants is that they would have the opportunity to sell material that otherwise would be merely copied and to create additional sources of revenue by selling material in different formats with an appropriate price structure. Authors could receive royalties for works translated into electronic form and distributed. Online publishers could sell information by the slice or byte. The publisher of a technical journal could sell a chapter instead of the entire work, for example.

Related technologies include encryption, digital watermarking, usage-metering software, secure payment mechanisms, and cryptographic containers for safe distribution.

Digital Vending Machines

Several companies—including AT&T, CD-MAX, InfoSafe Systems, Spyrus, Inc., and Wave Systems Corp.—are working on copyright protection schemes that are similar to digital vending machines.

As with any vending machine, customers would be free to browse the offerings and compare prices without having to actually buy anything. Once they had made their selection, the encrypted copyrighted material could be downloaded. Buyers would receive a key to unlock the material and use it in whatever ways were specified by their licensing agreements. There are two different delivery schemes: One alternative is to leave the material in plaintext. The other is to provide an application along with the material to decrypt the material; the buyer never gets an unencrypted version that can be accessed without the application.

Both approaches guarantee the copyright holder gets paid for the material that is copied, at least the first time it's used. It also gives buyers a chance to pay for only what they use—letting them buy a report a page at a time, for example, rather than acquiring the entire work.

This approach is merely a new wrinkle on an old idea. The publishers of type fonts have been offering a similar scheme for years, giving buyers an entire catalog of fonts on a CD-ROM and permitting consumers to purchase a font at a time.

However, vending machine programs do not necessarily provide protection for the material once it is in the hands of the buyer. There is nothing beyond the fear of prosecution for copyright infringement to prevent the buyer from reusing the material in ways neither covered in a licensing agreement nor approved by the copyright holder.

Publish for Pay

Wave Systems introduced its online "publish for pay" service in September 1996. The micropublishing service has two components: WINPublish, the selling side of the service, and WINPurchase, the buying side.

WINPublishers pay an annual $25 registration fee for the right to upload their documents in HTML to Wave's server, where they are encrypted and given whatever price tag the publisher demands. Information about the documents, such as titles and abstracts, are encrypted along with the documents. The documents, now portable, are posted to the seller's Web site and a site maintained by Wave. They also can be distributed on disk or by e-mail.

WINPurchasers register for the service by opening a credit card account on Wave's server. They receive software that plugs into their Netscape browsers so that whenever they click on a WaveEnabled file in their Web browser, they see its price. A second click triggers the plug-in to send the file to Wave's server, where it is decrypted. The transaction price is deducted from the buyer's account.

Wave takes a percentage of the transaction, ranging from 50 percent (for amounts of less than $3) to 10 percent (for amounts of $100 or more).

Digital Boxes & Other Containers

More advanced schemes are based on embedding protective mechanisms within the copyrighted material, which would remain even after the material is sold the first time. If a buyer passed the material on to someone else, the next person also would have to pay to use it.

Of several companies and organizations touting digital containers, including IBM, InterTrust (formerly Electronic Publishing Resources), and Xerox Corp., IBM is the only one to offer a working product.

Although approaches differ, the idea is the same: Copyrighted images, text, audio, video, and other media types are stored within a cryptographic envelope, box, or similar container that users can open only with a key. The envelope or box contains not only the document but also related information, such as an abstract, document price, and terms and rules for usage. A document can contain many different formats, such as text, HTML code, Joint Photographic Experts Group (JPEG) images, and more.

The protective mechanisms built into the leading cryptographic container technologies provide for the superdistribution of copyrighted content. A relatively new idea, *superdistribution,* lets content buyers reuse and even redistribute (for a fee) copyrighted material, as long as the copyright holder can collect fees from subsequent users. Subsequent sales net greater profits for the content owner, who does not incur additional costs for redistribution.

IBM Cryptolope Containers

IBM's cryptographic container technology, Cryptolope, is offered as part of its infoMarket service, which is a search service for customers and a rights and payments clearinghouse for content providers. It can be found at http://www.infomkt.ibm.com and http://www.cryptolope.ibm.com.

IBM infoMarket service already has partnerships with 29 information providers, including the Associated Press, ESPN Sports Ticker, and the technology companies Kodak, Netscape, and Verity.

With IBM's infoMarket, users can simultaneously search for and retrieve content—still images, text, sound, and video—from a distributed database in various formats hosted on a number of popular publishing platforms. This gives digital publishers greater control over how their content is presented to potential customers because they are not limited by the technical requirements and presentation formats of typical commercial online services.

Users who want to purchase, for example, a copy of the latest market research report from a publisher receive the contents in a sealed Cryptolope container. Once the content is purchased, the IBM infoMarket service transparently provides the customer with a private key to unlock the package. It can then be used according to the terms of the abstract. After content is downloaded, printed, or read, Cryptolope prevents subsequent efforts to copy or transmit the copyrighted information to others without the appropriate payment for its use.

IBM's Cryptolope package contains an encrypted form of a document, portions of which customers can read using Web browsers or editors. To actually buy a document, customers must use Netscape Navigator with its associated Cryptolope helper application or a custom application capable of interacting with the Cryptolope package. (Support for other browsers is under way.) The browser or custom application lets customers see an abstract of the document, price, rules for use, and so forth. Once end users agree to pay, their request goes to a clearing center to check permissions, and they get a key to unlock the document, which is contained within the Cryptolope package.

Multiple cryptographic technologies are used to help secure and authenticate the information contained within a Cryptolope container. In addition to document encryption, data in the Cryptolope container are cryptographically signed to prevent undetected alteration of any of the Cryptolope container information and identification of the originator of the container.

The Cryptolope package embeds a rules specification that is used in determining which users are allowed access to a document, what actions can be performed (view, print, save), and the costs associated with each action. At the time of content/service access, an evaluation is made based on user credentials, the requested action to be performed, and the user environment. This evaluation results in a list of user permissions granted, the cost for the action to be performed, and any usage restrictions.

Over time, additional information and functionality will be added to the Cryptolope container, including watermarking instructions and advertisements related to the document contained in the Cryptolope package. Cryptolope containers will be issued and handled by multiple issuing authorities, ensuring an open standard of Cryptolope containers is created and allowing a free market for the implementation of custom client applications.

Cryptolope buttons are part of every word processor or authoring system; clicking the button brings up controls authors could use to define usage terms and fees before sending the document on its way.

InterTrust DigiBoxes

InterTrust Technologies Corp., Sunnyvale, California, is touting what it calls the InterTrust Commerce Architecture, which provides a secure, end-to-end electronic commerce framework for content creators, distributors, users, and clearinghouses. The InterTrust architecture includes a digital lock box called the DigiBox and a Web server setup called the InterTrust Commerce Node.

The DigiBox secure container is a tamperproof electronic package that binds usage, payment, and metering controls to any kind of digital content. Content usage is effectively and efficiently controlled, and payment to all rights holders is automated. The payment scheme is highly flexible, permitting the copyright holder to set up different fee structures depending on how the material is used. One fee might cover the cost of reading the material; another, the cost of reprinting it as part of a magazine article; and yet another, using the material in a market research report that is to be resold.

With the InterTrust Commerce Node, the server deciphers DigiBox's encrypted information; reads the restrictions on use, payment, and distribution; and conveys this information to the customer.

Xerox Usage Rights Language

Like the other crypto container technologies, Xerox's approach to protecting copyrighted material also uses encryption to assign a series of permissions, licenses, and other information to the material. A protocol called the Xerox Usage Right Language describes what rights have been assigned to a particular digital work. These rights can be attached to the digital version of a book, musical recording, movie, computer program, or any other copyrighted material. The rights holder has considerable flexibility in tailoring the rights of each customer and fees owed. The rights holder could, for example, set limits on whether customers could make a backup copy of the work or lend it to someone else and could provide fees for each activity.

Xerox's approach differs from IBM's and other approaches in that it is based on using a trusted or security-conscious computer system capable of tracking the rights attached to each work and who has access to those rights.

The system employs a security processor that handles encryption and decryption and the creation and distribution of keys. It is also capable of detecting attempts to circumvent system security.

The chief advantage and drawback of the Xerox approach is that all activity must be channeled through the trusted system. That gives copyright holders the opportunity to interact directly with each customer and to know exactly what is being done with a given digital work. The downside is that having a focal point runs counter to the whole notion of a network, where services are distributed and accessible in a variety of places.

Standards Battle

IBM, InterTrust Technologies, Novell, and other organizations battling against copyright infringement formed a consortium in mid-1996 called the Electronic Rights Management Group. The group wants to formulate industry standards for the secure distribution of and payment for information published on the Net, under the management of the Information Industry Association.

Not long after the group was formed, however, the members started battling among themselves on what technologies will be used to form the basis of a standard. Each member is championing its own technology. Some of the technologies are proprietary, and there are no plans to make them compatible with other approaches.

IMPRIMATUR

A European commission also is working on developing standards to protect copyrighted material on the international level. Several European companies, research labs, and other organizations have formed a group called IMPRIMATUR, short for Intellectual Multimedia Property Rights Model and Terminology for Universal Reference. However, they haven't gotten much beyond developing a clever name for their project.

Privacy Is Good for Business

Consumer advocates are pushing federal regulators to clamp down on attempts by online service providers, digital merchants, advertisers, and marketers to gather information about Net travelers that can be used to fuel marketing campaigns. Several industry groups already have seen the handwriting on the wall, recognizing that without self-regulation, federal regulators will no doubt do it for them.

The Interactive Services Association, for example, has drafted and adopted a set of privacy guidelines. These guidelines cover four policies:

- Actively notifying customers that the service sells customer information
- Promptly removing customer names from mailing lists
- Reviewing the products and services of companies that buy ISPs' customer lists
- Limiting subscriber information to names and addresses or identifying them by their buying patterns only in broad terms

An industry group called the Coalition for Advertising Supported Information and Entertainment also is attempting to regulate itself in a bid to keep federal regulators from doing the job. The coalition released a manifesto of sorts that provides for certain consumer protections, such as requiring marketers to disclose their identities to consumers and to use personal information only in appropriate ways.

In a report entitled "Privacy and the NII," the National Telecommunications and Information Administration (NTIA) warned that in the course of using the NII,

> individuals will create information trails that could provide others, in the absence of safeguards, with the personal details of their lives ... There is a lack of uniformity among existing privacy laws and regulations for telephony and video services. In fact, similar services are governed differently depending on how they are delivered. And, other communications services like those available over the Internet are almost entirely unprotected. Furthermore, NTIA believes it will become increasingly difficult to apply existing privacy laws and regulations to communications service providers as services and sectors converge, and as new technologies evolve.

In its report, the NTIA proposed a framework based on two fundamental elements: provider notice and customer consent. Under this proposed framework, telecommunication and information service providers would notify individuals about their information practices, abide by those practices, and keep customers informed of subsequent changes to such practices.

Service providers would be free to use information collected for the stated purposes after obtaining the customer's consent. Two levels of consent exist: affirmative, which would require personal information, and tacit, for all other information.

The NTIA also suggests that the industry voluntarily adopt uniform privacy guidelines, while adding: "... if such private-sector action is not forthcoming, however, that framework can and should form the basis for government-mandated privacy regulations or standards."

The bottom line is that digital merchants and others doing business on the Internet will have to devote more attention to protecting the privacy of their customers. Merchants who already show concern for the privacy of their customers are no doubt going to have a competitive edge.

Cookies for Consumers

Until consumers complained about it, digital merchants could use "*cookies*," a record of how long a customer visited a Web site and what they did while they were there that is deposited on the customer's PC. Then, whenever the customer visits a merchant's site, the merchant can retrieve the cookie, analyze the shopper's last visit, and provide a view of the store customized to the customer's tastes.

Netscape Navigator users now have the option of blocking merchants from depositing a persistent cookie on the PC. A *persistent cookie* tracks customer shopping habits for weeks or months, rather than during a single visit.

This surreptitious tracking makes anyone who worries about privacy nervous. From the digital merchant's point of view, however, the cookies feature offers helpful services. You can tailor a pitch to each shopper. You can track which ads on a site attract the most attention. You can track a buyer's interest in certain products and, when he or she visits the site, display a message about new products in that category.

Persistent Cookies

A potential customer visits a merchant's site and expresses an interest in acquiring, for example, a certain type of collectible. The site creates a file or cookie with the preferences on the visitor's hard drive. The next time the visitor checks to see what new products are available, a list of products meeting the visitor's prequalified needs is displayed.

A person visits the site and decides to buy a few products, which are kept in a temporary cookie residing on the visitor's hard drive. Once the purchase is complete, the cookie is automatically removed.

If you plan to maintain cookies, you should tell visitors to your site and add that the information is protected and so is not intended for resale. Even better would be to ask visitors to complete a form rather than to take this information without informing them first.

Employers need to know that they also can use cookies to track employees' activities while using a company PC. If your company has a policy, for example, against employees downloading pornography from an adult site, you can use the cookie trail as grounds for letting the employee go.

Keeping Track

Cookies are only the beginning. Web servers, databases, and development toolkits will be able to record everything that a visitor does at your site. That means logging information about the visitor, words entered in a search request, which pages visited in what sequence, and sites visited and time spent at each. The information could be added to a database, analyzed, and used to dynamically create new pages tailored to the visitor's unique interests—all within seconds.

Request a Web page via your browser and you might get a JavaScript in return that can perform a variety of unwanted tasks such as launching an applet to retrieve your e-mail address and your cache file, which is basically a list of pages that you've looked at recently.

The Center for Democracy and Technology (CDT), an Internet civil liberties group, maintains a Web site (http://www.13x.com/cgi-bin/cdt/snoop.pl) that shows what type of information someone can glean from your perusing a Web site. The CDT site will tell what browser you're using, your computer monitor's resolution settings, the Internet access service provider you're using, the general geographic area you're calling from, and even the address of the last Web page you visited. When you next check your e-mail, you'll find a message waiting from the people who run CDT. Some browsers, such as Netscape Navigator 2.0, and 3.0 will give your e-mail address to any Web site that asks for it. What happens to your e-mail address after that is anyone's guess.

With your e-mail address, the site operator can use one of the many search engines to scan Usenet for postings. Those postings can be personal or can contain sensitive information about your company's affairs. If you give employees access, you should consider whether you want to permit employees to post messages containing your company's address.

Savvy digital merchants take advantage of these capabilities, but gathering it surreptitiously can come back to haunt them. Consider asking for the information directly, perhaps offering incentives to boost response. Require visitors to register before touting your site.

Floppy Copy Concerns

Software pirates steal in a year as much business software as McDonald's sells hamburgers. That's according to the Software Publishers Association (SPA), a trade group made up of top software publishers based in Washington, D.C. The SPA says a total of $8.1 billion worth of business application software was illegally copied in 1994. Most such thievery takes place in the United States, the SPA adds.

Software is protected by the Copyright Act and the Software Copyright Protection Bill, among others. According to Title 17 of the Copyright Act, only the copyright owner has the exclusive right to reproduce the copyrighted work and to distribute copies of the copyrighted work; anyone who violates any of the exclusive rights of the copyright owner is breaking the law.

You might have paid for a particular program, but the law says that you can't make copies or rent it to someone. However, you are allowed to make backup copies of your programs to protect your investment.

If you copy software that belongs to someone else and they learn about it, you can get into trouble. The law is pretty clear about what you can and can't do with copyrighted software. If you have questions or need advice, consult your attorney.

Many companies make more than just backup copies of their software. A company that I once worked for (who shall remain nameless, but you know who you are) bought a bunch of new computers but only a single copy of three programs that it needed for the new machines. These were fancy page layout and graphics programs, the kind that cost hundreds of dollars apiece. From the company's point of view, it was saving a lot of money, which is good for the bottom line. Besides, if the company didn't make copies, it wouldn't be able to buy all that it needed. This is the sort of rationalization that will one day get my former employer a visit from the SPA, a.k.a. the software police.

The SPA doesn't tolerate software piracy. It runs many hard-hitting magazine ads showing people in handcuffs and behind bars. In addition to admonishing readers "Don't copy that floppy," they urge employees to report their bosses if they suspect them of illegally copying software.

The SPA says it gets 800 calls a week on its hotline. They follow up on about 10 percent of the calls. If it suspects the employer is a large-scale software pirate, it calls the Federal Bureau of Investigation and local authorities.

If this happens, they will look for evidence that you purchased all software on your workstations and local area networks (LANs). If they find 10 copies of Microsoft Word but you have a receipt for only one copy, you'll be required to destroy the remaining copies and purchase nine replacements. You might also have to pay a penalty, typically equal to the retail price of the stolen software. Word sells for about $300 per copy, which would mean $5,400 for nine copies. For those with complete disregard for the law, penalties can be significantly higher. Under the Copyright Act, civil penalties can be as high as $100,000 for each infringed work, and criminal penalties can go to $250,00 and five years in jail for each infringed work

The Software Copyright Protection Bill makes it a felony to illegally copy 10 or more software programs or programs with a total retail value of $2,500 or more. Criminal penalties again are fines of up to $250,000 and imprisonment for up to five years. Not surprisingly, given the option of paying for the pirated software plus a penalty or getting embroiled in a complicated lawsuit, most companies settle out of court.

More companies today are making sure that the software they buy is not illegally copied. Licensing and metering software for networks is one key way companies can protect the software they buy. The SPA has a free software auditing package called SPAudit; which you can receive by calling 800-866-6585. To report cases of copyright infringement, the SPA hotline is 800-388-7478. You also can use their CompuServe forum by entering GO SPA.

Here are some tips to keep the software police at bay:

- Don't permit anyone to make illegal copies of software.
- Don't allow employees to load new software on their machines.
- Don't permit employees to download software from online services and bulletin board systems.
- Conduct an audit periodically to make sure that all of the software you're using is legitimate.

Digital Shrink Wrap

Microsoft has been encouraging software developers to enroll in what they call a digital shrink-wrap program. It's based on using digital certificates technology from VeriSign Inc. Microsoft's Authenticode program uses VeriSign's Digital ID technology to establish the identity of the company providing the software and to attest that the software has not been tampered with en route to the buyer.

VeriSign authenticates the publisher of the software and not the actual code. Signing the code with a digital signature is the next step in the program, according to VeriSign.

Developers participate in the program by submitting an application and undergoing a verification process administered by Microsoft, then obtaining a digital certificate from VeriSign. When developers post their software for downloading, they apply their digital signatures using Authenticode, which is free to the developers as part of Microsoft's ActiveX toolkit.

Authenticode is supported in Microsoft's Internet Explorer 3.0. Before downloading the software, the consumer's browser checks to see whether it has been certified. If not, the consumer can halt the download.

Individual developers pay VeriSign $20 per certificate; commercial developers pay $400.

Microsoft has submitted Authenticode for scrutiny by the World Wide Web Consortium in hopes that it will emerge as a standard.

Electronic Licensing & Security Initiatives

Stream International Inc., BBN, KPMG, and other companies, have formed the Electronic Licensing and Security Initiative (ELSI) with the aim of developing standards and establishing a clearinghouse that will make electronic distribution of software secure, accountable, quick, and inexpensive. Among those that have been given an opportunity to see the initial specifications to support the ELSI effort are AT&T, IBM, First Data, Microsoft, and Stream.

The ELSI will create an infrastructure to address an increasingly serious barrier to the evolution of software sales on the Internet: the ability to securely track software purchases in cyberspace, both cost efficiently and on a mass-market scale.

The participating companies will create an independent, open infrastructure for the software industry that will be something like a federal reserve bank for software, providing a secure distribution mechanism and a trusted repository for proof of software licensing.

The ELSI clearinghouse will create and manage tokens to provide secure transport and electronic proof of licensing over the Internet. The tokens also will provide end-to-end auditability and accountability of software licenses. By resolving the fundamental issues of security and licensing, token technology will become the foundation for other Internet-based value-added services, such as payment processing, electronic download of software, corporate asset management, software rental services, invoicing and royalty reporting, upgrade and fix management, password generation, registration services, and technical support validation.

ELSI's secure tokens will incorporate several security measures, including public-key encryption, certificate authority, nonrepudiation, digital signature, and a hierarchical trust model.

May You Have Many Employees

Okay, so you've set up a Web site and you're ready to go into business. But what about your employees? Shouldn't they have Internet access, too? They'll need to respond to e-mail requests for information, to monitor newsgroups for trends, to cruise the

World Wide Web to gather information and to keep an eye on the competition. I'll bet you can think of at least a dozen more reasons that it makes sense to give employees Web access.

First, think of the risks: Employees who are responsible for maintaining your Web site might harbor a grudge or innocently provide links to sites that the company does not endorse. For example, Kmart found that one of its employees had linked the company's home page to his personal Web page, which was in turn linked to a site that contained a spoof of the controversy surrounding indecent materials on the Internet.

The same employee who would never think to nail up a cheesecake calendar on his office wall might not give the same consideration to using his Internet access to download materials. An audit of computer use at Pacific Northwest National Laboratory in Richland, Washington, for example, revealed that nearly a hundred employees had used the lab's computers during off-hours to access Web sites specializing in pornography.

There are all sorts of alternative sex newsgroups and other sites that appeal to a wide range of sexual tastes, ranging from bisexual to bizarre. Many of these sites feature pictures and audio clips of a graphic nature. A sexual harassment suit may ensue if an employee uses a company computer to download one of these files.

Employees are increasingly apt to resort to using anonymous remailers—which permit them to conceal their e-mail address—to broadcast corporate secrets, without fear of being identified as the source of mischief. They've been used for a variety of illegal activities, including transmitting viruses and pornography, violating copyright laws, and harassing other Net users with sexually charged or otherwise offensive e-mail. Insiders at the Church of Scientology, for example, used an anonymous remailer to distribute copyrighted and confidential scriptures.

Hackers use the Internet all the time to carry out their activities. Have you ever considered that one of those hackers might be one of your employees? Also, many companies are linking to the Internet in order to maintain regular contact with suppliers and customers. Often, one company will have access to another company's database to check for product availability, to place orders, and so on. There's not much that anyone can do if one of your employees decides to exceed his or her authorization and start going through someone else's system, using equipment and connections you paid for.

It's also possible an employee might download a file—PostScript documents, Word macros, viruses, Trojan horses—that can overwrite files and cause you to lose data or open your Web server to other attacks.

Even a well-meaning employee can obtain false or misleading information from another site and then act on it. Perhaps a competitor decides to send your employees forged e-mail that appears to have been sent from you or post a false message on a newsgroup that results in lost business, low employee morale, or other damage.

Last, cruising the Internet can reduce productivity. Time can be wasted searching for material that's hard to find, using inaccurate information, or pursuing activities that aren't business related.

Make It a Policy to Protect Yourself

If you run a business, you must have a clearly stated policy covering precisely how information, computers, and related resources are to be used by employees. If your policy includes monitoring them, say so, in writing. If you have set ideas about what they shouldn't do with your company's computer resources, spell these out in a policy, too.

Your policy should spell out what you consider to be appropriate and inappropriate use of the Internet. If you don't want employees downloading copyrighted material, pornographic images, and other questionable materials, then state this explicitly in your policy.

This policy also must detail in firm terms the penalties for violating policy guidelines, or no one will take it seriously. One way to bolster security is to distribute a set of guidelines for computer-related activities the company considers proper and improper. Then, get the employees to buy into the policy.

Many large companies also create comprehensive policies that spell out in great detail how computers are to be protected, who is responsible for the various sorts of data that the company creates, what security controls must be implemented, and so on. That's not something the typical small company needs to do, however. Large companies have professionals who do nothing but create security policies and then go around enforcing them. If you run a smaller business yourself, you won't have time to do that.

The Right & Wrong of Using Computers

Many of the computer security policies I've come across devote a section or two to computer ethics before providing specifics.

An employee who duplicates a copyrighted software package, might not be dishonest but might view it as harmless. Having reported on too many instances in which employees did such things as planting programs to destroy valuable data or were clearly aware of what they were doing, I suggest you state explicitly what you consider acceptable and unacceptable behavior.

Top Down View of Policies

I've explained several different policies and identified several key issues they have in common. Although the end result is somewhat general, you can use the following information as the basis for developing your own policies.

You should state up front that the company's goal is to protect its computer systems and the information stored in them from accidental or deliberate unauthorized disclosure, modification, or destruction. Add to that your intent to put in appropriate security controls in order to achieve your stated goal. Last, note that you also intend to hold employees personally accountable for the information resources entrusted to them.

Having a written policy protects you from employees claiming they didn't know that certain activities were considered improper or that they didn't know you could terminate their employment if they violated the company's computer security policy. After formulating your policy, have your company's legal experts review it.

Here are some key areas that you should address in your policy:

- Permission
- Responsibilities
- Keep Passwords and Accounts Confidential
- Unauthorized Access to Files and Directories
- Unauthorized Use of Software
- Use for For-profit Activities
- Electronic Mail
- Harassment
- Attacking the System
- Theft
- Waste and Abuse
- Networks
- Enforcement
- Your Responsibility
- Workplace Monitoring

Permission

Your policy should state that the use of computer facilities by an employee must be authorized by the owner of the information or a senior manager. It should also say that the employee must obtain permission before using another employee's computer account or user ID from the owner of that account, who is responsible for its use. Employees should be told that all computer and electronic files belong to somebody and they should assume those files are private and confidential unless the owner has explicitly made them available to others.

Responsibilities

Employees should be told that they are each the owner of their data, and it is each employee's responsibility to ensure information is adequately protected against unauthorized access. That means each employee must avail him or herself of the access controls and other security measures the company has provided and take prudent and reasonable steps to limit access to their accounts.

Keep Passwords & Accounts Confidential

Advise employees to change their passwords frequently and avoid using their names, their spouses' or friends' names, or words that can be guessed easily. Also instruct them not to leave terminals unattended without logging off first.

Unauthorized Access to Files & Directories

Your policy should tell employees that they must not engage in any activity that is intended to circumvent computer security controls. These activities include attempting to crack passwords, discover unprotected files, or decode encrypted files. This also includes creating, modifying, or executing programs that surreptitiously penetrate computer systems.

Instruct employees that they must not access the accounts of others with the intent to read, browse, modify, copy, or delete files and directories unless a supervisor or other authorized person has given them specific authorization.

Advise employees not to use an account for any purpose not authorized when the account was established, including personal or commercial use.

Unauthorized Use of Software

Inform employees that they are prohibited from loading any software on any computer system without approval. That includes commercial, shareware, and freeware software. Further, they should be expressly prohibited from using company computers to make illegal copies of licensed or copyrighted software. Copyrighted software must be used only in accordance with its license or purchase agreement. Employees may not own or use unauthorized copies of software or make unauthorized copies of software for yourself or anyone else.

Also, employees are prohibited from using software that is designed to destroy data, provide unauthorized access to computer systems, or disrupt computing processes in any other way. Using viruses, worms, Trojan horses, or other invasive software is expressly forbidden.

The policy should inform employees that the company has installed antivirus software on all of its computer systems and employees are required to use it. They should be prohibited from tampering with this software or turning it off. Also, employees should be instructed to scan all disks for viruses or signs of other forms of malicious software before they are inserted into the company's computers.

Use for For-profit Activities

Ensure that your policy explicitly states that the company's computer systems are for the sole use of the company. Tell employees they are prohibited from using the company's computer systems for personal or private financial gain unless that use has been specifically authorized.

Electronic Mail

The policy should provide guidelines on the employees' use of the company's electronic mail system. For example, it should state that the e-mail system is to be used only for company-related business. Employees should be prohibited from transmitting fraudulent, harassing, or obscene messages and files. They also should be instructed not to send any electronic mail or other form of electronic communication by forging another's identity or attempting to conceal the origin of the message in any other way.

Harassment
Employees should be told not to use the company's computer systems to harass anyone. This includes the use of insulting, sexist, racist, obscene, or suggestive electronic mail; tampering with others' files; and invasive access to others' equipment. In addition, users of any electronic communication facilities—such as electronic mail, networks, bulletin boards, and newsgroups—are obligated to comply with the restrictions and acceptable practices established for those specific facilities. Certain types of communications are expressly forbidden. This includes the random mailing of messages; the sending of obscene, harassing, or threatening material; or the use of the facilities for commercial or political purposes.

Attacking the System
Use the policy to tell employees they must not deliberately attempt to degrade the performance of the company's computer system or subvert it in any other way. Deliberately crashing the system is expressly forbidden.

Theft
The policy should make clear that all hardware, software, and computer-related supplies and documentation are the sole property of the company. Employees should be told they must not remove them from company premises without proper authorization. Employees must dispose of all hardware, software, and computer-related supplies and documentation within the guidelines established by authorized company computer system personnel, not in the garbage. Note: You want to be sure employees don't simply toss old manuals, floppy disks, and similar objects into a garbage bin. Manuals should be shredded and floppies erased, for example, to remove any information that an outsider could use to penetrate the company's computer systems. Don't overlook recycling laser toner cartridges, which you can use to offset the cost of buying new cartridges.

Waste & Abuse

Instruct employees to avoid any activity around their workstations that may result in damage to their computers, software, or information. The policy should state that eating, drinking, or smoking while seated at your computer is not permitted. Include some mention that company computer systems are a valuable resource, and they should not be abused or wasted. That includes being considerate of coworkers if employees must share computer resources. Employees should be told to avoid monopolizing systems and connect time, disk space, and other computer resources. Finally, tell them that using the company's computer systems to store personal data or to play computer games is not permitted.

Networks

The policy should advise employees not to use the company-owned or any other network accessible by company computers—whether local, national, or international—for any activity other than company-related business. This includes, but is not limited to, "surfing" the Internet, engaging in online discussions in newsgroups and bulletin board services, attempting to access other computer systems without authorization, posting commercial messages, and transmitting viruses, worms, or other invasive software.

Enforcement

Make sure that employees are aware the company will investigate any alleged abuses of its computer resources. Mention in the policy that as part of that investigation, the company may access the electronic files of its employees. If the investigation indicates that computer privileges have been abused or policies violated, the company may limit the access of employees found to be using computer systems improperly. Further, flagrant abuses may be referred to senior managers or law enforcement authorities. Although the company wants to ensure that the privacy of all its employees is protected, in the course of its investigation, the company may reveal private, employee-related information to other employees.

Your Responsibility

Tell employees that they are responsible for their own actions. Inform them that their positions may be terminated in extreme cases of flagrant abuse or disregard of the company's computer-use guidelines. Mention too that employees also are required to participate in assuring the legal and ethical use of company computers and user accounts. Any violation of these guidelines should be reported to their supervisors or a senior manager.

Workplace Monitoring

The policy should note the company has the obligation to ensure that its computer resources are used properly and within the guidelines established by the company. In pursuit of that goal, the company reserves the right to monitor the system for signs of illegal or unauthorized activity.

Last Rights & Wrongs

Your policy also should state that employees may not engage in activities that abuse or misuse computer resources just because the particular activity is not expressly prohibited by the policy. Computer technology changes rapidly, as do the ways that employees are able to use, and perhaps abuse, the company's computer systems. No policy can cover all possibilities.

Caveat

A computer security policy is not a substitute for proper computer security controls. The policy's purposes are to demonstrate that you're serious about protecting the company's computer resources and to induce employees to become part of the solution rather than part of the problem. It also defines ground rules. In the event you do have a problem, the policy gives you a foundation on which to base corrective actions.

Policy Helpers

The National Institute of Standards and Technology, through its National Computer Systems Laboratory, publishes several special publications about information systems security, including an executive's guide to information policies. A list of current publications is available from Standards Processing Coordinator, National Institute of Standards and Technology, National Computer Systems Laboratory, Technology Building B-64, Gaithersburg, MD 20899, 301-975-2817.

For any computer security program to succeed, it must have support from senior management, or no one will take it seriously. Make sure everyone knows that the company's computer security policies have the blessing of those at the top. A computer security program is good for business. The main thing is that you have taken measures to protect the company's information and computers against fraud, disaster, and many other situations that could put your business out of business. Having a well-defined computer security policy can help boost the company's image with customers, suppliers, and other business partners.

Computer Awareness Training

Once you have developed your policy, communicate it to every employee. All new hires should receive a copy. Explain it to them in detail as part of their orientation. Employees also will need a refresher course about once yearly. Companies that foster security awareness say that training must be regular and that a refresher course every six months is not too often. Also, you must train new employees as soon as they are hired to impress upon them the importance of security before bad habits can begin. Managers must be part of the training equation as well. They should be asked to participate in and endorse programs to give these a stamp of legitimacy and importance.

Who Has the Right to Surf?

Clearly, not every employee needs to have Internet access. Decide who should have access and then make sure they understand that there are limits on what they may and may not do. In addition to formulating a policy, consider:

- Teaching employees Internet etiquette to avoid claims of defamation or sexual harassment and enforce a ban on sending any offensive messages to anyone. Check newsgroups for posts originating from company systems. If you find one of your employees is regularly participating in discussions in alt.sex.bestiality and has an e-mail address joeblow@*yourcompanyname*, you want to discourage that sort of activity.

- Limiting the amount of time that employees spend surfing the Internet. The fact is, surfing is a massive time-waster and productivity-killer. Many companies market software that tracks employee surfing and restricts what sites they can visit. Microsystems Software in Framingham, Massachusetts, for example, offers a product called Cyber Sentry you can use for this purpose. It is priced from $695 for 50 users to $1,295 for 250 users.

- Making sure your employees are aware that online activity—including their electronic mail—may be monitored.

- To avoid potential liabilities for copyright infringement, telling employees that information they download must be only for internal use.

- Keeping in mind that trying to control employees rather than educating them tends to be counterproductive.

- Realizing that if employees can download files, there's nothing to stop them from downloading viruses at the same time. Internet connection makes it even more critical that each workstation as well as your LAN is running antivirus software.

- Placing limits on what sorts of things that employees can do. However, if you close down too many I-way avenues, then you should rethink why you connected in the first place.

Appendix A

Using the Internet to Stay Ahead of the Bad Guys

There are megabytes—make that terrabytes—of information about electronic commerce and Internet security on the Internet and World Wide Web (WWW), if you know where to look. Start by doing a search using Yahoo, AltaVista, or one of the other search engines that are accessible from Netscape's home page (www.home.netscape.com) to get started.

I've compiled a list of popular Web sites, mailing lists, and other resources to help you learn more about protecting your electronic business. Keep in mind that this list is far from complete, as new sites open up every day.

Computer-Security-Related Organizations

The following organizations are sources of a wide variety of security-related information including advisories about newly discovered flaws in software with the potential of jeopardizing security, Frequently Asked Questions (FAQs), software tools and white papers, links to other relevant sites, and more.

Computer Emergency Response Team (CERT), Carnegie Mellon University
ftp://ftp.cert.org/pub/cert_advisories
http://www.sei.cmu.edu/SEI

Computer Incident Advisory Capability, Department of Energy
http://www.cs.purdue.edu/coast

Computer Operations, Audit, and Security Technology, Purdue University
http://www.cs.purdue.edu/coast/coast.html

Computer Professionals for Social Responsibility
www.cpsr.org

Computer Security Institute
http://www.gosci.com

The Computer Security Research Laboratory at the University of California at Davis
http://seclab.cs.ucdavis.edu/security.html

Electronic Frontier Foundation
http://www/eff.org

The Forum of Incident Response and Security Teams, National Institute of Standards and Technology
http://csrc.ncsl.nist.gov/first

Information Systems Security Association
http://www.uhsa.uh.edu/issa

Library of Congress Internet Resource Page, Internet Security
http://lcweb.loc.gov/global/internet/security.html

National Computer Security Association
http://www.ncsa.com

Safe Internet Programming, Princeton University
http://www.cs.princeton.edu/sip

World Wide Web Consortium, W3C
http://www.w3.org/pub/WWW/Security

Mailing Lists

Subscribing to e-mail lists is fairly straightforward, but there are slight variations from one list to another. Where I've indicated *your e-mail address*, enter your e-mail address exactly as you would to receive e-mail. Where I've indicated *your name*, enter your first and last name. Leave the subject line blank.

A word of caution: Some lists come to you in digest form, with all of the messages (usually a day's worth) in a single file. Other e-mail lists generate hundreds of messages a day, and you may soon find it difficult to sort through them all, especially if you subscribe to more than a few lists. When you subscribe, you will receive a notification that you have been added to the list, along with directions on how to unsubscribe.

Computer Security

The following mailing lists cover announcements about new security products and updates, new security holes, FAQs, and related topics:

Alert
To subscribe, send e-mail to:
mailto:request-alert@iss.net
In the body of the message, write:
subscribe alert

Best of Security
To subscribe, send e-mail to:
best-of-security-request@suburbia.net
In the body of the message, write:
subscribe best-of-security

COAST Security Archive
To subscribe, send e-mail to:
coast-request@cs.purdue.edu
In the body of the message, write:
subscribe coast *your e-mail address*

Risks
To subscribe, send e-mail to:
risks-request@csl.sri.com
In the body of the message, write:
subscribe

Encryption
The following are mailing lists devoted to encryption and related topics:

Cypherpunks
To subscribe, send e-mail to:
majordomo@toad.com
In the body of the message write:
subscribe cypherpunks *your e-mail address your name*

Firewalls
Internet Firewalls
This mailing list is a forum for firewall administrators:
To subscribe, send e-mail to:
majordomo@greatcircle.com
In the body of the message, write:
subscribe firewalls

Academic Firewalls
Another list about firewalls, this one maintained by Texas A & M University:
To subscribe, send e-mail to:
majordomo@net.tamu.edu
In the body of the message, write:
subscribe Academic-Firewalls

Hacking
The following lists cover topics of interest to hackers and those who keep up with what hackers are up to:

Computer Underground Digest
To subscribe, send e-mail to:
cu-digest-request@weber.ucsd.edu
In the body of the message, write:
sub cudigest

Phrack
To subscribe, send e-mail to:
phrack@well.com
In the body of the message, write:
subscribe Phrack

Privacy
The following mailing lists are devoted to computer privacy:

Computer Privacy Digest
To subscribe, send e-mail to:
comp-privacy-request@uwm.edu
In the body of the message, write:
subscribe cpd

Privacy Forum
To subscribe, send e-mail to:
privacy-request@vortex.com
In the body of the message, write:
information privacy

WWW Security
The following mailing lists cover various aspects of WWW security:

WWW Security
To subscribe, send e-mail to:
www-security-request@nsmx.rutgers.edu.
In the body of the message, write:
subscribe www-security *your_email_address*

Secure Socket Layer
To subscribe, send e-mail to:
ssl-talk-request@netscape.com
In the body of the message, write:
subscribe

Viruses
These mailing lists are devoted to discussion of viruses and alerts about new viruses:

Virus-L
To subscribe, send e-mail to:
listserv@lehigh.edu
In the body of the message, write:
subscribe virus-l *your-name*

Frequently Asked Questions (FAQs)
Here are some sources of FAQs covering various aspects of security:

Computer Security
The comp.security FAQ is posted every month to the newsgroup comp.security.misc.

Cryptography
A comprehensive FAQ on encryption from RSA Data Security:
http://www.rsa.com/faq

Hacking
The alt.2600 FAQ covers techniques used by hackers and is posted every month to the alt.2600 newsgroup.

Internet Firewalls
Firewall guru, Marcus J. Ranum's Internet Firewalls FAQ:
http://www.v-one.com/pubs/fw-faq/faq.htm

Internet Security and Related Topics
Several security-related FAQs maintained by Internet Security Systems, Inc., can be found at:
http://www.iss.net/sec_info/addsec.html

World Wide Web Security
The following WWW security FAQ is maintained by Lincoln D. Stein:
http://www.genome.wi.mit.edu/WWW/faqs/www-security-faq.html

Security-Related Usenet Forums
There are several newsgroups on Usenet devoted to discussions of privacy, encryption, and other aspects of security:
alt.privacy
alt.privacy.anon.server
alt.privacy.clipper
alt.security.pgp
alt-security.ripem
alt.security
alt.security.index
alt.security.keydist
alt.security.pgp
alt.security.ripem
alt.security.tscm
comp.org.eff.news
comp.org.eff.talk
comp.society.privacy
comp.security.announce

comp.security.firewalls
comp.security.misc
comp.security.pgp.announce
comp.security.pgp.discuss
comp.security.pgp.resources
comp.security.pgp.tech
comp.security.unix
comp.virus

Companies & Organizations Involved in Electronic Commerce

The following is a list of Web sites maintained by companies involved in electronic commerce:

Broadvision
Markets software to facilitate electronic commerce:
www.broadvision.com

Cardservice International
Credit card service provider for digital merchants:
www.cardsvc.com

CheckFree
Provider of secure credit card and check-processing software:
www.checkfree.com

Citicorp
Credit cards and other services:
www.citibank.com

CommerceNet
Consortium of companies and organizations involved in electronic commerce:
www.commerce.net

CyberCash
Developer of software for secure credit card transactions:
www.cybercash.com

DigiCash
Developer of an electronic cash system:
www.digicash.com

Electronic Commerce Resource Center
Electronic commerce resources and information:
www.ecrc.ctc.com

First Virtual Holdings
Developer of online electronic payment system:
www.fv.com

Mark Twain Banks
First U.S.-based bank to offer Digicash's e-cash:
www.marktwain.com

MasterCard
Credit cards and other services:
www.mastercard.com

Microsoft
Markets Web-server software for electronic commerce:
www.microsoft.com

NetBill Project
Micropayment research project at Carnegie Mellon University:
ini.cmu.edu

NetCheque
Electronic cash and cheque research project at the University of Southern California's Information Sciences Institute:
nii-server.isi.edu/netcheque

Netscape Communications
Markets Web-server software for electronic commerce:
www.netscape.com

Open Market
Markets Web-server software for electronic commerce:
www.openmarket.com

RSA Data Security
Developer and marketer of public-key encryption technology:
www.rsa.com

Terisa Systems
Developer and marketer of public-key encryption:
www.terisa.com

VeriFone
Provider of secure electronic payment software and related technology:
www.verifone.com

VeriSign
Digital signature certificate authority:
www.verisign.com

Visa International
Credit cards and other services:
www.visa.com

Appendix B

Firewall & Secure Web Server Buyer's Guide

Firewalls and secure Web servers are two key defenses available to digital merchants who wish to conduct business on the Internet yet protect their internal computer networks and Web sites from malicious outsiders. This appendix contains contact information for key firewall and secure Web server vendors in North America.

Firewalls

ACC Network Systems
8320 Guilford Rd., Ste. G
Columbia, MD 21406
410-290-8775

ANS CO+RE Systems
1875 Campus Commons Dr., Ste. 220
Reston, VA 22091
800-456-8267, 703-758-7700
Fax: 703-758-7717
E-mail: interlock@ans.netinfo@ans.net
FTP: ftp.reston.ans.net
http://www.ans.net/InterLock

Ascend Communications
1275 Harbor Bay Pkwy.
Alameda, CA 94502
510-769-6001
Fax: 510-814-2300
E-mail: info@ascend.com
http://www.ascend.com

Atlantic Systems Group
Incutech Center Bag Service 69000
Fredericton, N.B., Canada B3B 6C2
506-453-3505
http://www.ASG.unb.ca

BBN
150 Cambridge Park Dr.
Cambridge, MA 02140
508-873-2000
http://www.bbnplanet.com

Border Network Technologies, Inc.
BorderWareBorder Network Technologies
20 Toronto St., Ste. 400
Toronto, Ontario, Canada M5C 2B8
800-334-8195, 416-368-7157
Fax: 416-368-7789
E-mail: info@border.com sales@border.com
FTP: ftp.border.com
http://www.border.com

CheckPoint Software Technologies, Ltd.
One Militia Dr., Ste. 5
Lexington, MA 02173
800-429-4391, 617-859-9051
Fax: 617-863-0523
E-mail: Info@checkpoint.com
http://www.checkpoint.com

Digital Equipment Corporation
40 Old Bolton Rd.
Stow, MA 01775
508-496-8626
FTP: ftp.digital.com/pub
http://www.digital.com/info

enterWorks
19886 Ashburn Rd.
Ashburn, VA 20147
800-505-5144, 703-471-6000
http://www.enterworks.com

FireFox, Inc.
2099 Gateway Pl., Seventh Floor
San Jose, CA 95110
800-230-6090, 408-467-1100
Fax: 408-467-1105
E-mail: sales@firefox.com
http://www.firefox.com/Novix

Global Internet
755 Page Mill Rd., Ste. A101
Palo Alto, CA 94304
800-682-5550
http://www.globalinternet.com

Global Technology Associates
3504 Lake Lynda Dr., Ste. 160
Orlando, FL 32817
800-774-4GTA, 407-380-0220
Fax: 407-380-6080
http://www.gta.com

Harris Computer Systems/CyberGuard Corporation
2101 W. Cypress Creek Rd.
Fort Lauderdale, FL 33309-1892
800-666-4273, 954-973-5478
http://www.cyberguardcorp.com

IBM Corporation
P.O. Box 12195, B44A-B501
Research Triangle Park, NC 27709
919-254-5074
http://www.ibm.com

Information Resource Engineering
8029 Corporate Dr.
Baltimore, MD 21236
410-931-7500
Fax: 410-931-7524
E-mail: info@ire.com

J. River Inc.
125 North First St.
Minneapolis, MN 55401
612-339-2521
http://www.jriver.com

KarlNet Inc.
5030 Postlewaite Rd.
Columbus OH 43235-3950
614-263-KARL(5275)
http://www.gbnet.net/kbridge

Livermore Software Labs
1602 Mosay Stone
Houston, TX 77077
800-240-5754, 713-496-1580
http://www.lsli.com

Livingston Enterprises
6920 Koll Center Pkwy. #220
Pleasanton, CA 94566
800-458-9966, 510-426-0770

Milky Way Networks Corporation
2650 Queensview Dr., Ste. 225
Ottawa, Ontario, Canada K2B 8H6
613-596-5549
Fax: 613-596-5615
E-mail: info@milkyway.com
http://www.milkyway.com

NEC Technologies, Inc.
Internet Business Unit
110 Rio Robles Dr.
San Jose, CA 95134-1899
408-433-1226
Fax: 408-433-1230
http://www.privatenet.nec.com

NetPartners Internet Solutions
9665 Chesapeake Dr., Ste. 350
San Diego CA 92123
800-7231166, 619-505-3020
http://www.netpart.comWeb

Network-1 Software & Technology Inc.
909 Third Ave., Ninth Floor
New York, NY 10022
800-NETWRK1(638-9751)
http://www.network1.com

Network Systems Corp.
7600 Boone Ave., N
Minneapolis, MN 55428
612-424-4888
Fax: 612-424-2853
http://www.network.com

Network Translation
1901 Embarcadero Rd., Ste. 108
Palo Alto, CA 94303
415-494-NETS(6387)
http://www.translation.com

Norman Data Defense Systems Inc.
3028 Javier Rd., Ste. 201
Fairfax, VA 22031
703-573-8802
Fax: 703-573-3919

ON Technology Corp.
1 Cambridge Center
Cambridge, MA 02142
617-374-1400
http://www.on.com

Raptor Systems Inc.
69 Hickory Dr.
Waltham, MA 02154
800-932-4536, 617-487-7700
Fax: 617-487-6755
E-mail: info@raptor.com
FTP: ftp.raptor.com
http://www.raptor.com

Seattle Software Labs, Inc.
316 Occidental Ave., S, Ste. 300
Seattle, WA 98104
206-521-8340
Fax: 206-521-8341
http://www.sealabs.com

Secure Computing Corp.
2675 Long Lake Rd.
Roseville, MN 55113
800-692-LOCK(5625), 612-628-2700
Fax: 612-628-2701
E-mail: sales@sctc.com
FTP: ftp.sctc.com/pub
http: //www.sctc.com

SmallWorks Inc.
4401 Stony Meadow Ln.
Austin, TX 78731
512-338-0619
Fax: 512-338-0619
E-mail: info@smallworks.com
FTP: ftp.smallworks.com

SOS Corporation
40 Broad St., Ste. 2175
New York, NY 10004
212-809-5900
http://www.soscorp.com/products/Brimstone.html

SSC Incorporated
PO Box 55599
Seattle, WA 98155

Sterling Software
5215 N. O'Connor Blvd., Ste. 1500
Irving TX 75039-3771
800-700-5579
http://www.csg.stercomm.com

SunSoft Inc.
2550 Garcia Ave.
Mountain View, CA 94043
800-SUN-SOFT(786-7638), 512-434-1511
Fax: 512-218-3866
http://www.sun.com/sunsoft

Technologic Inc.
4170 Ashford Dunwoody Rd., Ste. 465
Atlanta, GA 30319
404-843-9111
Fax: 404-843-9700
http://www.togic.com

Trusted Information Systems Inc.
3060 Washington Rd.
Glenwood, MD 21738
301-854-6889
Fax: 301-854-5363
E-mail: netsec@tis.com
FTP: ftp.tis.com
http://www.tis.com

V-One
12300 Twin Brook Pkwy., Ste. 235
Rockville, MD 20852
301-881-2297
Fax: 301-881-5377
http://www.vone.com

Attack Simulators & Intrusion-detection Products

Axent Technologies, Inc./Raxco Inc.
2440 Research Blvd.
Rockville, MD 20850
301-258-2620
Fax: 301-330-5756

Internet Security Systems Inc.
2000 Miller Ct.
West Norcross, GA 30071
800-PROBE62(776-2362), 404-441-2531
E-mail: iss@iss.net

Secure Web Servers

The following companies, based in North America, market secure Web servers that provide support for the Secure Sockets Layer of Secure HyperText Transfer Protocol, among other security features.

America Online
8615 Westwood Center Dr.
Veinna, VA 22182-2285
800-879-6882
http://www.aolserver.com/server

Community ConnecXion Inc.
Berkeley, CA
510-601-9777
http://www.us.apache-ssl.com

FTP Software, Inc.
100 Brickstone Sq.
Andover, MA 01810
508-685-4000
http://www.ftp.com

The Great Lakes Area Commercial Internet, Inc.
414-475-6388
Fax: 414-475-7388
http://www.glaci.com

IBM
4205 S. Miami Blvd.
Research Traingle Park, NC 27709
800-426-2255
http://www.ics.raleigh.ibm.com

The Internet Factory Inc.
Pleasanton, CA
800-229-6020
Fax: 510-426-9538
http://www.artisoft.com

Luckman Interactive Inc.
1055 West Seventh Ave., Ste. 2580
Los Angeles, CA 90017
800-711-2676, 213-614-0966
http://www.luckman.com

Microsoft Corp.
One Microsoft Way
Redmond, WA 98052-6399
800-426-9400, 206-882-8080
Fax: 206-936-7329
http://www.microsoft.com

Netscape Communications Corp.
501 E. Middlefield Rd.
Mountain View, CA 94043
415-937-3777
http://www.home.netscape.com

Open Market Inc.
245 First St.
Cambridge, MA 02142
617-621-9500
Fax: 617-621-1703
http://www.openmarket.com

Oracle Corp.
500 Oracle Parkway
Redwood Shores, CA 94065
800-672-2537
http://www.oracle.com

O'Reilly & Associates
101 Morris St.
Sebastapol, CA 95472
800-998-9938

Process Software Corp.
959 Concord St.
Framingham, MA 01701
800-722-7770
Fax: 508-879-0042
http://www.process.ocm

Quarterdeck Corp./StarNine Technologies
2550 Ninth St., Ste. 12
Berkeley, CA 94710
800-525-2580, 510-649-4949
http://www.starnine.com

Questar Microsystems Inc.
19501 144th Ave NE, Ste 900A
Woodinville, WA 98072
800-925-2140
http://www.questar.com

SPRY, CompuServe Internet Division
3535 128th Ave., SE
Bellevue, WA 98006
800-557-9614, 206-957-8000
Fax: 206-957-6000
http://www.server.spry.com

Tandem
19191 Vallco Pkwy., M/S 4-40
Cupertino, CA 95014
408-725-6000

Index

A

Academic Firewalls mailing list   253
AccessData decryption software   92–93
ActiveX Controls, vulnerability to attack   183
Adelman, Leonard   82
AIDS Information Trojan horse   61
Alert mailing list   251
Anonymous FTP attacks   47–48
Anonymous remailers   238
Anonymous transactions
    DigiCash   142
    digital money   122, 128
Anti-Racketeering Act   20
Antivirus software   57–61
AO Saturn   37
Applications security policy, creating   214
Ardita, Julio Cesar   219–220
Arpanet   8
Asymmetric algorithms, definition   73
ATM cards
    Personal ATM (P-ATM)   133
    See also Digital money
Attack simulators
    Internet Scanner   203
    NetProbe   203–204
    Security Administrator's Tool for Analyzing Networks (SATAN)   202–205
    vendors, list of   266
Authentication
    definition   72
    with digital signatures   77–78
    See also Encryption
Authenticode digital shrink wrap   236

B

Banking industry   95
Banners, recommended wording   209–210
BBBOnLine CARE seal   103–104
Berners-Lee, Tim   10
Best of Security mailing list   252
Better Business Bureau Online Web site   103–104
Bonnie and Clyde example
    authentication   77–78
    digital signatures   77–78
    encryption   74–75
    RSA   83
    See also Encryption   83
Books, selling on the Internet
    See Copyright
Boot infectors   53
Broadvision Web site   256
Brochureware   3
Bul, Frans   38
Buying on the Internet
    See Electronic commerce

C

Cannabis virus   54
Cardservice International Web site   256
Cargill, Tom   179
Cash, alternatives to
    See Digital money
CBBB (Council of Better Business Bureaus) Web site   103–104
CDT (Center for Democracy and Technology)   233
Center for Democracy and Technology (CDT)   233
Central Intelligence Agency (CIA), attack on   12
CERN (European Particle Physics Laboratory)   10
CERT (Computer Emergency Response Team)   13–14, 65
    Web site   250
Certificates   108–109
    key-revocation certificate, creating   88–89
    and software copyright   236
    See also Encryption
CGI (common gateway interface)
    vulnerability to hackers   171–172
Chaos Merchants   161–162
Chaum, David   141
CheckFree Web site   256
Checksums   58
CIA (Central Intelligence Agency), attack on   12
Ciphertext, definition   73
Citibank system
    counterfeiting, defending against   153–154
    Money Modules   153
    Trusted Agent   154
    See also Digital money

Citicorp Web site 256
   attack on 36–39
Cleartext, definition 73
Clipper Chip 20, 91
   See also Encryption
Coalition for Advertising Supported Information and Entertainment 230–231
COAST Security Archive mailing list 252
Cohen, Fred 52, 164
CommerceNet Web site 256
Common gateway interface (CGI)
   vulnerability to hackers 171–172
Competitive intelligence gatherers 40
Computer crime
   See Crime
Computer Emergency Response Team (CERT) 13–14, 65
   Web site 250
Computer Incident Advisory Capability Web site 250
Computer Operations, Audit, and Security Technology Web site 250
Computer Privacy Digest mailing list 253
Computer Professionals for Social Responsibility Web site 250
Computer security
   FAQ 254
   mailing lists
      Alert 251
      Best of Security 252
      COAST Security Archive 252
      Risks 252
   Web sites
      Computer Security Institute 250
      Computer Security Research Lab, UC Davis 250
Computer Underground Digest mailing list 253
Consumer protection laws 129
Containers, digital 226–230
   See also Copyright
Content
   registering 221
   selling 223–230
   See also Copyright
Cookies 232
COPS 46
Copyright
   anonymous remailers 238
   Authenticode digital shrink wrap 236
   content
      registering 221
      selling 223–230
   Cryptolope 226–228
   DigiBox 228
   digital containers 223–230
   Electronic Rights Management Group 229–230
   e-mail 223
   HTML 221
   IMPRIMATUR 230
   industry standards 229–230
   InfoMarket 227–228
   law, changes to 220–223
   licensing software 237
   links, HTML 221
   micropublishing 225
   Microsoft Internet Explorer 236
   monitoring downloads 222
   penalties 235
   registering 221
   reporting violations 235–236
   shrinkwrap, digital 236
   software 234–237
   Software Copyright Protection Bill 235
   Software Publishers Association (SPA) 234–236
   source code, HTML 221
   SPA hotline 235
   SPAudit auditing package 235
   vending machines, digital 224–225
   violations, reporting 235–236
   Xerox Usage Right Language protocol 229
   See also Encryption
Copyright notices 221
Copyright symbol 221
Corporate liability 220
Council of Better Business Bureaus (CBBB) Web site 103–104
Counterfeiting, defending against
   Citibank system 153–154
   DigiCash 143
   digital money 122–123
Courtney intrusion detector 205
CRC (cyclic redundancy check) 58
Credit cards
   business objectives 101
   certificate authority (CA) 108–109
   dual signatures 107–108
   export restrictions 109, 115
   in-person purchases 100
   key-exchange pairs 107
   mail-order guidelines, applicability 101
   nonrefutability 102
   Secure Electronic Transaction (SET) standard 105–113
      merchant registration 110–111
   Secure HyperText Transfer Protocol (S-HTTP) standard 117–118
   Secure Sockets Layer (SSL) standard 114–117

Index 271

mailing list, subscribing to 254
security holes 115–116
signature pairs 107
telephone purchases 100
theft of card numbers 102–103
vGATE Internet gateway software 112–113
vPOS merchant software 112–113
See also Electronic Commerce
See also Encryption
See also Trusted Agent
Crime
  attack methods
    anonymous FTP 47–48
    competitive intelligence gatherers 40
    counterfeit digital money 122–123
    denial-of-service 16, 47
    e-mail, bombing 48–49
    e-mail, forging 50
    e-mail, stealing credit card numbers 102–103
    IP spoofing 44–45
    network scanning 46–47
    newsgroup posts, forging 50
    password sniffing 41–44
    Sendmail loopholes 45–46
    spamming 49
    synflooding 194–195
    Web servers 170
  defenses
    Computer Emergency Response Team (CERT) 13–14
    Council of Better Business Bureaus (CBBB) web site 103–104
    FBI security recommendations 207–209
  employees
    cost of 27–28
    disgruntled 28
    dishonest 28–29
    examples 30
    security policy 238–248
    statistics 17–18, 193
  examples
    Central Intelligence Agency (CIA), attack on 12, 162
    Chaos Merchants 161–162
    Citicorp, attack on 36–39
    Dangerfield, Rodney, attack on Web site 161–162
    Department of Justice, attack on Web site 12, 162
    employee crime 30
    Internet Liberation Front 49, 161
    Masters of Deception 48
    Netcom On-Line Communication Services, attack on 32
    Panix, attack on 16, 194–195
    Quittner, Joshua, attack on 49
    Swedish Hackers Association (SHA) 12, 162
    Wired magazine, attack on 49
  hackers
    and anonymous remailers 238
    Computer Underground Digest, subscribing 253
    definition 12
    e-mail scams 34
    FAQ 255
    laws against 12–13
    magazines for 16–17
    mailing lists 253
    Mitnick, Kevin 32
    Phrack, subscribing 253
    in popular culture 32
    social engineering 32–34
    techniques 32–35
    telephone scams 33–34
  legislation
    Computer Fraud and Abuse Act 13
    Critical Infrastructure Working Group 40
    National Information Infrastructure Protection Act 12–13
  mailing lists, subscribing to 251–254
  organized crime
    Levin, Vladimir 36–39
  reasons for 14–15
  spies 35–39
  terrorists 40
  See also Credit cards
  See also Digital money
  See also Encryption
  See also Web sites of interest
Cryptanalysts, definition 73
Cryptographers, definition 73
Cryptography FAQ 254
Cryptolope 226–228
CyberCash 134–140
  Web site 257
  See also Digital money
CyberCoins 135
CyberTrust digital certificate service 109
CyberWallet 135
Cyclic redundancy check (CRC) 58
Cypherpunks mailing list 252

D

Dangerfield, Rodney, attack on Web site 161–162
DARPA (Defense Advanced Research Projects Agency) 8

Data Encryption Standard (DES)
  See DES
Databases, encryption 92–93
Dean, Drew 179
Decryption
  definition 73
  See also Encryption
Defense Advanced Research Projects Agency (DARPA) 8
Denial-of-service attacks 16, 47
Department of Justice, attack on Web site 12, 162
DES (Data Encryption Standard)
  banking industry 81
  cracking 81
  electronic commerce 80
  export limitations 80
  history 79
  and RSA 83
  testing 92
  triple encryption 80
  See also Encryption
Diffie, Whitfield 75
DigiBox 228
DigiCash
  anonymous transactions 142
  counterfeiting, defending against 143
  digital signatures 142
  tolls, paying electronically 125
  Web site 257
  World Currency Access account, opening 144–145
  See also Digital money
Digital certificates 108–109
  and software copyright 236
  See also Encryption
Digital containers 226–230
  See also Copyright
Digital envelopes 77
Digital money
  anonymous transactions 122, 128
  CheckFree 140–141
  checks
    NetCash 155–157
    NetCheque 156–157
    NetChex 157–158
  Citibank system 153–154
  consumer protection laws 129
  counterfeiting, defending against 122–123
  CyberCash 134–140
  DigiCash 141–146
  DyniCash 125
  Electronic Funds Transfer Act (EFTA) 129
  Electronic Monetary System (EMS) 152–154
  e-wallets 124–126
  federal regulations 128–129
  First Virtual Holding, Inc. 146–152
  Games CyberCash, digital cash company 124
  how it works 119–122
  Joint Electronic Payments Initiative (JEPI) 128
  MasterCard Cash 126
  micropayments 123–124, 135, 155
  Mondex consortium 125
  NetBill, micropayment services 123–124
  NetCash 155–156
  NetCheque 155–157
  NetChex 157–158
  pocket change, electronic 136
  privacy concerns 128
  purses, electronic 124–126
  requirements 127–128
  road tolls, paying electronically 125
  Rocket Science, digital cash company 124
  smart cards 124–126
  standards 128
  stored-value cards 124–126
  Summer Olympics, smart card use 125
  VeriFone 133
  video games 124
  Visa Cash 126
  wallets, electronic 124–126
  See also Credit cards
Digital shrink wrap 236
Digital signatures 77–78
  and credit cards 107–108
  See also Digital money
Digital vending machines 224–225
Doligex, Damien 115
Double spending, defending against 122–123
Downloads, monitoring 222
Dual signatures 107–108
DyniCash 125
  See also Digital money

E

Ecash
  See Digital money
E-commerce
  See Electronic commerce
EDI (Electronic Data Interchange)
  vs. the Internet 21–22
EFTA (Electronic Funds Transfer Act) 129
Electronic commerce
  advantages 7
  anonymous transactions
    DigiCash 142
    digital money 122, 128

Index

NetCash 155
checks, paying with 118
content, selling 223–230
definition 6–7
disadvantages 7
liability for customer security 18–19
Web sites of interest 256–258
See also Credit cards
See also Digital money
Electronic Commerce Resource Center Web site 257
Electronic Data Interchange (EDI)
   vs. the Internet 21–22
Electronic Frontier Foundation Web site 250
Electronic Funds Transfer Act (EFTA) 129
Electronic Licensing and Security Initiatives (ELSI) 237
Electronic Monetary System (EMS) 152–154
Electronic pocket change 136
Electronic purses 124–126
Electronic Rights Management Group 229–230
Electronic wallets 124–126
E-mail
   anonymous remailers 238
   attacks, defending against 49
   bombing 48–49
   copyright 223
   credit card numbers, stealing 102–103
   employee security policy 243
   encryption
      Multipurpose Internet Mail Extensions (MIME) 93–94
      Privacy-Enhanced Mail (PEM) 93
      Secure-A-File software 93
      S/MIME 93–94
      software vendors, list of 94
   forging 50
   hackers, scams 34
   Multipurpose Internet Mail Extensions (MIME) 93–94
   privacy, Netscape Navigator 233
   Privacy-Enhanced Mail (PEM) 93
   Secure-A-File software 93
   Sendmail loopholes 45–46
   S/MIME 93–94
   software vendors, list of 94
   UDP port, blocking 189
E-money
   See Digital money
Employee crime
   cost of 27–28
   disgruntled 28
   dishonest 28–29

examples 30
security policy 243
statistics 17–18, 193
Employee security policy 238–248
   abuse of resources 245
   access to files 242
   anonymous remailers 238
   attacking the system 244
   computer ethics 240
   creating, guidelines 247
   downloading 248
   e-mail 243
   enforcing 245
   for-profit activities 243
   harassment 244
   Internet access 248
   monitoring users 246, 248
   network use 245
   passwords 242
   permissions 241
   pornography 238
   productivity 239, 248
   recommended content 241
   responsibilities 242, 246, 248
   theft 244
   training 247
   unauthorized use 242–243
   waste of resources 245
EMS (Electronic Monetary System) 152–154
Encryption
   Anti-Racketeering Act 20
   asymmetric algorithms, definition 73
   authentication
      definition 72
      with digital signatures 77–78
   banking industry 95
   Bonnie and Clyde example
      authentication 77–78
      digital signatures 77–78
      encryption 74–75
      RSA 83
   certificates 108–109
   ciphertext, definition 73
   cleartext, definition 73
   Clipper Chip 20, 91
   credit cards 107–108
   cryptanalysts, definition 73
   cryptographers, definition 73
   CyberTrust digital certificate service 109
   databases 92–93
   definition 71, 73
   digital envelopes 77
   digital money 70–71

digital signatures   77–78
electronic commerce   75–79
e-mail
   Multipurpose Internet Mail Extensions (MIME)   93–94
   Privacy-Enhanced Mail (PEM)   93
   Secure-A-File software   93
   S/MIME   93–94
   software vendors, list of   94
export restrictions   20–21, 94–96
frequently asked questions (FAQ)   254
identification, definition   71
Kerberos   90
   See also NetCheque
keys
   digital envelopes, creating   77
   IDEA, size   85
   Pretty Good Privacy (PGP), size   86–87
   public, finding   78–79
   size   73–74
mailing lists
   Academic Firewalls   253
   Cypherpunks   252
   Firewalls   252
as munitions   94–96
national standards   91
nonrepudiation, definition   72
one-key cryptography, definition   73
plaintext, definition   73
policy, creating   97–98
privacy, definition   71
proprietary algorithms   91–93
public-key cryptography
   certificate authority (CA)   108–109
   and credit cards   107
   definition   73
   and electronic commerce   75–79
   finding public keys   78–79
   public-key servers   78–79
RIPEM   90
secret-key cryptography, definition   73
security loopholes   97
Simple Mail Transfer Protocol (SMTP)
   networks   94
single-key cryptography, definition   73
symmetric algorithms, definition   73
Usenet newsgroups, list of   255–256
uses of   5–6
verification, definition   72
VeriSign digital certificate service   109
wire-tapping   91
word processor files   92–93
See also Copyright
See also Credit cards

See also DES
See also Digital money
See also PGP
See also RSA
See also SET
See also S-HTTP protocol
See also SSL
European Particle Physics Laboratory (CERN)   10
E-wallets   124–126
Executable files, definition   53
Export restrictions
   credit cards   109, 115
   Data Encryption Standard (DES)   80
   encryption   20–21, 94–96
   Pretty Good Privacy (PGP)   84
   Secure Electronic Transaction (SET) standard   109
   Secure Sockets Layer (SSL) standard   115

F

FAQ (frequently asked questions)
   computer security   254
   cryptography   254
   encryption   254
   firewalls   255
   hacking   255
   Internet security   255
   WWW security   255
Farmer, Dan   46
FBI security recommendations   207–209
Felten, Ed   179
File infectors   53
File Transfer Protocol (FTP)
   UDP port, blocking   189
File-change detectors   58
Finger
   UDP port, blocking   189
Firewalls
   address and machine name handling   201
   administration   201
   application-level gateways   190
   applications, customizing for proxies   211
   auditing   201
   authentication   195–197, 200
   circuit-level gateways   190
   configuration practices   212
   COPS   210
   Crack   210
   Cracklib   210
   defending against attack   192–193
   definition   26, 185–186

Index

dual-homed gateways   190
encryption
   link-level   198–199
   network-level   199–200
FAQ   255
features, how to compare   200–202
flexibility *vs.* security   191
hackers   194–195
identification of outsiders   195–197
known security loopholes, checking for   210–211
mailing lists, subscribing to   252–253
monitoring for system changes   212
objectives   187
one-factor security   196
one-time password generators   196–197
packet-filtering routers   188–191
   UDP ports, blocking access to   189–190
Passwdplus   211
password checkers   210–211
passwords   196–197
personnel   202
pricing   201–202
proxies   200–201
reusable passwords   196
SATAN   211
screened-host firewalls   190
screened-subnet firewalls   190
smart cards   196–197
SOCKS   211
supported protocols   186
Tiger   212
TIS Internet Firewalls Toolkit   212
tokens   196–197
Tripwire   212
trusted outsiders   195–197
two-factor security   196–197
UNIX, checking for known loopholes   212
Usenet newsgroups, list of   255–256
vendors   202, 259–265
viruses   194
vulnerability to attack   192
Firewalls mailing list   252
First Virtual Holdings
   buying items   148–149
   keyboard-capture software   97
   online mall, web site   151
   opening an account   149–150
   selling items   149–151
   Trojan horse, password grabber   147–148
   VirtualPIN   148–149
   Web site   257
   See also Digital money

Forrester Research
   See Statistics
Forum of Incident Response and Security Terms
   Web site   250
FTP (File Transfer Protocol)
   UDP port, blocking   189

G

Gabriel intrusion detector   206
Games CyberCash, digital cash company   124
   See also Digital money
Guerrilla freeware   84

H

Hackers
   anonymous remailers   238
   Computer Underground Digest   253
   definition   12
   e-mail scams   34
   frequently asked questions (FAQ)   255
   laws against   12–13
   magazines for   16–17
   mailing lists, subscribing to   253
   Mitnick, Kevin   32
   Phrack   253
   in popular culture   32
   social engineering   32–34
   techniques   32–35
   telephone scams   33–34
   See also Crime
Hellman, Martin   75
Heuristics   57
HomePort San Diego Marketplace Web site   4
Hopwood, David   179
Hostile Applets Home Page   180
HTML (HyperText Markup Language)
   copyright   221
   definition   11
HTTP (HyperText Transfer Protocol), definition   10
Hyperlinks
   copyright   221
   definition   11

I

IDEA (International Data Encryption Algorithm)   84
IMPRIMATUR   230
Industrial espionage
   See Crime
IndustryNet Marketplace Web site   4

InfoHaus Web site   4
InfoMarket   227–228
Information Systems Security Association Web site   250
Interactive Services Association   230
International Data Encryption Algorithm (IDEA)   84
Internet
   civil liberties   233
   history of   8–10
   security FAQ   255
   size   9–10
   vs. EDI (Electronic Data Interchange)   21–22
   WWW users   11
   See also Electronic commerce
   See also Statistics
Internet Liberation Front   49, 161
Internet Payment Wallet   136
Internet Protocol (IP)   8
Internet Scanner attack simulator   203
Internet Security Scanner (ISS)   46–47
Internet worm   63–64
InterTrust Commerce Node   228
InterWeb Web site   4
Intranets
   defending against attacks   175–176
Intrusion detectors
   Courtney   205
   Gabriel   206
   Netstalker   207
   OmniGuard/Intruder Alert (ITA)   206
   Pingware   207
   rule-based anomaly detectors   206
IP (Internet Protocol)   8
IP spoofing   44–45
ISS (Internet Security Scanner)   46–47
Italian virus   54

J

Java
   applet sandbox   178–179
   Applet Security Manager   178
   applets
      definition of   18–19
      hostile, list of   180–181
      VirtualTag, legal issues   18–19
   defending against attacks   178–179
   risks of   177
   security loopholes   179–180
JavaScript, vulnerability to attack   182
JEPI (Joint Electronic Payments Initiative)   128
   See also Digital money
Jerusalem virus   54

Joint Electronic Payments Initiative (JEPI)   128
   See also Digital money

K

KDC (key-distribution center)   90
Kerberos
   security loopholes   96
   tickets   90
   See also NetCheque
Key rings, creating   87–88
Key-distribution center (KDC)   90
Key-exchange pairs   107
Key-revocation certificate, creating   88–89
Keys
   digital envelopes, creating   77
   IDEA, size   85
   Pretty Good Privacy (PGP), size   86–87
   public, finding   78–79
   size   73–74
   See also Encryption
Korolkov, Eugene and Katerina   37–39

L

Lachmanov, Alexi Michailovich   38
LaDue, Mark   180
Legislation
   Anti-Racketeering Act   20
   Communications Decency Act (CDA)   218
   Computer Fraud and Abuse Act   13
   consumer protection   129
   copyright, changes to   222–223
   Critical Infrastructure Working Group   40
   digital money   129
   against hackers   12–13
   National Information Infrastructure Protection Act   12–13, 222–223
   Software Copyright Protection Bill   235
   See also Copyright
   See also Crime
   See also Digital money
Levin, Vladimir   36–39
Libel   218–219
Library of Congress Internet Resource Page   250
Licensing software   237
Logic bombs   64

M

Macintosh servers, vulnerability to hackers   165
Mailing lists, subscribing to
   computer security
      Alert   251

Index   277

Best of Security   252
COAST Security Archive   252
Risks   252
encryption
   Academic Firewalls   253
   Cypherpunks   252
   Firewalls   252
hacking
   Computer Underground Digest   253
   Phrack   253
privacy
   Computer Privacy Digest   253
   Privacy Forum   253
viruses
   Virus-L   254
WWW security
   Secure Socket Layer   254
   WWW Security   254
Mark Twain Banks   144–145
   Web site   257
Marketplace Web site   4
MasterCard Cash   126
MasterCard Web site   257
Masters of Deception   48
Merchant Cash Register   135
Merchant Server features   168
Merchant Shopping Basket feature   168
Merchant Workbench feature   167
Merchants, electronic
   See Electronic commerce
Michelangelo virus, trigger date   53
Micropayments   123–124, 135, 155
   See also Digital money
Micropublishing   225
   See also Copyright
Microsoft Internet Explorer
   Java security loopholes   179
   Microsoft Word templates, security loopholes   184
   security concerns   176–177
   software copyright protection   236
Microsoft Merchant System   166–169
Microsoft Web site   257
Microsoft Word Basic viruses   54
Mitnick, Kevin   32
Mondex consortium   125
Money
   See Digital money
Money Modules   153
Morris, Robert Tappan   63–64
Morris worm   63–64
Multipartite viruses   52
Munitions, encryption as   94–96

N

National Computer Security Association Web site   251
National Institute of Standards and Technology   247
National Science Foundation (NSF)   9
National Telecommunications and Information Administration (NTIA)   231
NCSA seal of approval   174
NetBill Project
   micropayment services   123–124
   Web site   257
NetCash   155–156
NetCheque   155–157
   Web site   257
NetChex   157–158
Netcom On-Line Communication Services, attack on   32
NetProbe attack simulator   203–204
Netscape Communications
   Secure Sockets Layer (SSL) standard   113–117
   Web site   258
Netscape Navigator, security holes
   exportable version   115
   Java   179–180
   Java applets   116
   JavaScript   182
   random-number generator   96, 116
Netstalker intrusion detector   207
Network File System (NFS)
   UDP port, blocking   189
Networks
   scanning attacks   46–47
   security policy, creating   214–215
Newsgroup posts, forging   50
NFS (Network File System)
   UDP port, blocking   189
No Trespassing signs, recommended wording   209–210
Nonrepudiation, definition   72
NSF (National Science Foundation)   9
NTIA (National Telecommunications and Information Administration)   231

O

Olympics, smart card use   125
   See also Digital money
OmniGuard/Intruder Alert (ITA)   206
One-key cryptography, definition   73
Online malls
   HomePort San Diego Marketplace   4
   IndustryNet Marketplace   4
   InfoHaus   4

InterWeb   4
Marketplace   4
Shopping2000   4
Village Potpourri Mall   4
Open Market Web site   258
Operating systems
    security policy, creating   213–214

P

Panix, attack on   16, 194–195
Pass phrase, creating   87
Password sniffing   41–44
P-ATM (Personal ATM)   133
    See also Digital money
Persistent cookies   232–233
Personal ATM (P-ATM)   133
    See also Digital money
Pgp -kg command   86
PGP (Pretty Good Privacy)
    AUTOEXEC.BAT, modifying   86
    commercial version   89
    and Data Encryption Standard (DES)   85
    and digital signatures   89
    documentation   85
    export restrictions   84
    installation considerations   86–89
    International Data Encryption Algorithm (IDEA)   84
    key rings, creating   87–88
    key-revocation certificate, creating   88–89
    keys, generating   86–87
    obtaining   85–86
    pass phrase, creating   87
    pgp -kg command   86
    pgp2.6   85
    pgp26a.zip   85
    pgpwin.zip   85
    plaintext message, deleting   88
    public key, adding to server   88
    random keystrokes   87
    and RSA   84
    SET command   86
    setting directory path   86
    time zone   86
    user name   87
    versions   85
    ViaCrypt   89
    -w (wipe) option   88
    winpgp.zip   86
Pgp2.6   85
Pgp26a.zip   85
Pgpwin.zip   85

Phrack   16–17
    subscribing   253
Ping-Pong virus   54
Pingware intrusion detector   207
Plaintext, definition   73
Pocket change, electronic   136
Polymorphic viruses   57
POP (Post Office Protocol)
    UDP port, blocking   189
Pornography   218
Post Office Protocol (POP)
    UDP port, blocking   189
Pretty Good Privacy (PGP)
    See PGP
Privacy
    buyers   19
    Center for Democracy and Technology (CDT)   233
    Coalition for Advertising Supported Information and Entertainment   230–231
    Computer Privacy Digest mailing list   253
    cookies   232
    customer consent   231
    definition   71
    digital money   128
    guidelines   230
    Interactive Services Association   230
    Internet civil liberties   233
    mailing lists   253
    mailing lists, subscribing to   253
    National Telecommunications and Information Administration (NTIA)   231
    persistent cookies   232–233
    Privacy Forum mailing list   253
    provider notice   231
    Usenet newsgroups, list of   255–256
    user data, gathering   232–233
Privacy Forum mailing list   253
Proprietary algorithms   91–93
Proxies
    SOCKS tools   191–192
    See also Firewalls
Public-key cryptography
    certificate authority (CA)   108–109
    credit cards   107
    definition   73
    electronic commerce   75–79
    finding public keys   78–79
    public-key servers   78–79
    See also Digital money
    See also Encryption
    See also PGP

See also RSA
See also SET
Public-key servers   78–79
Publishing
   content, selling   223–230
   See also Copyright
Purses, electronic   124–126

Q

Quittner, Joshua   48–49

R

RIPEM   90
Ripper virus   54
Risks mailing list   252
Rivest, Ron   82
Rocket Science, digital cash company   124
Rosen, Sholom   152
Routers, definition   8
RSA
   benefits   83
   in Bonnie and Clyde example   83
   history   82
   licensees, list of   83–84
   prime numbers   83–84
   vs. Data Encryption Standard (DES)   83
   See also SSL
RSA Data Security Web site   258
Rule-based anomaly detectors   206

S

Sacrificial lamb configuration   174–175
Safe Internet Programming Web site   251
Sandberg, Christopher   129
SATAN (Security Administrator Tool for Analyzing Networks)   46–47, 202–203
Scanners   57
Schiffman, Allan M.   118
Secret-key cryptography, definition   73
Secure Electronic Transaction (SET) standard
   certificate authority (CA)   108–109
   dual signatures   107–108
   export restrictions   109
   key-exchange pairs   107
   merchant registration   110–111
   signature pairs   107
   VeriFone, Inc.   112
   vGATE Internet gateway software   112–113
   vPOS merchant software   112–113
   Web site   105

Secure HyperText Transfer Protocol (S-HTTP) standard   117–118
Secure Sockets Layer (SSL) standard
   export restrictions   115
   mailing list, subscribing to   254
   security holes   115–116
Security Administrator Tool for Analyzing Networks (SATAN)   46–47, 202–203
Security holes
   checking for   210–212
   e-mail   45–46
   encryption   97
   Java   179–180
   Java applets   116
   JavaScript   182
   Kerberos   96
   Microsoft Internet Explorer
      Java   179
      Microsoft Word templates   184
   Microsoft Word templates   184
   Netscape Navigator
      exportable version   115
      Java   179–180
      Java applets   116
      JavaScript   182
      random-number generator   96, 116
   random-number generator   96, 116
   Secure Sockets Layer (SSL) standard   115–116
   UNIX Sendmail   45–46
Security-related organizations, list of Web sites   250–251
Selling on the Internet
   See Electronic commerce
Sendmail
   security loopholes   45–46
   UDP port, blocking   189
SET (Secure Electronic Transaction) standard
   certificate authority (CA)   108–109
   dual signatures   107–108
   export restrictions   109
   key-exchange pairs   107
   merchant registration   110–111
   signature pairs   107
   VeriFone, Inc.   112
   vGATE Internet gateway software   112–113
   vPOS merchant software   112–113
   Web site   105
SHA (Swedish Hackers Association)   12, 162
Shamir, Adi   82
Sharper Image, The   3–4
Shopping
   See Electronic commerce
   See Online malls

Shopping2000 Web site 4
Shrink wrap, digital 236
S-HTTP (Secure HyperText Transfer Protocol)
    standard 117–118
Signature pairs 107
Signatures, digital
    See Encryption
Simple Mail Transfer Protocol (SMTP) networks 94
Single-key cryptography
    definition 73
    See also DES
    See also Encryption
Slatalla, Michelle 48
Smart cards 124–126
    VeriFone reader and writer 133
    See also Digital money
Social engineering 32–34
Software
    Electronic Licensing and Security Initiatives (ELSI) 237
    licensing 237
    Software Copyright Protection Bill 235
    Software Publishers Association (SPA) 234–236
    virus-activity monitors 59
Source code, copyright 221
SPA hotline 235
Spamming 49
    See also Crime
SPAudit auditing package 235
Spies 35–39
SSL (Secure Sockets Layer) standard
    export restrictions 115
    mailing list, subscribing to 254
    security holes 115–116
Statistics
    EDI use 22
    employees
        crime 17–18
        security breaches 193
    firewalls
        security breaches 192
        use of 186–187
    foreign spies, FBI estimates 36
    Internet, credit card use 99
    online malls, number of 4
    paperwork, cost of 21
    sales figures, Internet 1–2
    security breaches
        cost of 13–14
        employee 193
        firewalls 192
        via the Internet 25
    security measures, use of 25–26
    software piracy, cost of 234
    terrorists attacks on Pentagon computers 40
    viruses, number of 51
Stealth viruses 51
Stefferud, Einar 148
Stein, Lee 148
Stored-value cards 124–126
    See also Digital money
Storefront in a box 165–166
    See also Web servers
Swedish Hackers Association (SHA) 12, 162
Symmetric algorithms, definition 73
Synflooding 194–195

T

Telephone scams 33–34
Terisa Systems
    Secure HyperText Transfer Protocol (S-HTTP)
        standard 113, 117–118
    Web site 258
Terminate and stay resident (TSR) 59
Terrorists 40
Time bombs 64
Tolls, paying electronically 125
TradeSecret 22
TradeWeb 22
Tripwire 46
Trojan horses 61–62
Trusted Agent 154
TSR (terminate and stay resident) 59
2600 magazine 16

U

UDP (User Datagram Protocol) ports, blocking 189–190
UNIX
    security tools Web site 46
    Sendmail
        security loopholes 45–46
        UDP port, blocking 189
UNIX-to-UNIX copy program
    UDP port, blocking 189
Usenet newsgroups
    security-related 255–256
User Datagram Protocol (UDP) ports, blocking 189–190

Index

V

Vending machines, digital 224–225
Venema, Wietse 46
Vera Cruz virus 54
Verification, definition 72
VeriFone Web site 258
VeriSign, Inc.
    digital certificate service 109
    digital shrink wrap 236
    Web site 258
VGATE Internet gateway software 112–113
ViaCrypt 89
Video games 124
Village Potpourri Mall Web site 4
VirtualPIN 148–149
    See also Digital money
Virus-activity monitors 59
Viruses
    anonymous remailers 238
    antivirus software 57–61
    definition 52–54
    disinfectant 59–61
    examples, list of 54
    file-change detectors 58
    and firewalls 194
    first known 52
    launchpads 52
    logic bombs 64
    mailing list, subscribing to 254
    Microsoft Word Basic viruses 54
    multipartite viruses 52
    number of 51
    payloads 53–54
    polymorphic viruses 57
    preventing 59–61
    removing 59
    scanners 57–58
    statistics 51
    stealth viruses 51
    symptoms 56
    time bombs 64
    transmission 55
    triggering 53
    Trojan horses 61–62
    virus-activity monitors 59
    Virus-L mailing list 254
    vs. programs 52
    Word Basic viruses 54
    worms 62–63
Virus-L mailing list 254
Visa Cash 126
    See also Digital money
Visa International Web site 258
Voronin, Vladimir 38
Vova 36
VPOS merchant software 112–113

W

-w (wipe) option 88
Wallach, Dan 179
Warning banners, recommended wording 209–210
Web browsers
    ActiveX Controls, vulnerability to attack 183
    Java
        applet sandbox 178–179
        Applet Security Manager 178
        defending against attacks 178–179
        hostile applets, list of 180–181
        risks of 177
        security loopholes 179–180
    JavaScript, vulnerability to attack 182
    Microsoft Internet Explorer
        Java security loopholes 179
        Microsoft Word templates, security loopholes 184
        security concerns 176–177
        software copyright protection 236
    Netscape Navigator
        e-mail privacy 233
        exportable version 115
        Java security loopholes 116, 179–180
        JavaScript security loopholes 182
        random-number generator 96, 116
        security concerns 176–177
Web servers
    attack methods, list of 170
    common gateway interface (CGI)
        vulnerability to hackers 171–172
    firewalls 174–175
    Internet service providers (ISP), deciding to use 164–165
    InterTrust Commerce Node 228
    intranets, defending against attacks 175–176
    Macintosh, vulnerability to hackers 165
    Microsoft Merchant System 166–169
    NCSA seal of approval 174
    sacrificial lamb configuration 174–175
    secure
        features 165–166
        vendors, list of 266–268
    storefront in a box 165–166

UNIX
    defending against attacks   172–174
    vulnerability to hackers   165
Web sites of interest
    attack simulators, vendors   266
    Better Business Bureau Online   103–104
    Broadvision   256
    Cardservice International   256
    CheckFree   256
    Citicorp   256
    CommerceNet   256
    Computer Emergency Response Team (CERT)   250
    Computer Incident Advisory Capability   250
    Computer Operations, Audit, and Security Technology   250
    Computer Professionals for Social Responsibility   250
    Computer Security Institute   250
    Computer Security Research Lab, UC Davis   250
    Council of Better Business Bureaus (CBBB)   103–104
    cryptography FAQ   254
    CyberCash   257
    DigiCash   257
    electronic commerce   256–258
    Electronic Commerce Resource Center   257
    Electronic Frontier Foundation   250
    firewalls
        FAQ   255
        vendors, list of   259–265
    First Virtual Holdings   257
    Forum of Incident Response and Security Terms   250
    Hostile Applets Home Page   180
    Information Systems Security Association   250
    Internet security FAQ   255
    Library of Congress Internet Resource Page   250
    Mark Twain Bans   257
    MasterCard   257
    Microsoft   257
    National Computer Security Association   251
    NetBill Project   257
    NetCheque   257
    Netscape Communications   258
    online malls
        HomePort San Diego Marketplace   4
        IndustryNet Marketplace   4
        InfoHaus   4
        InterWeb   4
        Marketplace   4
        Shopping2000   4
        Village Potpourri Mall   4
    Open Market   258
    RSA Data Security   258
    Safe Internet Programming   251
    Secure Electronic Transaction (SET) standard   105
    security-related organizations, list of   250–251
    Terisa Systems   258
    UNIX security tools   46
    VeriFone   258
    VeriSign   258
    Visa International   258
    Web servers, secure, vendors   266–268
    World Wide Web Consortium   251
    WWW security FAQ   255
Winpgp.zip   86
WINPublish, micropublishing service   225
Wired magazine, attack on   49
Wire-tapping   91
Word Basic viruses   54
    See also Viruses
Word processor files, encryption   92–93
World Currency Access account, opening   144–145
    See also Digital money
World Wide Web Consortium Web site   251
World Wide Web (WWW)
    demographics   11
    history   10–11
    security
        frequently asked questions (FAQ)   255
        mailing lists, subscribing to   254
    See also Copyright
    See also Electronic commerce
    See also Encryption
Worms   62–63

X

Xerox Usage Right Language protocol   229

Z

Zimmerman, Phil   84

discover the award-winning online magazine for Netscape users!

Navigate!™

for Netscape Navigator users at all levels:

- interviews with industry experts
- easy tutorials for the latest Netscape software
- in-depth articles on timely topics
- exciting site reviews
- software treasures

Navigate!
the online magazine for Netscape™ users

http://www.netscapepress.com/zine

Follow the leader!

Hot on the heels of the runaway

international ***bestseller*** comes the

complete Netscape Press line:

easy-to-follow tutorials;

savvy, results-oriented ***guidelines***;

and targeted titles that zero in on

your *special interests*.

All with the ***official***

Netscape seal of approval!

http://www.netscapepress.com

Netscape Press is an imprint of **VENTANA**.

OFFICIAL
Netscape Plug-in BOOK
$39.99
1-56604-468-5

OFFICIAL
Online Marketing with Netscape BOOK
$34.99
1-56604-453-7

OFFICIAL
Netscape Navigator GOLD 3.0 BOOK
$39.95
Win 1-56604-420-0
Mac 1-56604-421-9

International Bestseller
250,000+
in its first edition!

NETSCAPE PRESS

OFFICIAL Netscape Navigator 3.0 BOOK

"Destined to become the bible to the world's most popular browser."
—*PC Magazine*

$39.99
Windows 1-56604-500-2
Macintosh 1-56604-512-6

The definitive guide to the world's most popular Internet navigator

BY PHIL JAMES
FOREWORD BY MARC ANDREESSEN

International Bestseller! More than 250,000 in print!

OFFICIAL Multimedia Publishing FOR Netscape

Make your Web pages come alive!

$49.95
1-56604-381-6

OFFICIAL Netscape Guide to Online Investments

The Complete Reference for Online Banking and Financial Management

$24.99
1-56604-452-9

OFFICIAL Netscape Beginner's Guide TO THE Internet

Your First Book on the Net & Navigator

$24.99
1-56604-522-3

OFFICIAL Netscape Guide TO Internet Research

$29.99
1-56604-604-1

OFFICIAL HTML Publishing FOR Netscape

Your complete guide to Web design and production

$39.95
Win 1-56604-288-7
Mac 1-56604-417-0

Design Online!

Interactive Web Publishing With Microsoft Tools
$49.99, 818 pages, illustrated, part #: 462-6

Take advantage of Microsoft's broad range of development tools to produce powerful web pages; program with VBScript; create virtual 3D worlds; and incorporate the functionality of Office applications with OLE. The CD-ROM features demos/lite versions of third party software, sample code.

Looking Good Online
$39.99, 450 pages, illustrated, part #: 469-3

Create well-designed, organized web sites—incorporating text, graphics, digital photos, backgrounds and forms. Features studies of successful sites and design tips from pros. The companion CD-ROM includes samples from online professionals; buttons, backgrounds, templates and graphics.

Internet Business 500
$39.95, 450 pages, illustrated, part #: 287-9

This authoritative list of the most useful, most valuable online resources for business is also the most current list, linked to a regularly updated *Online Companion* on the Internet. The companion CD-ROM features a hyperlinked version of the entire text of the book.

The Comprehensive Guide to VBScript
$39.99, 864 pages, illustrated, part #: 470-7

The only encyclopedic reference to VBScript and HTML commands and features. Complete with practical examples for plugging directly into programs. The companion CD-ROM features a hypertext version of the book, along with shareware, templates, utilities and more.

Books marked with this logo include *Online Udates*™, which include free additional online resources, chapter updates and regularly updated links to related resources from Ventana.

Web Publishing With Adobe PageMill 2
$34.99, 450 pages, illustrated, part #: 458-2

Here's the ultimate guide to designing professional web pages. Now, creating and designing pages on the Web is a simple, drag-and-drop function. Learn to pump up PageMill with tips, tricks and troubleshooting strategies in this step-by-step tutorial for designing professional pages. The CD-ROM features Netscape plug-ins, original textures, graphical and text-editing tools, sample backgrounds, icons, buttons, bars, GIF and JPEG images, Shockwave animations.

Web Publishing With Macromedia Backstage 2
$49.99, 500 pages, illustrated, part #: 598-3

Farewell to HTML! This overview of all four tiers of Backstage lets users jump in at their own level. With the focus on processes as well as techniques, readers learn everything they need to create center-stage pages. The CD-ROM includes plug-ins, applets, animations, audio files, Director xTras and demos.

Web Publishing With QuarkImmedia
$39.99, 450 pages, illustrated, part #: 525-8

Use multimedia to learn multimedia, building on the power of QuarkXPress. Step-by-step instructions introduce basic features and techniques, moving quickly to delivering dynamic documents for the Web and other electronic media. The CD-ROM features an interactive manual and sample movie gallery with displays showing settings and steps. Both are written in QuarkImmedia.

Web Publishing With Microsoft FrontPage 97
$34.99, 500 pages, illustrated, part #: 478-2

Web page publishing for everyone! Streamline web-site creation and automate maintenance, all without programming! Covers introductory-to-advanced techniques, with hands-on examples. For Internet and intranet developers. The CD-ROM includes all web-site examples from the book, FrontPage add-ons, shareware, clip art and more.

Make it Multimedia

Microsoft SoftImage|3D Professional Techniques 🌐
$69.99, 524 pages, illustrated, part #: 499-5

Here's your comprehensive guide to modeling, animation & rendering. Create intuitive, visually rich 3D images with this award-winning technology. Follow the structured tutorial to master modeling, animation and rendering, and to increase your 3D productivity. The CD-ROM features tutorials, sample scenes, textures, scripts, shaders, images and animations.

LightWave 3D 5 Character Animation f/x 🌐
$69.99, 700 pages, illustrated, part #: 532-0

Master the fine—and lucrative—art of 3D character animation. Traditional animators and computer graphic artists alike will discover everything they need to know: lighting, motion, caricature, composition, rendering ... right down to work-flow strategies. The CD-ROM features a collection of the most popular LightWave plug-ins, scripts, storyboards, finished animations, models and much more.

3D Studio MAX f/x 🌐
$49.99, 552 pages, illustrated, part #: 427-8

Create Hollywood-style special effects! Plunge into 3D animation with step-by-step instructions for lighting, camera movements, optical effects, texture maps, storyboarding, cinematography, editing and much more. The companion CD-ROM features free plug-ins, all the tutorials from the book, 300+ original texture maps and animations.

Looking Good in 3D 🌐
$39.99, 400 pages, illustrated, part #: 434-4

A guide to thinking, planning and designing in 3D. Become the da Vinci of the 3D world! Learn the artistic elements involved in 3D design—light, motion, perspective, animation and more—to create effective interactive projects. The CD-ROM includes samples from the book, templates, fonts and graphics.

To order any Ventana title, complete this order form and mail or fax it to us, with payment, for quick shipment.

TITLE	PART #	QTY	PRICE	TOTAL

SHIPPING

For all standard orders, please ADD $4.50/first book, $1.35/each additional.
For "two-day air," ADD $8.25/first book, $2.25/each additional.
For orders to Canada, ADD $6.50/book.
For orders sent C.O.D., ADD $4.50 to your shipping rate.
North Carolina residents must ADD 6% sales tax.
International orders require additional shipping charges.

SUBTOTAL = $ _____
SHIPPING = $ _____
TAX = $ _____
TOTAL = $ _____

Or, save 15%—order online.
http://www.vmedia.com

Mail to: Ventana • PO Box 13964 • Research Triangle Park, NC 27709-3964 ☎ 800/743-5369 • Fax 919/544-9472

Name _____
E-mail _____ Daytime phone _____
Company _____
Address (No PO Box) _____
City _____ State _____ Zip _____
Payment enclosed ____ VISA ____ MC ____ Acc't # _____ Exp. date _____
Signature _____ Exact name on card _____

Check your local bookstore or software retailer for these and other bestselling titles, or call toll free: **800/743-5369**